Lucrecia Martel |

Contemporary Film Directors

Edited by Justus Nieland and Jennifer Fay

The Contemporary Film Directors series provides concise, well-written introductions to directors from around the world and from every level of the film industry. Its chief aims are to broaden our awareness of important artists, to give serious critical attention to their work, and to illustrate the variety and vitality of contemporary cinema. Contributors to the series include an array of internationally respected critics and academics. Each volume contains an incisive critical commentary, an informative interview with the director, and a detailed filmography.

A list of books in the series appears at the end of this book.

Lucrecia Martel |

Gerd Gemünden

**UNIVERSITY
OF
ILLINOIS
PRESS**
URBANA,
CHICAGO,
AND
SPRINGFIELD

© 2019 by the Board of Trustees
of the University of Illinois
All rights reserved
1 2 3 4 5 C P 5 4 3 2 1

♾ This book is printed on acid-free paper.

Frontispiece: Lucrecia Martel in 2018

Library of Congress Cataloging-in-Publication Data
Names: Gemünden, Gerd, 1959– author.
Title: Lucrecia Martel / by Gerd Gemünden.
Description: [Urbana, Illinois] : University of Illinois Press, [2019] | Series:
   Contemporary film directors | Includes bibliographical references,
   filmography, and index.
Identifiers: LCCN 2019018163 (print) | LCCN 2019980226 (ebook) | ISBN
   9780252042836 (hardcover) | ISBN 9780252084669 (paperback) | ISBN
   9780252051692 (ebook)
Subjects: LCSH: Martel, Lucrecia, 1966– —Criticism and interpretation.
Classification: LCC PN1998.3.M36855 G46 2019 (print) | LCC PN1998.3.M36855
   (ebook) | DDC 791.4302/3309282—dc23
LC record available at https://lccn.loc.gov/2019018163
LC ebook record available at https://lccn.loc.gov/2019980226

Contents

Acknowledgments ix

A POETICS OF THE SENSES | 1

Drowning in Indolence: *La ciénaga* 29

Touching Tales: *La niña santa* 50

Dazed and Deceitful: *La mujer sin cabeza* 69

Leaving Salta: Recent Shorts and a Lost Film 89

The Myopia of Colonialism: *Zama* 105

INTERVIEWS WITH LUCRECIA MARTEL | 135

Filmography 149

Bibliography 155

Index 183

Acknowledgments |

Daniel Nasset, acquisitions editor at the University of Illinois Press, enthusiastically supported the project from the beginning, as did series editors Jen Fay and Justus Nieland, whose profound knowledge of Martel's oeuvre had a positive impact throughout the writing and review process. Haden Guest and B. Ruby Rich participated in a 2016 manuscript review, under the umbrella of the Leslie Center for the Humanities at Dartmouth, and gave invaluable comments on an earlier draft. Early fans and eloquent advocates of Lucrecia Martel in this country, their insights, and their thoughts helped make this a better book, as did the feedback of my colleague Julio Ariza, who shared his deep knowledge of contemporary Argentine culture. Patricia Barbieri, at Lita Stantic Productions, provided me with the fabled script of *La ciénaga*. Christoph Hochhäusler generously shared a recording of his and Nicolas Wackerbarth's extensive 2018 *Revolver Live* conversation with Lucrecia Martel in Berlin. Esther Allen pointed me to important early texts by Antonio Di Benedetto. David Oubiña and Aldo Palparella kindly gave permission to reprint David's 2009 interview with Lucrecia Martel. Deborah Oliver of Ab Initio Consulting & Publishing was a most mindful editor. At Dartmouth, Jill Baron, librarian for Romance languages and Latin American studies, tracked down resources with the skimpiest of information. Ashley Manning ('17), my research assistant under the Dartmouth College Presidential Scholarship program, helped reconstruct the production history of *El Eternauta*. Chris Iványi, digital arts lab specialist, provided crucial assistance with illustrations while Peter Ciardelli, audiovisual specialist, offered timely help with VHS frame grabs. Noah Isenberg, bad hombre y muy amigo, gave advice, feedback, and much more along the long way to the completion of this project. The biggest gracias of all goes to Silvia Spitta, my first reader, my collaborator on the interview with Lucrecia, the real source of my interest in Latin American cinema, and *so* much more. To her I dedicate this book.

Lucrecia Martel |

A Poetics of the Senses |

Film images affect primarily the spectator's senses,
engaging him physiologically before he is in a position
to respond intellectually.

—Siegfried Kracauer, *Theory of Film*

So Much Water

Lucrecia Martel's most recent feature, *Zama*, opens to the titular hero striking a pose of grandeur, wearing a tricornered hat and bearing a sword, while standing proudly before an immense river. We soon learn that the waters behind him bear the sole promise for his future, namely a ship delivering the longed-for transferal from this backwater of the Spanish colony to the town where his wife and children live. As it turns out, this vessel never arrives, but through several ironic twists of fate, at the end of the film his boat finally does come in: badly injured and clinging on to dear life, the hero finds himself in a dugout canoe, slowly moving deeper into the wilderness and farther away from his planned destination, and history itself—an image of hope, not despair, as Martel has insisted.

Rivers feature prominently at the beginning and the end of the *Zama*, and most of the story is set close to shore. While the source for the film, Antonio Di Benedetto's 1956 novel, does not name the town in which Zama is posted, detailed descriptions of streets and buildings clearly identify it as the city of Asunción, set on the confluence of the Pilcomayo and Paraguay Rivers, which form the Paraná, a river that has fascinated Martel throughout her career (as I explore in more detail). The novel opens with the first-person narrator's description of an image that is not depicted in Martel's film but that clearly informs the spirit of her adaptation:

> I left the city and made my way downriver alone, to meet the ship I awaited without knowing when it would come in. I reached the old wharf, that inexplicable structure. The city and its harbor have always been where they are, a quarter-league farther upriver. I observed, among its pilings, the writhing patch of water that ebbs between them. A dead monkey, still whole, still undecomposed, drifted back and forth with a certain precision upon those ripples and eddies without exit. All his life the water at forest's edge had beckoned him to a journey, a journey he did not take until he was no longer a monkey but a monkey's corpse. That water that bore him tried to bear him away, but he was caught among the posts of the decrepit wharf and there he was, ready to go and not going. And there we were. There we were: Ready to go and not going. (2016b, 7)

Ahí estábamos por irnos y no: the stagnation and indeterminacy that rules Zama's life, of a journey not taken, of missed opportunities, of futility and decay, is a predicament that governs the lives of many of Martel's key characters. And indeed, it is a state of being that is always closely intertwined with water, an unmistakable leitmotif in all of Martel's feature films and most of her shorts. Just take the swimming pool, which in her first three features, often referred to as the Salta trilogy, assumes a larger symbolic function. Life revolves around the brackish waters of the dilapidated swimming pool in *La ciénaga/The Swamp* (2001), where the drunk adults lounge around at the film's opening and where Mecha injures herself. The big thermal pool of the hotel in *La niña santa/The Holy Girl* (2004) is Amalia and Josefina's favorite hangout; this is where the teenagers share their secrets and where, at the film's end, we watch them idly drifting in the warm waters unaware of the catastrophe about to descend on the adults in the hotel. A newly constructed swimming

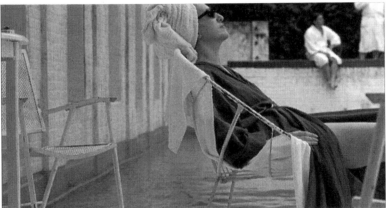
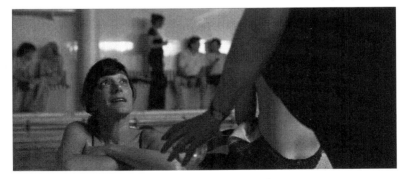

Figure 1. Pool life in *La ciénaga*, *La niña santa*, and *La mujer sin cabeza*

pool also figures prominently at the beginning of *La mujer sin cabeza/ The Headless Woman* (2008), where Vero meets up with her friends, members of a class that turns its back toward those who serve them, even to the extent of covering up a crime. A ten-minute profile by EICTV (Escuela Internacional de Cine y Televisión, Cuba) features Martel, cigar in hand, explaining her career trajectory while seated alongside a large swimming pool with the Caribbean ocean in the background—a clear sign of how carefully the filmmaker manages her own image as well.

In interviews Martel has commented that the swimming pool particularly suits her concern with depicting the life of the upper-middle classes. Due to the scarcity of public swimming pools in Argentina, they function as markers of class. Only the very wealthy own private pools, while access to other pools is often through membership to a costly private club. As I explain below, the swimming pool is also Martel's favorite metaphor for conveying her concept of sound. But not only swimming pools, water in general is ubiquitous in Martel's work. Indeed, few directors can claim to have made water such a central and varied theme in their oeuvre. As B. Ruby Rich comments in regard to *La ciénaga*, "[water] is ever-present in the air, for instance, as an oppressive humidity; frozen into ice to be secured from the maid or the bedside freezer; drawn in the bathroom, where José and Verónica shower incestuously; drained from the horrifyingly fetid swimming pool, and refilled; or in its alcoholic form, a potion for the middle-aged and elixir for the young, sip after sip of danger and relief" (2001).

In brief, water becomes the single most important symbol to encompass the major themes, moods, and tonalities of Martel's oeuvre, as well as their formal registers. Emphasizing the fluidity or blurring of borders, it defies fixed, concrete identities and desires. At times foreboding or ominous, water is often the source of acousmatic sound—we feel it, we sense it, but we don't see where it comes from. At others, water connotes exuberance and sensuality, channeling multidirectional desires that break the limits imposed by patriarchy, Catholicism, or normative heterosexuality.

The ubiquity of stagnant waters in Martel's films is also symbolic of her resistance to the ever-increasing speed of mainstream storytelling; her goal is to force viewers instead into a new relationship with the cinematic image. "I want the opposite of junk food," Martel once remarked, "which you have to chew fast because if you slow down you realize it is shit" (quoted in Aldazábal 2004).[1] Martel's more recent critique of television series, which have come to dominate networks or streaming platforms such as Netflix, Hulu, and HBO, equally eschews a form of filmmaking where the dominance of the script comes at the expense of a storytelling that appeals to other senses (Diz and Lerer 2017). For her, the narrative model set by US companies, which has been adopted worldwide without challenge, has led to an impoverishment that is a de facto step backward, not forward (Urritia 2018; Costa 2018). And in a post-screening conversation with Esther Allen, she wryly commented, "plot is only the seafoam on top of a wave" (2018b)—what interests her is the teaming ocean beneath. Accordingly, the plots that drive her films tend to be minimal, indeterminate, and unresolved and are often located off the beaten track.

An important key to Martel's filmmaking is a short text she prepared in 2013, written for the Buenos Aires film journal *Las naves* in response to the editors' request to describe her approach to filmmaking.[2] The statement was published as the first of thirty-nine so-called manifestos by various international filmmakers that made up the journal's 2013 inaugural issue. It reads as follows:

> Sometimes, but rarely, in a fragment of a dialogue, in the coincidence of sounds, in an incomprehensibly familiar image, the artifice of reality appears.
>
> All of our power and the mystery of the end lie in these cracks.
>
> Making movies allows me to look for these cracks and sometimes, but rarely, find them.
>
> But they don't last long and I forget them. (Martel 2013)[3]

For a filmmaker decidedly averse to making programmatic declarations about her films and their intended meanings, this manifesto—if we may actually call it that—occupies a unique space among Martel's written and spoken comments on her films. Here, she summarizes in a few sentences the essential components of her commitment to filmmaking: an emphasis on the fleeting and the ephemeral; the primacy of subjective perspective; the significance of sound and of the fragment; and the insistence on the experiential immediacy of reality. Filmmaking, she believes, enables us to discover the cracks (*rajaduras*) in the everyday, which in turn offer a glimpse into the constructedness of what we call reality—the fact that reality is made, not given—and how the individual pieces are assembled.

These revelations, it needs to be emphasized, are the viewers' experiences when watching Martel's films, and not those of the filmmaker and her crew as they are working on the set. While open to discoveries when in production, Martel is generally averse to improvisation, choosing locations carefully and designing the soundscape before she sets up the camera. If her films may at times seem improvised, this is still the result of careful planning, as Martel has asserted that "there is very little difference between the script and the film" (Bernini et al. 2001, 127).

One can get a very good sense of Martel's working methods through Manuel Abramovich's documentary *Años luz/Light Years* (2017), in which he followed her on the set of *Zama* during the spring of 2015. The film takes its title from an e-mail Martel sent Abramovich, in which she responds to his request to film her by stating "I'm light years away from being a protagonist in a film." Luckily for him—and Martel's public—this was not her last word. Not your usual making-of, *Años luz* is a very personal portrait of a woman deeply immersed in her work. We watch Martel directing actors, exchanging notes with her team, and at times getting irritated with Abramovich's distracting presence on the set. As in his 2017 documentary *Soldado/Soldier*, Abramovich favors an observational stance with little camera movement. He carefully captures Martel's perfectionism, her obsession with such details as the pronunciation of a certain word or the use of an accent or an intonation, or the exact placement of animals in the frame (who are oblivious to direction). Here her sense of humor also comes through, as when she dryly comments on the interference of airplane noise: "Is today national aviation day?"

The result of such meticulous insistence on each and every detail are films that are of a piece. They provide access to a reality otherwise beyond reach, training viewers for registering the uncertainty and contingency of life—filmmaking, for Martel, is always a form of discovery and preservation. Repeatedly, she has underscored the revelatory power of film: "We are confined to a certain way of perception," she observed, "and what cinema allows you to do is to distort this perception a little

6 | **Lucrecia Martel**

bit, and for me, with luck, in this distortion, between what the film does and what the spectators do, a certain type of revelation can occur . . . a small revelation, not a big truth" (quoted in Sabat n.d.).[4]

Martel's films—and this is the central premise of my interpretation—insist on the ephemeral, fortuitous, fragmentary, and endless quality of human experience. For her, film is not just a visual medium; it also encompasses a strong aural and haptic dimension that physically involves viewers and viscerally affects their engagement with the screen. Feeling, touching, and smelling not only are foregrounded as acts performed by her characters, but they are also forms of sensory perception induced in the viewer. It is as if we could smell the decay and sweltering heat embalming the estate of La Mandrágora or Zama's outpost in the hinterlands, or the sulfuric steam rising from the pools in *La niña santa*. The skin, as an organ that transmits heat, moisture, touch, and pressure, becomes a central focus. In *Zama*, the skin is a canvas for body paint, arms dyed in green, or torsos covered in a bright red powder, proudly displayed by the black and indigenous characters. But the skin also conveys vulnerability and the record of violence: note the many cuts and bruises of the characters in *La ciénaga*; the skin is the site of impact of the sexual molestation in *La niña santa*; and the skin registers the violence that causes death by an automobile in *La mujer sin cabeza*. The decomposing arm of the leader of the search party, in *Zama*, displays a palette of putrefaction, ranging from red and blue to dark purple and finally black. Time and again, the skin points to the fragility and vulnerability of the human body. Yet the skin is also the conduit of the sensual and the erotic—often coded in Martel's films as a "forbidden" sexuality, with overtones of homosexuality, incest, or miscegenation.

Because of its illicit and frequently incestuous desire across family members, class barriers, and generations Martel's cinema clearly has a queer vision (Rich 2013; Galt 2013; White 2015). To be sure, her stories are not coming-out dramas, melodramas of sexual awakening and liberation, or other narratives that revolve centrally around sexual identity. Instead, deviant desire is always present under the surface or as a backstory. In Martel, "lesbian desire is neither tragic nor scandalous," notes Rich, "but always there [. . .]. She offers a wondrous example of how queer cinema, done right, is cause for a radical expansion of possibility. She parses queer questions, not queer answers" (2013, 180). Because her films value style more than representation, and because they resist deciphering the psychological motivations of her characters, they do not fit the mold of tales that advocate consciousness-raising or elevating visibility.

Martel's stylistic choices create fundamental epistemological uncertainties in the service of moral fables that force viewers to question their values and beliefs. Like many contemporary Latin American directors, Martel addresses highly political topics, including religion and the role of the Roman Catholic Church, patriarchy, same-sex or incestuous desires, fraught gender relations, privileges associated with race and class, and the role of memory in post-dictatorship Argentine society. What is unique about her films, however, is how they demand that viewers formulate their own ethical stance. Repeatedly, we find ourselves among, not above, Martel's characters, forcing us not so much to judge their shortcomings but rather to imagine our own behavior under similar circumstances.

Martel has repeatedly described herself as post-Catholic, by which she means that she was brought up in a very Catholic environment (even though her father allegedly is an atheist and her mother does not believe in virgins, only in what the virgins believe in) and attended a Catholic school, but at some point she was confronted with doubts about the church and eventually lost faith. In conversation with Mónica Yemayel, Martel shared an anecdote from when she was fifteen that describes the beginnings of this crisis: "I was a volunteer with 'Acción Católica,' and one day I found myself wearing a beige sweater with a Dior label and a gilded little necklace, talking against abortion in front of some very lively young women who were already mothers. And I, who had no idea what screwing was, was lecturing them. Imagine how they looked at me. And I thought, 'what is this nonsense'?" (Yemayel 2018). The notion of post-Catholicism is a major theme that informs her work on many layers, manifesting itself as a profound epistemological skepticism that influences everything from the narrative to the mise-en-scène, the editing, and the handling of sound. In the Salta trilogy, Catholic rituals and practices are invoked time and again but emptied of their redemptive purpose; they have become hallow and meaningless. The apparition of the virgin on a water tank, in *La ciénaga*, becomes a news story, worship and prayer in *La niña santa* is infused with sexual tension, and the faith-based meeting, which Vero attends at the beginning of *La mujer sin cabeza*, introduces us to agnostic Aunt Lala, who converses with spirits. For Amalia, serving god appears to be completely compatible with satisfying sexual desire. In lieu of religious faith, belief in the supernatural has a hold over many of Martel's characters, as becomes evident in the tale of the African Rat, which proves fatal for little Lucho, or the girls' visit to a fabled scene of an accident in *La niña santa*. The ritual Zama undergoes near the end of the film, when he and his fellow men have been captured by an indigenous tribe, is a quasi-religious experience whose meaning remains opaque to us (and most likely to Zama, as well), and that can be read as an anti-Catholic gesture, or even a form of colonialism in reverse.

Post-Catholicism also sheds some light on Martel's surrealist impulses, which manifest themselves in either parodic or horrific mode. Consider the strange incidents that puncture the Salta trilogy (a naked man falling down several stories in *La niña santa*, or a tooth growing in the middle of Lucho's palate), or the surrealism of her later shorts, *Muta* and *Pescados*, and the final part of *Zama*. Along the same lines, Martel's penchant for horror often borders on the surreal or the supernatural, while also conveying the sensation that there is no god to save us. As Martel explained in her interview with us, *Zama* is intentionally devoid of references to religion and the Catholic Church, a fantastic counterfactual projection onto the past. The film conveys Zama's experience that there is no hope, which is very un-Catholic, even if it appears that he finds his peace in the end. Yet what seems like a loss can also be a gain. The Christian hope for redemption, and for an afterlife, lets you endure all kinds of misery—poverty, lack of control over your life, servitude—but once you take that hope away, people might confront that which represses them. The release from Catholic eschatology can itself become a reason for hope; one's destiny is not in the hands of god but your own. Martel's films are rarely ever that optimistic, but they also do not make false promises.

Martel and the New Argentine Cinema

Since about the turn of the millennium, Lucrecia Martel has emerged as one of the leading directors of the highly acclaimed New Argentine

Cinema, as well as one of the most celebrated female auteurs in Latin America. While her oeuvre to date consists of a mere four features, her style has been hailed as that of an iconoclast (Matheou 2010a). The script of her first feature, *La ciénaga* (2001), won the Sundance Institute/NHK Filmmakers Award, and the film subsequently won the Alfred Bauer Prize at the Berlin Film Festival for a feature that opens new perspectives.[5] Her next features, *La niña santa* (2004) and *La mujer sin cabeza* (2008), both screened in the competition for the Palme d'Or in Cannes. After a hiatus of nine years, her latest feature to date, *Zama*, was premiered in Venice in 2017 to wide international acclaim. Closer to home, her films won important prizes in Cuba, Brazil, Uruguay, and her native Argentina. While Martel's international fame rests on these features, she has also worked for television and made numerous shorts, including *Rey Muerto/Dead King* (1995), a spoof on the Western that won first prize at the Havana Film Festival and marked her international breakthrough. Her reputation has been furthermore enhanced by the fact that she served as a member of the jury for film festivals in Venice, Cannes, and Berlin. In 2019, Martel served as president of the international jury at Venice, which in its announcement hailed her as "Latin America's most important female director and one of the top female directors worldwide" (Vivarelli, 2019). An early fan and supporter of her work was Pedro Almodóvar, whose company El Deseo coproduced *La niña santa*, *La mujer sin cabeza*, and *Zama*.[6]

Born in 1966 in Salta into a large middle-class family—she is one of seven brothers and sisters—Lucrecia Martel began experimenting with a video camera her father bought when she was sixteen.[7] In interviews she has stated that in these home movies she adopted the position of a silent observer, taking extended footage of friends and family around her until they became oblivious to being filmed and behaved without self-awareness—a strategy she artfully re-creates in her feature films, where the camera "simply acts as if it were another character, present but unseen, neither an objective onlooker nor identifiable as one of the cast" (Page 2013, 79). In others, she persuaded her four brothers and two sisters to act in her invented scenarios.

In 1986, at the age of nineteen, Martel moved to Buenos Aires, arriving with somewhat undefined career goals. David Oubiña cites chemical engineering, history, zoology, art history, and forensic photography as among her short-lived interests (2009b, 91). Finally, she enrolled in

Figure 2. A teenage homemade Western

animation courses at the Escuela de Cine de Animación de Avellaneda (AVEX) and later at ENERC (Escuela Nacional de Experimentación y Realización Cinematográfica/National School of Experimental Film Direction). During this period, she shot her first shorts, including the animated *El 56* (1988), *La otra*/The Other (1989), *Piso 24*/Floor 24 (1989, another animation), and the 21-minute *Besos rojos*/Red Kisses (1991). After the success of *Rey Muerto*, in 1995, she began working in television, at first overseeing a children's program and subsequently directing the documentaries *Encarnación Ezcurra* (1998) and *Las dependencias: Silvina Ocampo*/The Servants (1999), both under producer Lita Stantic. Winning the Sundance Institute/NHK Filmmakers Award for *La ciénaga* allowed her to eventually complete her first feature film, and to make the transition to being a full-time independent filmmaker.

Together with Pablo Trapero, Martín Rejtman, Adrián Caetano, and Lisandro Alonso, Lucrecia Martel today counts as one of the key figures of the New Argentine Cinema, a body of diverse films that has emerged since the late 1990s. As with other important national new waves of the 1960s and 1970s, such as the Nouvelle Vague in France, the Cinema Novo of Brazil, or the New German Cinema, this latest movement in Argentine cinema owes its coherence not least to the extensive attention of both national and international critics. While it may lack the strong stylistic affinities of the Romanian New Wave, or the programmatic rigor of the Dogme95 movement in Denmark, the label is widely acknowledged as legitimate, and even if in the accounts of some critics certain aspects of the movement are contested and emphases differ, a remarkably coherent narrative has emerged.

What unites this diverse body of film are new forms of production and distribution, and the division of labor among various filmmakers. Rejecting the national precursors of the 1970s and 1980s, particularly the auteurism of established directors such as Eliseo Subiela and Fernando Solanas, these new filmmakers favor working in collectives and outside the established national industry, however modest in scale that industry may be.[8] It is a cinema created by, and addressed to, new social groups, seeking to find a new language and a new diction. To reach these groups, it presents viewers with new actors, sometimes lay actors as in Rejtman's or Trapero's early films, who often employ a new acting style that turns away from a classic portrait of manners, or what in Argentina is called *costumbrismo*, and toward "actorship more concerned with observation and ostentation than action" (Andermann 2012, 130). Taking leave from the country's strong melodramatic tradition, these new films largely avoid an exaggerated display of emotions, favoring a dead-pan or introverted affect that challenges viewers to seek meanings rather than to recognize them.

While there are important exceptions, this is a cinema that, at least initially, has worked largely outside established genres. Location shooting takes precedence over studio productions, introducing viewers to spaces in the larger Buenos Aires metropolitan area not previously seen on film: less frequented parts of the downtown area, the suburbs, or the metropolitan periphery. In the films of Martel, it is the provinces of northern Argentina that are portrayed in a new, and often less idyllic, light. A shared feature of these films is their commitment to avoiding clichés and commonplaces, instead demonstrating a desire for telling stories that have not been told, and in ways that haven't been seen or heard. As Gonzalo Aguilar has remarked, "instead of a message to decode, these movies offer us a world: a language, an atmosphere, some characters . . . a *brushstroke*—a brushstroke that does not respond to questions formulated insistently beforehand but sketches out its own questioning" (2008, 16).

As with other important film movements, a number of decisive factors, both pertaining to the nation's film culture as well as to transnational forces—particularly European and North American film festivals—enabled the emergence of the New Argentine Cinema. In Argentina, important new legislature, the founding of numerous film schools, the creation and revival of national festivals, and the increasing importance of film criticism proved decisive. Most of these developments are a direct result of the profound changes in the Argentine film industry and cultural sphere at large since the mid-1990s, and they have affected the conception, production, distribution, and reception of films and their overall rapport with audiences. Key among these developments was the 1994 passage of the Ley del Cine (film law), which guaranteed state support for national productions, and which specifically introduced provisions, both in terms of funding and exhibition, for debut films (*óperas primas*). Apart from lessening the financial risk of budding filmmakers, the law's most concrete impact was increased emphasis on the screenplay, which has become the filmmakers' calling card for securing funding. Martel's script for *La ciénaga*, which ultimately benefitted from a Sundance/NHK award, is a case in point. In a film that employs willfully disorienting camerawork and that emphasizes inertia, immobility, and tenuous relationships among its principal characters, the screenplay, in fact, provides a rigorous and multilayered framework that brings together seemingly meandering plotlines.

There is a certain irony in the fact that during the presidency of Carlos Menem (1989–99), which pushed a neoliberal agenda and advanced the privatization of many key industries, the film industry became one of the most protected sectors. Menem envisioned a film industry that could rival US blockbusters by producing high-budget Argentine genre films featuring major stars. For this purpose, the INCAA (Instituto Nacional de Cine y Artes Audiovisuales/National Institute of Cinema and Audiovisual Arts) was revamped so as to financially support films that follow this model. Because film was now considered a national treasure, INCAA was also charged with funding new directors and their *óperas primas*, including guaranteeing the distribution of their films and helping with the conversion of video to film under its quota system. As a result, the low-budget films of the New Argentine Cinema emerged simultaneously and alongside such prestige-driven and nationally and internationally highly successful films as Fabián Bielinsky's *Nueve reinas/Nine Queens* (2001) and *El aura/The Aura* (2004), as well as Juan José

Campanella's *El hijo de la novia/Son of the Bride* (2001), *Luna de Avellaneda/Avellaneda's Moon* (2004), and the Academy Award–winning *El secreto de sus ojos/The Secret in Their Eyes* (2009)—incidentally, but not coincidentally, all starring Ricardo Darín.

In tandem with these developments intended to revamp film funding, production, and distribution in Argentina, film criticism began to play a decisive role in promoting certain directors, often embedding them in an artistic discourse that shaped the reception of their films in very specific ways—a discourse that has often frustrated filmmakers like Martel who feel that a certain label has been put on them from above. At the same time, directors are well aware that they benefit from a stamp that widens the recognition of their works in an international context, no matter how appropriate that label may ultimately be. Journals such as *Film, Sincortes*, and *Haciendo cine*, which have strong online presences, have joined such established publications as *El amante* to play an increasingly important role in promoting young directors. Among particularly influential critics we find Quintín, who directed the BAFICI (Buenos Aires International Independent Film Festival) from 2001 to 2005; Andrés di Tella, a filmmaker in his own right; and Fernando Martín Peña, a collector, historian, and host of the TV show *Filmoteca: Temas de Cine*, who in 2008 discovered the extended version of Fritz Lang's silent sci-fi classic *Metropolis* (1927). However, it also fair to say that Buenos Aires–based film criticism had a keen self-interest in promoting this new movement, gaining respectability while capitalizing on the films' national and international successes, and even securing the films' inclusion in prominent festivals. As Joanna Page has pointed out, particularly *El amante*'s advocacy of a new generation thus turned into a self-fulfilling prophecy (2009, 3).

Yet another important factor in the resurgence of Argentine cinema in the late 1990s has been the founding of several film schools, which have provided the training ground for the new generation of filmmakers. The most prestigious include the private Fundación Universidad del Cine (FUC), and ENERC, which Martel attended and which falls under the umbrella of INCAA. As a consequence, this period saw a dramatic increase in the number of students enrolled in production classes and of films produced and released per year (Falicov 2003). While in 1997 there were twenty-seven feature films produced in Argentina, by 2004 that number had reached 69 (Aguilar, 216f.). According to Andermann, by 2010 the New Argentine Cinema included more than four hundred films, a number comparable to that of the New German Cinema (1966–82).

Cinema and Crisis

The rise of the New Argentine Cinema coincided with Argentina's turn to a neoliberal economy under President Menem. Menem pegged the Argentine peso to the US dollar, which ultimately resulted in "a phantom stability and hints of welfare" and ended abruptly and dramatically with the 2001–2 economic crisis, when the Argentine bank system all but collapsed (Fiorucci and Klein 2004, 11). The political, economic, and social fallout reached unheard of dimensions, even in a country with a long history of crises. The GDP fell almost 20 percent between 1998 and 2002, which led to widespread protests and food riots. Unemployment almost tripled in the buildup to the crisis, hitting 21.5 percent in 2002. Another important factor was an ideological crisis: Argentina has long considered itself the most Western and European of Latin American countries, and at the beginning of the twentieth century was among the wealthiest nations in the world. The 2001 crisis, which had no equal in other South American countries, suddenly turned Argentina into the poor neighbor of Brazil, Chile, Uruguay and Peru.

But as is often the case, the arts flourish in times of crisis, partly because so many social problems cry out for artistic expression, and partly because artists learn how to make a virtue out of necessity. Indeed, many of the most celebrated films made during the years of the crisis and its fallout were made on extremely low budgets. It is perhaps no coincidence that almost all feature films of the movement reference the crisis in some oblique way—unemployment, debt, a widening gap between the rich and the poor, and a dramatic rise of the precariat are recurring themes. Its victims and losers are most directly portrayed in José Gaggero's *Cama adentro/Live-In Maid* (2004), which revolves around the downward mobility of a middle-aged bourgeois woman and the changing relation to her maid, or in his *Vida en Falco/*Life in a Falcon (2005), a documentary about a homeless man who lives in an abandoned car, the titular Ford Falcon. Caetano's *Bolivia* (2001) focuses on the migrant experience of displacement and the scarcity of labor in

A Poetics of the Senses | 15

the capitol; here the pessimistic portrayal of social descent is offset by the human dignity bestowed on the menial tasks performed by Andean foreign workers. The downbeat comedy *Los guantes mágicos/The Magic Gloves* (Rejtman 2006) centers on the increasingly absurdist exchange of goods, money, and social identities in an economy gone insane.

Martel's features, too, chronicle the fallout of the crisis, though in more circuitous ways. The three films that make up the Salta trilogy, all set in northeastern Argentina, where Martel grew up, revolve around families from the provincial bourgeoisie at specific moments of conflict—be it the social decline of plantation owners drowning in their own inertia (in *La ciénaga*), the sexual awakenings of a teenager caught up in religious mysticism (in *La niña santa*), or the existential crisis of a female dentist trying to cover up a hit-and-run collision (in *La mujer sin cabeza*). Focusing on the decline of the domestic sphere during the postcrisis years, Martel's films dissect the indolence and parochialism of the life of the middle class in the provinces and unearth the decay that lies just beneath the surface. In the process, they also confront viewers with the latent, everyday racism that pervades family and labor relations. The films' somber mood is augmented by subtle but persistent hints at incest; death, too, is omnipresent.

Yet while political issues surface in Martel's films as well as those of her peers, the political is articulated here quite differently than in the films of preceding generations. Clearly, Caetano, Rejtman, Trapero, and Martel share an aversion to the Argentine post-dictatorship cinema of the 1980s, which relied heavily on allegory to tell veiled tales of torture, trauma, and political opportunism. As Aguilar has argued, the films of the New Argentine Cinema reject the political imperative (what to do) and the identitarian imperative (what we are like) that were crucial for the films came before it (2008, 16). Instead, the new films display thematic ambiguities and narratives of dispersion that challenge viewers to establish new modes of reception and identification. They employ film as a medium of opacity rather than transparency, favoring an anti-explanatory approach that demands viewers make up their own minds. If the characters find themselves within stories whose meaning are beyond their grasp, so do we, the spectators: the comfort denied to them is not afforded to the viewers, either.

Rather than dwelling on the nation's history, the New Argentine Cinema is mostly concerned with the present, and most of the films convey minimalist stories about characters unencumbered by the past. Argentine film criticism has echoed this disconnection with the past by claiming that its twenty-first-century cinema owes very little to national predecessors. The filmmakers, too, have often considered themselves a generation of orphans, thereby denying any indebtedness to precursors—a common move presaged by other new waves. If there are acknowledged influences, they come from European art cinema (Italian neorealism, Robert Bresson, and Michelangelo Antonioni are frequently cited) and American independent auteurs like John Cassavetes or Richard Linklater. Martel, in turn, has referred to the films of David Cronenberg and David Lynch, which, like hers, have a penchant for the uncanny and horror.

On the whole, however, Martel has been reluctant to accept the label New Argentine Cinema, even if, at least on the festival circuit, she has profited from such branding. Repeatedly, she has stated that she considers the term "absurd" (Bettendorf and Pérez Rial 2014a, 192) or that she feels more like a holdover from, or the tail (*coletazo*) of, the old Argentine cinema (García and Rojas 2004, 14). Indeed, there are numerous ways she differs from her above-cited peers. In contrast to their general disavowal of national film history, Martel has talked about Argentine directors she cherishes, indicating that the notion of being orphans may be overstating the case. In particular, she has singled out Leonardo Favio, a member of the so-called 1960s generation (*generación del sesenta*), which has at times been compared to the generation of the 1990s (Ulrich 2011; F. Peña 2003). Equally important for Martel is the significance of María Luisa Bemberg, particularly her standing in Argentina's film industry: "Bemberg showed our generation how as a woman one can make successful films and that was an enormous influence" (García and Rojas 2008, 10). And elsewhere she has added Torre Nilsson as an important precursor (Bettendorf and Pérez Rial 2014a, 192).

Argentine critics have by and large cited Italian neorealism as one of the most formative influences of the New Argentine Cinema, often referencing as prime examples Rejtman's *Rapado/Cropped Head* (1992), Trapero's *Mundo grua/Crane World* (1999), and Caetano's *Bolivia* (2001). Indeed, Martel shares with them, and with neorealism in general, a preference for location shooting and the casting of lay actors, many of them children and adolescents. Yet Martel's dark ruralism invokes a mood and tone distinctly different from the above titles; hers is a highly constructed, artificial realism that makes no claim to authenticity. In further contrast to the above directors, from her first feature onward Martel has used established stars such as Graciela Borges and Mercedes Morán, but cast them against character and opposite nonprofessional actors, thus portraying well-known actors in a fresh light. Yet another difference to most filmmakers of the New Argentine Cinema is Martel's approach to genre conventions, which is highly original and idiosyncratic. Elements from, say, horror or the melodrama are frequently evoked. These enunciations create an atmosphere yet desist from employing the respective genres' narrative conventions—at times they feel like teasers that do not deliver. The result is often an open-ended form that challenges viewers to provide their own sense of closure. *Zama* can be seen as a radical reworking of the colonial frontier story that defies the conventions set by both Argentine and international period dramas.

Perhaps the single most consequential difference is that Martel has worked from the beginning with noted producer Lita Stantic while her peers self-produced or coproduced their first film or films. A figure of enormous standing, Stantic has played a fundamental role in Argentine cinema, and she is one of the few who straddle the generational divide from the early 1980s to the present. First teaming up with María Luisa Bemberg, the powerful duo broke the gender barrier with a series of highly acclaimed films, including *Momentos* (1981), *Señora de nadie/Nobody's Wife* (1982), *Camila* (1984), *Miss Mary* (1986) and *Yo, la peor de todas/I, Worst of All* (1990). Stantic's only film as director is the drama *Un muro de silencio/A Wall of Silence* (1993), which stars Vanessa Redgrave as a British director making a film about a woman whose husband was disappeared during the military dictatorship and who herself was kidnapped and detained in a clandestine camp. Set in 1989, the year of the *indulto* (amnesty laws) that pardoned the military leaders put on trial four years earlier, the film is a powerful exploration of the role of memory and justice in post-dictatorship Argentina that draws on Stantic's own traumatic experience of the disappearance of her partner, Pablo Szir. Apart from her work as producer and director, Stantic is also an influential figure in the larger cultural sphere. A former president of the Cámara Argentina de la Industria Cinematográfica/

Board of Argentine Industrial Cinematography (1986–96), she is also the founder of the Festival del Cine y la Mujer/Festival of Women Filmmakers. During the years of censorship, she worked with Cine Liberación to hold underground screenings of banned films (Galt 2013, 70). Most importantly for Martel's context, however, is Stantic's role as one of very few established producers to take on the projects of younger directors (apart from Martel, she has also worked with Trapero, Caetano, and Diego Lerman), reinventing herself in the process and becoming a crucial facilitator whose real impact on the latest generation has still not been fully acknowledged.

Martel first met Stantic while working for television; it was Stantic who encouraged her to submit the screenplay of *La ciénaga* to the Sundance script competition. Martel's decision to work with established stars clearly shows Stantic's influence; the choice is unique among her peers, who turned to casting big names only once they had achieved a certain international recognition. Because of Stantic's role as producer, Martel's directorial debut was not really a low-budget affair (as most other directors' were), and its backing by private investors such as Cuatro Cabezas was an extraordinary achievement for an *ópera prima*, as Quintín has observed (2000, 24). With *Zama*, Martel and Stantic parted ways, because Martel felt that the landscape for independent international coproductions had changed dramatically over the recent years, to a point that Lita Stantic's mode of production was no longer in keeping with the times and Martel's own ambitions.[9]

A Beginning in Shorts and Television

Martel first gained international prominence on the festival circuit when her short *Rey Muerto* took first prize at the Havana Film Festival. The film had originally been released in Argentina as part of the omnibus film *Historias breves/Short Histories*, a compilation of ten shorts assembled by FUC graduates and released by INCAA in 1995 (incidentally the year the Dogme95 manifesto was published). Among the featured directors were several now considered key members of the New Argentine Cinema, including Caetano, Gaggero, Bruno Stagnaro, and Daniel Burman, and *Historias breves* is now widely considered the movement's first official sign of life. *Rey Muerto* was a particular standout in this compilation, a cri de coeur that first drew attention to Martel's unique voice.

Evoking the sensibility of a spaghetti Western, with its wind-swept dusty roads, barren landscape, slow-motion photography, and overdrawn macho masculinity, the film tells the story of a woman named Juana who, together with her three children, runs away from her abusive husband. In a showdown on a country road, he catches up to her and confronts her, but before he can lay a hand on her she shoots him in the head. Bathed in the warm light of the proverbial sunset, the liberated Juana and her children safely cross a bridge, presumably toward a better future awaiting on the other shore.

The film's title is the name of a (fictitious) small town in the Salta region where the film is set (this will also be the setting for the estate in *La ciénaga*), but it also references the defeat of the patriarch at the film's end—as the husband holds his bloody head in agony, we cut to a sign bearing the town's name, a tongue-in-cheek comment on the feminist dimension of this unconventional Western. Unlike Martel's later features, this short tells its story in bold strokes that quickly establish the sharp contrast between the aggressive husband and his vulnerable wife whose getaway plans challenge his control over her. In a series of small vignettes, we watch him bragging with his buddies in a local bar, shooting wildly at flying ducks, or, in a flashback (the only one in Martel's entire oeuvre), striking violently at his wife when he catches her preparing a meal in the company of another man. Juana, in the meantime, is seen furtively walking down what looks like the main street of US westerns, exposed to the gaze of the barber, the neighbors, and her husband's buddies, who quickly get word to him and initiate a hot pursuit. But Juana has expected as much. She has pawned her last household items and purchased a gun with the modest proceeds, with which she shoots him. When the fatally wounded husband sinks to the ground, it is for the viewer to decide whether he cries out in agony or mere surprise.

Like traditional Westerns, *Rey Muerto* creates its suspense by intercutting scenes of the weaker party's slow getaway with the rapidly encroaching threat of the strong assailant; mere onlookers, the cowardly town people passively stand by, fearing for both Juana's safety and their own. Loud rhythmic salsa music propels the action forward, juxtaposed with ominous drums that heighten the suspense. As in most Westerns, "good" wins over "evil," but the reversal of gender roles, in which the weak female upends the strong male, provides a fresh outlook. While

Figure 3. Juana (Sandra Ceballos) confronts her abusive husband in the feminist spaghetti Western *Rey Muerto*

Martel's feature films will frequently reference elements of the horror film, none of them espouse the conventions of an established popular genre to the same extent as this short. *Rey Muerto*'s playful subversion of stereotypes, both on the visual level as well as on the level of narrative, is indeed unique. In interviews Martel has underscored her fondness for both American and European Westerns, which were among the few international films that were screened in her hometown. Another important aspect of the film is its sense of humor, signaled by the title's double entendre, which recalls slapstick traditions but also the early films of Quentin Tarantino, who had just burst onto the scene one year earlier with *Pulp Fiction*. Humor will also inform her later films, but there it is transformed into a subtle and embedded humor that conveys a general and profound sense of unmooring and being off-kilter.

Rey Muerto stands out among Martel's works that predate *La ciénaga* not only because of the visibility it brought her, but also because it's the only film from this period she still acknowledges. The shorts that came

A Poetics of the Senses | 21

before and the television work that followed she now considers inferior and simplistic.[10] And indeed, looking back at them, the cinematography, sound design, editing, and the frequent use of voice-over or talking heads very much bear the marks of a film student and beginning television director and display yet none of the sophistication of her later features. Nevertheless, some thematic concerns, which have remained constant throughout her career, are already present, including her interest in gender identity, the role of women in Argentine society and history, or the relation between servants and their masters. Hardly ever discussed by critics, they are well worth a second look.

La otra (1990) is a nine-minute snapshot of a group of Buenos Aires drag queens, or *transformistas*, mostly comprised of brief interviews and clips of their performances. Like transvestites, the members of this loosely defined group wear women's makeup, false eyelashes, dresses, and high heels when they sing and perform, but they are careful not to create the illusion of a complete gender reversal. As one dancer explains, it is a performance that relies on "transforming into a woman without stopping being a man," thus emphasizing the playfulness of gender manipulation. Martel's first work for television, and her first collaboration with producer Lita Stantic, was *Encarnación Ezcurra* (1998), a portrait of María de la Encarnación Ezcurra y Arguibel, the much-revered wife of the politician Juan Manuel de Rosas. A powerful but controversial politician and army officer who governed Buenos Aires Province and who led fights in the provinces against the indigenous population, Rosas was aided in his ambition by the savvy and unconditional support of his wife, a gun-carrying, independently minded woman who kept him abreast by letters of political intrigue and latest development. The film is comprised of a voice-over reading excerpts from nineteen letters they exchanged, as well as newspaper articles of the time, which are set against footage of various Argentine silent and classic films, their slapstick creating a humorous contrast to the more somber voice-over. Interspersed is the commentary of four historians, filmed in the back-seat of a driving car, who hold forth about various aspects of Ezcurra's political and personal life. Focusing on the 1830s, only two decades after Argentine independence and three after the events depicted in *Zama*, this somewhat clumsy, made-for-television film allows us to grasp how radically different Martel's representation of history has become in the years since. Nevertheless, as a document to an exceptional and influential woman too often ignored by historians, *Encarnación Ezcurra* must in itself count as an attempt to rewrite history.

Exceptional and influential are also adjectives that describe the Argentine writer and poet Silvina Ocampo, the subject of Martel's follow-up *Las dependencias* (1999), also produced for TV by Stantic as part of the *Historias de vida* series. While famous already during her lifetime, Ocampo kept a low profile in public and was extremely camera shy (she considered herself ugly, we learn); as if to preserve this sense of privacy, Martel choses to tell the poet's story through the perspectives of her private secretary and her seamstress, who both joined the household at a young age and worked for Ocampo for many years. Ocampo had an intimate relationship with both of them, wrote them letters from her travels in Europe, and even offered her secretary the informal *tú* instead of the formal *Usted*. Conversations of the two employees describing their experiences are contrasted with footage of two literary giants—Ocampo's late husband, Adolfo Bioy Casares, and his friend Jorge Luis Borges, who visited the house every day—establishing a beautiful interplay between the public, literary world and the intimate realm of the household. Yet there can be no doubt which aspect really interests Martel: the film's title references the servants' quarters, and indeed Martel's emphasis already points to the Salta trilogy, even though Ocampo's servants are white and educated (the seamstress, we learn, actually emigrated from Spain and, like her *patróna*, also wrote poetry). Ocampo has described her predilection for the life of the servants in her poem "La casa natal," and Martel's attraction to Ocampo's poetry rests on a shared interest in "the subterranean power struggles between parents, children and servants" (Page 2009, 186).

Formally, too, *Las dependencias* is cut from a different cloth than *Encarnación Ezcurra*. The color cinematography is broken up by black-and-white tracking shots of a camera moving through the stairways and rooms of a largely empty house while we listen to Ocampo's voice reciting poetry. The unmoored camera work and the disembodied voice evoke an eerie and slightly uncanny sensation that will be a hallmark of the Salta trilogy. "All of Ocampo's stories have seamstresses," a voice-over tells us, creating a moment of self-reflexivity that is further amplified when we realize that Martel wears the same style of glasses Ocampo did.

A Poetics of the Senses | 23

Rarely considered in discussions of Martel's oeuvre, *Las dependencias* is a remarkably sure-footed and mature work that announces many of her central themes as well as her aesthetic sensibilities.

A Cinema of and for the Senses

As the German critic and writer Siegfried Kracauer noted in *Theory of Film* (quoted in the opening epigraph to this section), the act of watching films impacts spectators on many different levels, fully engaging the senses in comprehensive ways that not only precede but also precondition any intellectual reckoning. Before we understand, we experience. Watching Martel's films, I contend, is at times an especially hypnotic and deeply immersive experience, often continuing long after they have ended. Because of their pronounced affective dimension, her films engage *all* senses and thus challenge the primacy of the visual. The director makes a number of aesthetic and narrative choices to create this profound impact. On the most general level, Martel's cinema revolves around a radical reorganization of time and space. Her films rarely use establishing shots, conventional transitions between scenes are mostly omitted, and dialogue is not a motor for plot advancement. Her camera prefers to capture people from oblique angles to obstruct identification, and it frequently adopts the perspective of a child to render what is shown with a sense of curiosity and uncertainty (most notably so in *La ciénaga*). Montage techniques emphasize the unresolved, the truncated, and the elliptical. Sound often undercuts visual information, thus further deactivating the power of the image.

Indeed, Martel's highly original use of sound has become a widely acknowledged trademark of her films. All her films include densely layered soundscapes in which human voices, ambient noises, and ominous or eerie sounds create a thick and often disorienting environment. Sounds are usually heard before their sources are seen, if they are seen, and identified, at all. Martel cites aesthetic, political, and economic reasons for her idiosyncratic approach. One characteristic of sound is its epistemological primacy: "It seems to me that visually we are far more colonized [than in terms of hearing]. [. . .] Sound is still more loose. One hears a lot more than one sees" (quoted in Porta Fouz 2008, 22). Elsewhere, she has added, "Sound is the first thing that comes to us as humans. [. . .] the sound environment we grew up in determines us and shapes us [. . .] visual aspects definitely come second" (quoted in Oumano 2011, 39).

Martel's penchant for horror also comes into play here: while it is possible to close one's eyes during frightening scenes, covering one's ears is nearly impossible. In conversation with Matthijs Wouter Knol during the 2013 Berlinale Talent Campus, she explained the pragmatic dimension of favoring sound, emphasizing that a clear concept of the soundscape allows her to film more economically. When she comes to the set, this concept is firmly in place and the position of the camera is then developed accordingly. While Martel has changed cinematographers with each film, she continues to work with the same sound editor, Guido Berenblum, a task she generally considers undervalued and far more challenging than operating the camera.

To illustrate how she understands the working of sound, Martel has turned again to the metaphor of the swimming pool. "When you are in a swimming pool," she has commented to Demetrios Mattheou, "you are surrounded by water and you can feel it because its presence has an impact on your breathing. You cannot ignore that you're under water. Sound makes you feel this sensation" (2010, 310; see also Bettendorf and Pérez Rial 2014a, 188). In a 2015 featurette, "Siete notas sobre cine"/"Seven Notes on Cinema," which she made for the Criterion DVD of *La ciénaga*, she further explains that the movie theater is like a pool turned on its side, with the waterline representing the screen, while viewers find themselves submerged in the water. While the image on the screen is two-dimensional, she contends, the sound is actually tactile and hence the only three-dimensional part of the cinematic experience.

The primacy of sound also determines the use of music, which she uses sparingly and almost always diegetically, favoring songs by her Salteño compatriot Jorge Cafrune, as well as those of José Larralde. Non-diegetic music meant to enhance emotions and provide narrative structure and smooth transitions clearly contradicts the environment of unease her films try to create: "Music always allows the viewer to anticipate and even prejudge what's next. Sound only allows the simultaneity of the experience" (quoted in Matheou 2010b). *Zama* was her first feature to break with this practice, but even here the music does not guide the audience but rather surprises them, creating a slight sense of parody and incongruity.

Dialogue in Martel's films is often little more than another unintelligible element of the dense soundtrack. Even when we can understand what her characters are saying, their language will sound strange to residents of Buenos Aires because of a rather distinct intonation, accent, and argot. Much of the humor of these films, which is closely tied to language, is lost on foreign audiences. As Martel has often underscored, her use of dialogue is heavily influenced by how people in Salta speak, including her own family home, but it is inflected by the prose of writers such as Horacio Quiroga, whose uncanny and unsettling tales take place predominantly in the northern provinces of Argentina (Page 2013; Schroeder 2016, 266–81).

In sync with the disorienting arrangement of sound and space is the unique treatment of time. Martel's films contain few concrete markers of the passage of time such as shots of dawn or dusk, the consummation of meals, or even references to what time, day, or month it might be. With the exception of *Zama*, her features are all set in the present, yet they make almost no reference to current events. Typically, Martel's films do not cover long periods of time, focusing instead on only a few days in their protagonists' lives. The places they inhabit seem hermetically sealed off from the rest of the world (such as the estate in *La ciénaga* or the crumbling hotel in *La niña santa*), creating a sense of claustrophobia or abandonment—sensations that Martel's films seek to reproduce in the viewers. *Zama*'s outpost at the end of the world marks a culmination, and ultimately a revolt against, this retreat from life.

Equally unique is Martel's treatment of the narrative. A repeated strategy is to remove the plot from the center of attention and focus instead on the nondramatic moments on the margins. In *La ciénaga*, for example, extensive screen time is taken up by observing a group of liquored-up adults lounging around a brackish swimming pool while their unsupervised children are repeatedly shown lying on their beds, absorbed in semi-erotic daydreaming. The languid camera movements and the siesta-pace editing create a sensation of real time; indeed, the camera often lingers on its subjects significantly longer than would be necessary to deliver narrative information. These strategies evoke sentiments of premonition and doom, thereby recalling some of the generic attributes of horror, further referenced in titles such as *La ciénaga* and *La mujer sin cabeza*, which sound like those of cheap horror movies.

Another distinctive feature is the films' narrative minimalism. Characters engage in activities that have no causal relation to the plot, structuring conflicts are underdeveloped, and endings are unresolved. Martel's films abound with narrative ellipses—important things are simply left out, a practice that culminates in *Zama* (adapted from a highly elliptical novel). *La mujer sin cabeza* revolves entirely around the question of whether or not its female protagonist, Vero, has run over a child while driving along a dusty country road. There is some evidence that she did, but the question remains unanswered. Instead, the film shows how this incertitude affects Vero and those around her as they try to cover up a crime that may not even have been committed.

Consequently, Martel's narratives are puzzles in which not all pieces ultimately fall into place. (Martel has claimed that some of her characters are a mystery even to her.) Devoid of any narrative omniscience—be it through the use of a voice-over or conventional establishing shots—they are reluctant to provide information about their respective characters' past, their personal histories, and even their relation to one another. The dialogue, too, rarely conveys vital information that explains the characters' motivations or propels the plot. The general lack of character development is underscored by a minimalistic and restrained acting style that eschews the melodramatic traditions of Argentine cinema. The overall effect of Martel's aesthetic choices is to call into question the facile promise of realism or naturalism and to keep viewers on edge: "What I want to achieve in my films is a form of estrangement that is completely invisible. It is a state of permanent suspicion, a situation in which we do not know on which level of reality or fantasy we are, or when we're crossing from one to the other" ("Siento que tengo que superarme" 2004). Martel's reference to levels (*planos*) points to a favorite term of hers, namely layers. "What I mean by layers," she told Amy Taubin in 2009, "is a form of accumulation, which makes plot no longer necessary in its classical sense. I work with a number of elements that are tied together, and each one of them is present in each scene in different positions, different perspectives, foreground or background" (2009b). Apart from sound, the mise-en-scène, shallow-focus photography, and the recurrent use of objects are key factors in the continuous rearrangement of these layers, creating an intra- and inter-filmic network of cross-references that often becomes evident only after multiple viewings.

More than ten years after completing the Salta trilogy, the powerful impact of Lucrecia Martel's work can be felt not only in Argentina, but in all of Latin America and indeed globally. While it has been particularly influential in the development of a queer cinema in Latin America, it has also, as Deborah Martin summarizes, "paved the way for a new wave of Argentine women filmmakers making films about children and marginal sexualities, and/or using tactile and immersive film language and experimentation with sound to destabilize the cultural hegemony of the visual, the masculine and the adult" (2017, 242). In the immediate wake of the Salta trilogy, there have been Lucia Puenzo's *El niño pez/The Fish Child* (2009) and Julia Solomonoff's *El ultimo verano de la boyita/The Last Summer of La Boyita* (2009), as well as films by Albertina Carri and Celina Murga that show not only thematic connections but also affinities with Martel's penchant for water metaphors, for Martel's idiosyncratic reordering of time and space, and for her elliptic narratives.

Clearly cementing both Martel's singularity as well as acknowledging her extraordinary influence, critic A. O. Scott observed in a review of the 2018 New York Film Festival that great filmmakers are genres unto themselves, citing the Chilean film *Muy tarde para morir joven/Too Late to Die Young*, by Dominga Sotomayor Castillo, as an example for a film that "might belong to a genre called Lucrecia Martel." "Its oblique narrative strategy and close scrutiny of family dynamics," Scott goes on to note, are reminiscent of the Argentine's work (2018). Eric Kohn, in a IndieWire review of the same film, describes it as "*Captain Fantastic* meets Lucrecia Martel" (2017). A similar claim could be made with regard to *Los perros/The Dogs* (Marcela Said, 2017) and *La reina del miedo/The Queen of Fear* (2018), for which the well-known Argentine actor Valeria Bertuccelli, in her directorial debut, teamed up with Fabiana Tiscornia, who had served as assistant director on *Zama*. Said's second feature scrutinizes the hypocrisy and inner rottenness of upper-class Chileans who harbor a dark secret about their activities during the military junta, clearly recalling *La mujer sin cabeza*; in turn, *La reina del miedo*, about a young actor (Bertuccelli) stuck in her own fame, evokes the quagmire of Martel's middle-aged women. And in both the Chilean and the Argentine films dogs bark incessantly and a stagnant pool figures prominently.

Drowning in Indolence: *La ciénaga*

> The film depicts a society [. . .] that lives vaguely hoping that nothing will ever change, and in terror of everything repeating itself, indefinitely.
>
> —Lucrecia Martel, director's statement, 2001

The celebrated opening of Lucrecia Martel's *La ciénaga* introduces *in nuce* the themes, locations, major personae, and structuring oppositions that inform much of the rest of the film, creating a mood of premonition that hints at decay, forbidden sexuality, impending violence, and latent horror. The film opens onto a gray sky over a densely wooded hill before cutting to a close-up of a mound of luscious red peppers lying in the sun. Rumbling clouds and thunder announce an imminent storm. The first credits fade onto the screen, dissolving quickly to make space for an extreme close-up of a wineglass being refilled with red wine, the loud clinking of ice cubes amplified by the screaming of birds and the chirping of cicadas. Another set of credits appears—introducing the major stars, Graciela Borges and Mercedes Morán—while diegetic sound gives way to an uncanny, low-frequency rumble. We return to a woman in a bathing suit holding the glass of wine—Mecha, played by the just announced Borges—but breaking with conventions, her face fills only part of the frame as she gets up to drag her lawn chair across the deck of a swimming pool with brackish water; Gregorio, her husband (Martín Adjemián), and other guests follow suit, the camera pitilessly scouring the sagging flesh of their midriffs while the soundtrack uncomfortably amplifies the screeching of metal along the concrete deck.

Another quick set of credits is followed by a cut to moving curtains casting a shadow on the dimly lit wall of a bedroom in which Momi, Mecha's younger daughter (Sofia Bertoletto), and Isabel, the maid (Andrea López), are taking a siesta. Caressing Isabel, Momi begins to softly pray, thanking God for giving her Isabel and kissing the sleeve of the servant's uniform like the beads of a rosary. Outside, Mecha and Gregorio are drowsily looking toward the hills from which loud clapping noises are heard—are they thunder or gunshots?—while Mecha wonders with whom Joaquín (Diego Baenas), her younger son, might be hunting out there. We cut to a handheld camera that follows a boy with a rifle swiftly moving through the dense underbrush of the forest, racing after loudly barking dogs who have tracked down a cow trapped in a deadly swamp. Joaquín takes aim to relieve the doomed animal, but before we find out whether he actually pulls the trigger, we cut back to the parents lazily drowsing alongside the putrid pool, oblivious to both children's potentially dangerous pursuits.

The three locations contrasted in the opening minutes—the bedroom, the greenish pool, and the hillside forest with its deadly quicksand—will provide key settings for much of *La ciénaga*; they are all part of La Mandrágora (lit. the mandrake), the farm and summer residence of Mecha's large family, situated in the province of Salta, and surrounded by the Yungas forests that extend over the eastern slope of the Andes. All three locations embody stagnation, lack of motion, and entrapment, with the title-giving swamp adding a threatening dimension to this immobility. Furthering the paralysis is the steamy ambience of the height of summer, a humid and sultry affair in this part of the country, which people try to endure through extended siestas and poolside lounging, as well as the intoxicating effects of alcohol (further enhanced by the symbolism of the mandrake, a plant revered for its anesthetic or hallucinogenic effects, which, according to legend, lets out a scream when plucked).

Just beneath these impenetrable surfaces, something is brewing. The three arrested images—Momi confessing her love to the sleeping Isabel; the smashed Mecha and Gregorio staring toward the mist-covered hills; Joaquín pointing his rifle at the trapped cow—all signal an eruption ready to occur at any moment. Only moments later, having gathered up an armful of empty glasses, Mecha will fall near the pool—the glasses break, the wine spills, Mecha begins to bleed, and the thunderstorm erupts: different but related fluids are suddenly, and violently, released at the same time. Indeed, the entire film is one extended premonition of a catastrophe waiting to happen. When it finally occurs, it does so unrelated to any of the ominous forebodings that litter the film, catching the characters as well as the viewers completely off guard, and radically questioning the meaning of life and death.

The disquieting and disorienting opening sequence sets a mood that wavers between sensuality, dread, paralysis, and impending catastrophe. Indeed, the slithering fonts of the credits and its accompanying low-frequency rumble, the invisible presence of a visceral threat, and the mother's stupor that fogs her perception while not entirely blinding it are ingredients common to cheap horror films. As the film progresses, this is borne out by the zombielike existences of Mecha and Gregorio, by the repeated flowing of blood, and by the development of sexual desires that push against taboos on homosexuality, incest, and racial mixing. But unlike in "real" horror films, no monster or evil force will attack—the threat that looms large over La Mandrágora will remain outside the frame for the entirety of the film. When death does strike, it does so in an almost banal and meaningless form that renders it even more cruel.

The uncanny sensation that Lucrecia Martel creates in the opening sequence results from careful aesthetic choices. With the absence of any establishing shots, viewers are left to their own devices to map the relation of the various locations, as well as those between the characters introduced. Even after repeated viewings, it remains impossible to determine the exact layout of Mecha's meandering house and its many bedrooms, or its proximity to the city. (In an interview, Martel has asserted that she *never* mentions city names in her films [B. Brooks 2011], and the names of the village of Rey Muerto and the town of La Ciénaga are entirely fictional.) Never once do we witness characters traversing spaces between important locales, further rendering futile any attempt to understand the lay of the land. The characters' restricted movements are paralleled by that of the camera, which makes almost no use of traveling shots, zooms, slow-motion photography, or flashback narration (all prominent in the over-the-top *Rey Muerto*). The lack of traditional modes of orientation is further augmented by the disquieting use of sound, which repeatedly assumes a primacy over the visual. While sound connects spaces that are physically separated—the dragging lawn chairs are audible in Isabel's room, while the gunshots from the hill are heard everywhere—it often contradicts, rather than complements, the visual information, literally drowning out what we see, thus following Robert Bresson's advice about sound: "What is for the eye must not duplicate what is for the ear" (1986, 50).

The color palette, too, relies on strong, denaturalizing contrasts. It is dominated by the complementary colors of red and green—represented by the red peppers (which, as we later learn, are the main crop of the farm and the family's source of income), the wine, and the blood, and the green hills and putrid water of the pool—while warmer, more harmonious tones are largely absent. Throughout the film, the grayish color of a sky heavy with rain clouds provides the main background for the exterior shots, while the respective interiors of Mecha's and Tali's house are predominantly dark, enhancing the film's overall sense of claustrophobia and asphyxiation.

When people come into view, they appear at the edge of the frame (Mecha), in near darkness (Momi), or are seen from behind (Joaquín), and their identity is barely sketched. Indeed, the entire make-up of Mecha's and her cousin Tali's extended families is never fully established, leaving viewers in a mild state of confusion throughout the film. Similarly, the meandering narrative avoids dramatic plot points (with one important exception), choosing to follow one main character before abandoning her in favor of another; instead of pursuing a narrative arc or a sense of closure, the film's movement is circular, leaving viewers at the end exactly where they started.

Yet while the term *plot* may be too strong a word to summarize the events of *La ciénaga*, certain narrative strands do evolve. The film revolves around Mecha, a matriarch who presides over a family of four children, a good-for-nothing husband, and several maids, all spending a sweltering summer on the hacienda La Mandrágora, and around her cousin Tali (Morán), who also has four children and lives in a nearby city. At the beginning of the film, the two women meet by coincidence in the city hospital, where Mecha is being treated for the cuts to her chest due to her drunken fall, while Tali's son Luciano is being patched up for leg injuries. Throughout the film, the two extended families intermingle, with several subplots developing but none really moving forward: the boys go hunting in the hills surrounding the farm; Mecha's oldest son, José, visits from Buenos Aires; the girls shop in the city for a shirt for one of the brothers; the television reports the sighting of the Virgin on a water tank; Mecha and Tali make plans for a shopping trip to Bolivia that never materializes; and at the end, Luciano, Tali's youngest son, falls off a ladder in the courtyard of his house, his death providing a sudden and apparently meaningless ending to a story that rejects any sense of closure.

If this summary indicates that *La ciénaga* stubbornly refuses any linearity, this resistance becomes even clearer when we contrast it with Martel's own idiosyncratic synopsis:

> February in the northeast of Argentina. The sun cracks the earth and tropical rains. In the mountains, some of the soil turns into swamps. These swamps [*ciénagas*] are deadly traps for heavier animals, yet for the lucky vermin they are hotbeds. This story is not about swamps, though, but about the town La Ciénaga and its surroundings. About 90 km from there is the village Rey Muerto and close to there is the farm the Mandrake. The mandrake is a plant that was used as a sedative, before there was ether and morphine, when it was necessary to alleviate people from serious pain, such as an amputation. In our story, it is the name of a farm where red peppers are harvested, and where Mecha spends her summer, a woman in her fifties with four children and a husband who dyes his hair. But that's something to be quickly forgotten after a few drinks. Although, as Tali says, alcohol enters through one door but doesn't leave through the other. Tali is Mecha's cousin. She also has four children, and a husband who loves his house, hunting, and his children. She lives in La Ciénaga, in a house without swimming pool. Two accidents bring the two families together in the countryside, while they are trying to survive a hellish summer.[11]

It is striking that this so-called synopsis reveals next to nothing about the film's plot nor its protagonists, and, as noted, the film itself indeed avoids any direct reference to the geographical markers given above. With its suggestive imagery of sweltering heat, deadly swamps, and plants associated with witchcraft, the passage is rich in atmosphere but poor in dramatic development; only the last sentence provides a nod toward creating suspense, as if to comply with the all-important mandate of "pitching a story" (the reader is invited to wonder, "How *will* these families actually survive this summer?")—a half-hearted promise on which the actual film never really makes good.

The depiction of a crumbling family of elevated status has a strong tradition in Argentine cinema, accounting for some of the best films the country has produced. Among them, particularly Leopoldo Torre Nilsson's *La casa del angel/The House of the Angel* (1957) and *La caída/ The Fall* (1959) stand out, both after screenplays by Beatriz Guido and starring Elsa Daniel. Nilsson's *Fin de fiesta/The Party Is Over* (1960) first established Graciela Borges as a melodramatic actor, a form of stardom that clearly serves as invisible backstory for Martel's has-been Mecha. Several critics have particularly pointed to the influence of María Luisa Bemberg's *Miss Mary* (1986), as has Martel herself (Quintín 2000, 28).[12] The two films invite comparison not only because both revolve around the declining fortunes of a large family, but also because both were produced by Lita Stantic, and because Bemberg and Martel both stand out as celebrated female auteurs within a male-dominated field.

Set in the late 1930s, during the so-called Infamous Decade, when a democratically elected government was replaced by conservative forces under General José Félix Uriburu, Bemberg's film depicts in extended flashbacks the life of an English governess, Miss Mary, who has been hired by an aristocratic landowner to educate his son and two daughters. With its focus on female childhood against the backdrop of a colonial legacy, the film offers a scathing critique of the hypocrisy of Argentine patriarchy. One victim of this system is the figure of the mother, significantly also called Mecha. Like Martel's character, Bemberg's is a matriarch who suffers from her husband's adultery and who hides her frustration behind large sunglasses. Bemberg has commented that *Miss Mary* is a film about "a great emptiness" and that her Mecha figure wilts under "the crippling circularity of her existence" (Torrents 1990, 174, 171), a description that certainly fits the Mecha of *La ciénaga*, though with the important exception that Martel's character has seemingly only herself to blame.

As notable as the similarities are the ways in which the two films differ, which bring into relief Martel's idiosyncratic style of directing. Relying on an omniscient form of storytelling, *Miss Mary* is explicit in rendering the reasons for the decline of the estate and the family, thus putting viewers in a position to render judgment. Not only does the film look back on a period now long gone, it also shows why and how it had to end, insisting on a separation between past and present, all of which Martel avoids. In *La ciénaga*, the stranglehold of the past extends into the present, and the future looks bleak as well. If in *Miss Mary* the lines between oppressor and oppressed are clearly drawn, in Martel's film this relationship is constantly changing. "All characters, including the

Figure 4. Another alienated matriarch named Mecha: Nacha Guevara in María Luisa Bemberg's *Miss Mary*

children, participate in some way in the perverse exercising of power," observe Schwarzböck and Salas (2001, 12).

While *Miss Mary* is the portrait of a certain era, which Bemberg paints with both a critical eye and a certain sense of nostalgia, *La ciénaga* is set in the here and now and carefully avoids any reference to specific current events. Yet many critics, particularly in Argentina, have read *La ciénaga* as a film about the decline of the provincial bourgeoisie, which in turn is a stand-in for a stagnant and paralyzed society. According to such a reading, the dysfunctional middle-class family and its dilapidated country estate become an image of a societal pillar beyond repair. For David Oubiña, the film is an indirect portrait of "what remains of Argentina after the military rule of the 1970s and the socioeconomic decline of the '80s and '90s" (2009b, 61). Paola Arboleda Ríos is even more specific and claims that the film's references to a social and psychological crisis are rooted in more recent events, namely the negative impact of the neoliberal agenda of the Menem presidency. "*La ciénaga* deals, in an allegorical manner, with the social effects of the economic disasters

Argentina faced since the late 1990s," she observes, "the corporate take-over of the finances of the State, the privatization of the social security system, corruption at high levels, including the judicial system, excessive presidential expenses, high salaries of government employees, and permanent tax frauds. These economic failures led Argentina to national bankruptcy" (2011, 51). The New Argentine Cinema in general has been understood as very critical of the fallout of neoliberalism, even if these films rarely contain specific references to current events or refrain from articulating concrete political messages, as the films from preceding decades were prone to do. Martel herself has at times invited such allegorical readings only to reject them on other occasions. As Joanna Page has argued, allegorical readings may indeed "occlude a more radical understanding" of the politics of Martel's films (2013, 71) and, accordingly, she has shifted the discussion toward a different understanding of the political. In her view, it is more productive to "move from questions of interpretation to questions of construction" (2013, 72), focusing in particular on Martel's narrative strategies and their affinities to folktales and oral traditions, a topic about which Martel has extensively spoken in interviews and workshops.

La ciénaga does not follow a linear plot but instead consists of numerous smaller vignettes in which various individual characters come to the fore only to soon retreat again into the background. When Martel was awarded the Sundance award to further develop the screenplay, she reportedly was advised to focus on only one of the several strands and to give the story a tighter structure, which she refused: "I didn't want this to be the story of an alcoholic woman or the falling apart of a family" (Lalanne 2002, 74). Instead, the completed film features competing stories that create a rich tapestry, revealing a meticulously layered screenplay that is the exact opposite of improvisation or *cinema trouvé*.[13] Martel's refusal to create teleological narratives seeks other means to weave a web of meanings by relying on certain recurring motifs. In particular, Martel's use of water assumes the function of a leitmotif. Just consider the significance of reoccurring objects such as ice cubes, water balloons, or wet towels; water-related fluids such as wine, blood, and mud; visual clues such as characters filmed behind glass blurred by water drops; or recurring sounds like the dripping of water, the clinking of ice cubes, or thunder clap. The most important locations involve water, such as the

Figure 5. A rare joyous release of emotion in *La ciénaga*

pool and the swamp, the water tank on which the Virgin appears, and the dam, where the sudden release of gushing water creates one of the film's most exuberant and joyous scenes.

Among these, the swamp claims center space, as it combines both the fluidity of water and the stagnation of sand, both of which combine into a deadly place for animals and, by extension, humans. If Lucrecia Martel's film is primarily a film about standstill and asphyxiation, underneath the surface we constantly sense a threatening undercurrent—a "hotbed," as Martel describes it in her plot summary cited above. As she has explained elsewhere, this undercurrent is governed by the laws of desire: "I wanted the film to oscillate between two poles—the drowsiness and the voluptuousness. This is possibly the most profound drama of the film" (Lalanne 2002, 75). As the opening sequence is quick to show, one such undercurrent is Momi's doubly taboo infatuation with Isabel, an attraction that both her sister and older brother do not approve of (the first time José calls her "Momi sucia," or dirty Momi, is when he watches her lying in bed with Isabel, leaving it open whether he is referring to her lack of hygiene or her attraction to the indigenous maid). José's own sexual attractions are not beyond reproach, either. His mistress, Mercedes, is his father's former lover, a woman significantly older than he (the actor who plays her, Silvia Baylé, being some twenty years older than Juan Cruz Bordeau, who plays José), and apparently a former

A Poetics of the Senses | 37

schoolmate of Tali's, who remembers her as a woman who "never sleeps alone." While Mecha despises her, she is also dependent on Mercedes's skills as a businesswoman managing the proceeds of the pepper harvest, the sole source of income of the farm. Once José returns to the farm, he trades Mercedes's companionship for that of his mother, quite literally taking his father's place, who has just been booted out of the bedroom by Mecha. The Oedipal overtones of this triangle reach almost parodic dimensions in a scene in which José, lying next to Mecha, has a phone conversation with Mercedes, during which he (accidentally?) calls his lover "Mecha," the colloquial form of Mercedes, thus blurring the line between his mother and his lover, who, after all, is Mecha's former rival for Gregorio's affection and possibly now for José's affection as well. Mercedes tells José to return to Buenos Aires, which José promises to do, only to then cuddle up with his mother, who comforts him by saying "get some rest." The scene is given yet another ironic twist by virtue of the fact that Bordeau is the real-life son of Graciela Borges.

Since the bed is the primary location for both rest and sexual activity, it becomes indeed the film's most important location. Shots of people lounging in bed in various configurations are abundant. While for Mecha the bed becomes a place of retreat (there are strong hints that she will follow her mother's example and withdraw entirely to her bedroom), it is here that the multiple forms of desire are negotiated. José claiming

Figure 6. Everyone congregates in Mecha's bed in *La ciénaga*

a spot in his mother's bed is only one of many invasions within the extended family. Joaquín, too, lounges on Mecha's bed, as does Tali when she comes to visit and help Mecha dab cream on her lacerated cleavage. Momi likes to lie next to Isabel in the maid's bed, but she also enters Verónica's, who in turn claims a spot next to José, an intrusion he fights only half-heartedly. Indeed, the sexual tension between him and Verónica is particularly explicit. In one scene, José steals her panties, puts them over his head and runs away, only to be pursued by his sister, a chase that ends with both of them wrestling in the mud. When Verónica takes a shower to clean herself, José inserts his muddy shoe into the stall, her naked body separated from her brother's only by a thin shower curtain. It is a highly sensual scene that wavers between family comedy, whiffs of incest, and the creepy undertones of the knife-wielding shower scene in Hitchcock's *Psycho*. Yet while sexual desire is a constant presence and cause for tension, *La ciénaga* contains no scenes of actual sexual activity. There may be constant build-up, but there is no release.

This sense of being contained or trapped is most powerfully conveyed through Martel's configuration of time and space. Spatial relations between important locations—the town, the farm, the various rooms of the house—are intentionally left vague, leaving viewers permanently disoriented. A similar effect is reached through how the film establishes temporal relations, which results in the sensation that time is standing still. There are few markers of the passage of time such as sunrise or sunset (indeed, the sun is always covered by the same gray, sweltering sky), shared meals, or the following of daily routines. A digital clock always blinks 12:00. No one works, no one seems to have any chores or obligations; the days are mostly spent horizontally, with few activities interspersed. The only indication of how much time passes between the beginning and the end of the story are how fast Mecha's and José's wounds are healing, suggesting a span of less than a week. Everyone seems to wait for something, but what?

While *La ciénaga* refrains from telling one unified story, the very act of storytelling itself is central to the film. It is a process that is marked, as Martel has commented, by "digressions, repetition, the superimposition of ideas: all those things that take place in speech are structures that we can use in filmmaking" (Martel 2009), and by what Page calls polytemporality, "a layering of times in which the past is often seen with the

Figure 7. Momi sublimates desire in *La ciénaga*

hindsight of the present, or the present and future are prefigured and anticipated" (2013, 72).[14] The story of the African rat, which is first told by one of the girls, is a case in point. It revolves around a woman who picks up a stray dog in the streets and brings it home, where she places him with her cats. The next morning she finds the cats gone and the dog covered in blood. When she takes the dog to the vet, the vet chops him in half, revealing that the dog is actually an African rat with a double row of sharp teeth. When it is first recounted at the pool, the story appears to be rather random, but is later revealed to be the reason for Luciano's tragic death. While this death strikes viewers as meaningless, on closer inspection it becomes clear that it has been foreshadowed several times: when Luciano is first treated at the hospital for cuts to his leg and we understand that he's prone to accidents (Tali tells her husband, "he's done it again"); when he is mesmerized by the dead rabbit on the kitchen counter; when he stands right in the line of fire as two boys take aim to shoot the trapped cow; when during a game he is told to play "dead"; and when he holds his breath for a frighteningly long time. Indeed, a special association between him and the African rat is established by virtue of the fact that he is growing a tooth where none should be. As Martel explains, Luciano's death is typical of oral narration: "When an event that has already happened is recounted, precedents and causes are found, which go right back to the person's birth, as if he or she were condemned from the very beginning. In the face of the terrible or the unexpected, a desire always rises to find a scheme in which to place it. To me, that is the structure of orality" (quoted in Oubiña 2009a, 68).

The story of the African rat also recalls the fantastic and supernatural tales of Horacio Quiroga, a writer Martel has frequently cited as an inspiration for her films.[15] Quiroga has often been considered a main influence for the magical realism of Gabriel García Márquez and Julio Cortázar, but Martel uses him very differently. While magical realism is mostly defined as the appearance of the unreal or the fantastic in a realist setting and leads to a blending of the natural and the supernatural, Martel insists that reality itself is a construction and not a given into which a second reality can intrude (Rich 2001). There are, therefore, no different registers of the real but only one reality of which the fantastic is an important, ever-present part. According to this logic, the story of the African rat is just as much a construction of reality as everything else that

A Poetics of the Senses | 41

surrounds the characters in La Mandrágora, even if the consequences it has for Luciano may be of greater impact.

The significance Martel gives to capturing the impact of orality also pertains to the dialogue of the screenplay, which does not follow the usual pattern of he says, she says, but appears superimposed, with lines spoken on top of each other. Characters tend to speak past each other and fail to listen, and the telephone frequently rings but often remains unanswered (as Mecha repeatedly complains, even though she herself refuses to pick it up even when it's at arm's length). Significantly, the dialogue rarely reveals major plot points nor advances the story, but is mostly indicative of the state of mind of certain characters. The editing further underscores this impression by not cutting at the beginning or the ending of scenes but often joining conversations in medias res. "The idea was not to have beginnings for scenes," explains Martel, "instead, we had scenes that felt like interruptions of situations that had already begun. If you know the origin and the end of a situation, you de-dramatize it a lot" (quoted in Bernini et al. 2001, 136). The effect of this technique is twofold: on the one hand, viewers experience a certain confusion ("what have I missed?"), similar to the one created by the avoidance of establishing shots or shots that connect spaces ("where are we?"); yet on the other hand, the difficulty in understanding what is being conveyed can also be liberating, because it can give way to enjoying how exchanges are put together rather than deciphering what they actually convey.

The proximity to oral traditions is further invoked by Martel's frequent use of elliptical storytelling—important parts of the story are simply left out, tasking the viewer to fill in the gaps. In particular, it is her use of off-space that stands out—what is not shown or told is as important as what appears in the frame. In one scene, we witness how Luciano stands in the line of fire as two boys take aim to shoot the trapped cow. From there, we cut to the farm with people standing around the pool while a shot rings out from the hills, leaving us to wonder if Luciano might have been killed. Rather than cutting back to the mountain, viewers are left to worry, until a few minutes later Luciano appears in a different scene completely unhurt, as if he had never been in any danger. Another example of this discontinuity occurs when we watch Momi dive into the dirty pool; the camera shows us her underwater perspective but it withholds her resurfacing—has she been caught in something hiding on the murky bottom? Tellingly, these moments of prolonged suspense—yet another nod toward the horror film—are never really resolved. They play with our fears, mocking us for having experienced genuine concern or fright when none was warranted, eventually turning us into viewers who stop caring, just like the characters we are watching.

As Martel has repeatedly asserted, it is particularly in her native Salta that the forms of storytelling invoked in the film are still going strong, and many of the characters are allegedly composites of members of her extended family. Certain forms of speech such as the tendency to create new words—Mecha invites Tali's children "que vengan a piletear" (lit. to come swimming-pooling)—are typical of the region. Martel's above-quoted summary of *La ciénaga* equally highlights that the Salta region serves as more than simply a location or a backdrop; rather, La Mandrágora appears to be a character in the film that has a profound influence on the rest of them.

At the same time, it needs to be underscored that the Salta region is not depicted in a naturalistic way. The heavy symbolism of the opening scene, with its "anti-naturalist sound effects" (described as such by Martel during the 2013 Berlinale workshop), works hard to dispel any expectations that we might be in for an "authentic" portrait of the customs of the people in the provinces. Instead, we are privy to watching a type, a social class that exists in many places. "The mentality in Salta is similar to that of any place in Latin America," Martel has suggested "My film is not regional, it's not about the people of Salta, it's not folkloric. You hardly even see Salta" (quoted in Rangil 2005, 100). Yet while the story of the *La ciénaga* and its characters may take place elsewhere as well, the location does matter. The Salta region, which borders Bolivia, is a geographically and politically volatile area, and one that is largely absent in most other Argentine films, which privilege life in the capital of Buenos Aires. Martel shot in the eastern part of the state, with its low jungle and humid atmosphere, not in the picturesque west, famous for its rock formations and high peaks (prominently featured in the road rage episode from *Relatos salvajes/Wild Tales* [Damián Szifrón, 2014]), so as to avoid any touristic associations.

As has been observed, the Salta region recalls William Faulkner's South, not only because of its sweltering heat but because in both regions status and social class are largely determined by race. With a relatively large native population, Salta is a visible challenge to Argentine self-understanding as a nation of immigrants who descended from the boats to settle the uninhabited pampas, allegedly a space without people for a people without a space. For Argentines to see themselves as displaced Europeans, they must marginalize or render invisible the indigenous population, as their presence challenges the desired homogeneity of the nation, something that is clearly not possible in Salta. Already by virtue of its setting, *La ciénaga* thus questions the foundational fiction of contemporary Argentine national identity.

Indeed, the fraught relation between Mecha's white middle-class family and their indigenous servants is a central aspect of the film. Already in the opening sequence, the complexities of this relation are introduced when we witness Momi's affection for Isabel, which violates both the strong hetero-normativity of macho society as well as the taboo regarding the mixing between the white middle-class *patrona* (mistress) and the indigenous *empleada* (maid). As we later understand, this affection is partly the result of parental neglect, as Isabel has assumed the responsibilities of Momi's parents, telling her what to wear, when to take a shower, and not to swim in the pool. (In turn, Momi and Verónica repeatedly assume the responsibilities of the adults, such as taking care of the injured mother and driving her to the hospital, even though both are too young to have a driver's license.) On the other hand is Mecha's open disdain for Isabel, whom she suspects of stealing towels, and whom she repeatedly insults with racial slurs. Mecha's impending dismissal of Isabel, of which Momi learns from Verónica, presents a further threat to Momi's affection, and leads her to tell her sister that she wants to be with Isabel and nobody else.

Mecha's son Joaquín has clearly learned the lessons of his mother, as he enunciates the difference between whites and Indians in the most emphatic way. Yet ironically he is the one who most mimics the behavior of the indigenous—he eats the fish about which he complains; he derides how "they" fondle animals while doing it himself; and his derogatory comment that "they" live on top of each other is an apt description of his own home. It is here that the film's scathing critique of the latent racism of the provincial middle class reaches almost satirical proportions, something which led audiences in Salta to accuse Martel of showing the worst side of society (Martín Morán 2003, 234).

44 | Lucrecia Martel

Compared to Joaquin's hatred of the *collos*, Momi seems to be free of racial prejudice, but as Ana Peluffo has rightly observed, Momi's relationship with Isabel both transgresses and reproduces the ideology of racism (2011, 218). When Momi feels slighted by Isabel, she calls her *china carnavalera*, which the subtitles translate as "party girl," but which, with its reference to carnival when all rules are put into abeyance, is more adequately rendered as "wild Indian girl," a slur her mother also uses. While Isabel has to supply Mecha with ice for her wine, she has to supply Momi with affection; both mother and daughter make demands without reciprocating. And like Mecha, Momi suspects Isabel of theft when she catches her looking through her things, only to observe that Isabel has found her *own* bracelet in Momi's closet, which Momi pretends to have only borrowed—despite her rebellion against her parents, Momi is reproducing her mother's behavior of blaming the indigenous staff for their own failings.

Isabel's volatile position between her own community, represented by her boyfriend El Perro (the dog), and that of Mecha's household, becomes particularly evident in a scene in which Verónica and Momi, accompanied by Isabel, are buying a shirt in town for their brother José. When Isabel spots El Perro outside the store, she exits. From behind the window Momi spies on the two flirting and then suggests bringing El Perro into the store to have him model the shirt. In this scene, Martel uses depth of field to emphasize the different locations of three groups—the girls in a store that caters to the middle class; the *collos* men outside, next to a street vendor; and Isabel coming and going. Every time the door opens, diegetic cumbia music is briefly heard, only to recede again when it closes, further emphasizing the barriers between the spaces and the groups that inhabit them. Even more revealing is how El Perro is made the subject of both female and male gazes: asked by Verónica to try on the shirt, he strips off his own T-shirt, and his muscular torso is carefully inspected by both Momi and Isabel, as well as by his incredulous buddies looking in through the glass door. After El Perro has tried on the shirt, Verónica furtively smells it and turns up her nose. The scene makes it clear that the race barriers between Isabel and these young middle-class women clearly outweigh any gender solidarity that might exist between them. Verónica's gesture of disgust and Momi's cunning ridiculing of El Perro, her rival for Isabel's affection, already point toward Isabel's departure from La Mandrágora at the end of the film. Isabel decision to do so makes her the only person in the film to actually change her life. Yet as she silently sheds tears while packing her things, we realize that this change may not be for the better, and that a pregnancy, as Mecha suspects, may have made this choice a necessity.

It is important to note here that the film's perspective on matters of race strictly follows that of its middle-class protagonists; the film never makes any attempt to speak "on behalf of" the indigenous population by assuming a point of view apart from that of the middle-class characters. We are not privy to Isabel and El Perro's conversations; when the camera grants them some privacy, as in the dance scene during the carnival in La Ciénaga, their dialogue is drowned out by the loud music. Martel has repeatedly insisted that her stories are told from the perspective she herself knows best, and she considers any attempts to create omniscient or empathetic portrayals to be preposterous and patronizing (Rangil 2005, 103).

The repeated insistence on racial difference is certainly a leftover from colonial thinking, which particularly in the provinces has gone unchallenged for generations. Yet this insistence takes on new significance against the background of the fall from grace of Mecha's family. Their economic decline makes them cling to symbols of status (such as employing maids) precisely because the resources to do so are dwindling. As long as appearances are kept, the family can continue to dwell in a parallel universe. (What happens when the bubble bursts and the tables are actually turned is a scenario poignantly explored in José Gaggero's *Cama adentro/Live-In Maid* as well as in the Bolivian film *Zona Sur* [Juan Carlos Valdivia, 2009]). As Martel notes in her director's statement, "the film depicts a society that has lost its traditions but which cannot afford the security that could make up for it" (2001). The inhabitants of La Mandrágora live within a culture of class and racial entitlement, but with dwindling access to resources. They are stuck in the past not because they refuse to give up on traditions, but because traditions have become meaningless and nothing new has taken their place.

Neither Gregorio nor Mecha are ever shown leaving La Mandrágora (except when a resisting Mecha is taken to the hospital), as if the same spell had been cast over them as the one that afflicts the dinner guests in Luis Buñuel's *El ángel exterminador/The Exterminating Angel* (1962).

When Tali and her family first visit La Mandrágora, she has to break open the padlock of the gate, as if entering the enchanted grounds of Sleeping Beauty, except that no one will ever wake from their slumbers here. The sensation of stagnation and asphyxiation that engulfs the inhabitants of the estate comes even more into view when compared with Tali's vibrant family, which at least initially appears to be the healthy counterexample to her cousin's dysfunctional family. In contrast to the vain and self-absorbed Gregorio, Tali's husband, Rafael, is a caring father who dotes on the children, while Tali appears to be sane vis-à-vis the alcoholic Mecha. Yet on closer inspection it becomes clear that Rafael is a domineering and controlling man who talks badly about Mecha's family behind her back, and who preempts his wife's plans to get away to Bolivia for a few days, presumably because the road is too dangerous (ironically, his own house turns out to be a far deadlier place). Tali seems the most sympathetic of all adults, but she, too, is not above uttering racist slurs, and her gossip reveals her superficiality; in the end, it is she who leaves the ladder propped up that leads to Luciano's death, surely engulfing her in a paralyzing guilt that will trap her even more than Mecha's resignation.

In contrast to the unflattering portrayal of the adults, the children seem to invite more empathy, often providing the main perspective for viewers. Throughout *La ciénaga*, the camera is frequently placed at a lower height than that of the average adult and more akin to the perspective of children, thus forcing us into their point of view. Martel has described her camerawork as that of "spying with a lot of curiosity" (quoted in Knol 2013), which is also typical of how children view the world. Several critics have observed that particularly Momi's perspective comes closest to providing guidance for viewers. Repeatedly, we find point-of-view shots of Momi lustfully observing Isabel or registering disdain about her parents' behavior, making her the character that most invites viewers' identification. While Oubiña describes Momi as the only character who returns to lucidity at the end of the film (2009b, 35), for Laura Podalsky, Momi's plunge into the murky pool becomes a visual metaphor for "penetrat[ing] the surface of the dirty reality ignored by others" (2007, 117). Yet assigning Momi such a privileged position overlooks that she herself is repeatedly called "dirty Momi" and that the narrative abandons her for long stretches; when the camera assumes her perspective again, at the end of the film, it does so with less flattery, signaling that whatever may have set her apart from the others no longer exists.

If there is one child who is clearly distinct from the others, it is not Momi but Luciano, who is the only one portrayed as innocent. In contrast, Luciano's hyperactive sister enjoys bossing and scaring him, and José, a grown man who no longer resides at home, reverts to teenage behavior when he returns, endlessly lounging in beds and provoking a fight with El Perro over Isabel. As noted earlier, Joaquín is particularly savage and racist, and in very disconcerting ways Momi begins to reproduce her parents' behavior, just as her other siblings do. A clear indication of all children's latent aggression and propensity for violence, regardless of age, is the fact that many bear scars (be it the subtle scar on Verónica's chin or Joaquín's disfigured eye) and that they incur numerous injuries throughout the film, from Luciano's cut leg, Joaquín's and Martin's (Tali's older son's) scratched faces, to José's broken nose. Yet these experiences seem to be of no consequence—like the parents, the children no longer seem willing or able to learn.

By contrast, when the gravest accident happens, Luciano's fall from the ladder, no blood is spilled. If throughout the film there is hardly a shot with no fewer than two characters in it, at the moment of his death Luciano is all by himself and seen only from a distance, as if the camera were endowing the victim with a certain dignity. Instead of staying on him, the camera quickly cuts to the vacant spaces around him (the patio, the kitchen, the living room), now eerily devoid of all the activity and sounds that previously filled it, just as Fritz Lang did in *M* (1931) to signal the murder of young Elsie. It is the only scene of this kind, clearly a dramatic high point to which, in ways that only become clear in hindsight, the narrative has been building.[16]

Like the numerous accidents, the miracle of the appearance of the Virgin represents a promise of change, yet it equally fails to make an impact. On three occasions, different ensembles of characters are shown watching the television newscast, making it an important event that unites disparate groups. Tali comes across as gullible when she excitedly comments on the reports of her friend Teresa, who witnessed the apparition when it was "very fresh." In the end, Momi too visits the place (yet another trip not recorded by the camera) but fails to see anything. Religion may be an important part of the social fabric in the Salta region, but it is hardly a redeeming force (both José and his girlfriend, Mercedes, wear crucifixes but never pray or speak about religion). The television coverage reveals that in an environment starving for a savior there are no true believers. In the end, the appearance of the Virgin is just another supernatural story, like that of the African rat, which people take at face value but which ultimately has no real impact. As Aguilar has observed, the introduction of television coverage is a frequent tool in the New Argentine Cinema (2008, 24). At first we may suspect that it inflects the film with a documentary aspect that stands in contrast to Martel's heightened realism, yet we quickly note that television is no conveyor of truth. Instead, it caters to the viewers' superficial religious fanaticism, and it turns them into consumers who purchase what they see advertised, as does Mecha, who orders a mini fridge for her bedroom retreat. If the film for the most part withholds any direct social critique, it here clearly debunks the overt manipulation by the mass media, revealing the false promise of authenticity to which it responds with a carefully constructed realism that challenges any consumer attitude viewers might bring to the cinema.

La ciénaga is a horror movie in which the real monstrosity is the apathy of the middle-class families. Its emphatic circular structure is only fully revealed at the end. The very last shot of the film, of the misty hills surrounding the farm, repeats the film's first and is accompanied by the same sound of thunderclap. Throughout the film, there have been strong hints that Mecha will end up a recluse like her mother, while José will likely become a second Gregorio. In the final scene, this parallel between generations is extended to include Momi and Verónica. Now it is Momi whom we watch noisily dragging a lawn chair along the pool, as her parents did earlier, and sitting down next to Verónica, who wears the same dark sunglasses her mother always wears, a symbol of a refusal to acknowledge reality. As it turns out, Momi, too now partakes of this blindness. In what will be the concluding line of the film (she also spoke the film's very first words), she tells her sister that she went to see the appearance of the Virgin, but without success: "I didn't see anything." The gesture not only imitates the willful ignorance of her parents, it also alludes to the cruelty of Luciano's death, which was witnessed by nobody, a reiteration of the parental neglect that pervades the film, of which Momi has now become a part. Indeed, the swamp will devour them all.

Touching Tales: *La niña santa*

> What is important now is to recover our senses. We must learn to see more, to hear more, to feel more [. . .] In place of a hermeneutics, we need an erotics of art.
>
> —Susan Sontag, "Against Interpretation"

> *La niña santa* is sort of a surgical story that intends to draw a line between live tissue and moral prosthesis.
>
> —Lucrecia Martel, director's statement, 2004

In the densely populated realm of *La ciénaga*, we follow the comings and goings of two large families and their interlocking fates over a period of a few days. Among the many secondary characters who populate their shared orbit, we find "el gringo," the nickname of the doctor whom both Mecha and Tali seek out at the beginning of the film, and at whose office Tali's plan to visit Mecha and her family is first formed. "El gringo" appears only in a few short scenes and we never learn much about the origin of this nickname, which in Argentina refers to Italians, not Americans: Is he someone who moved from a different region to Salta, where a *porteño* already counts as foreigner? Does his nickname signal some strange form of reverse racism, according to which a high educational standard equals a quasi-European origin? And what is his real name?

Like many other characters in *La ciénaga*, "el gringo" remains marginal and mysterious, but a doctor does become a central figure in Lucrecia Martel's follow-up feature, *La niña santa* (2004). According to Martel, both films inhabit the same world. "I had the idea for *La niña santa*," she explains, "from a song that the children sing in *La ciénaga*, 'Doctor Jano, cirujano' [surgeon] [. . .] *La niña santa* is a story within *La ciénaga*" (Romero 2005, 159). We never learn whether the Dr. Jano from the children's song is indeed "el gringo," but the one who features prominently in *La niña santa* is not a surgeon but an otolaryngologist—an ear, nose, and throat specialist. Indeed, the act of hearing and listening becomes a central theme in Martel's second feature, underscored (again) by a richly textured soundtrack that assembles a wide array of sources. The significance of the sonic is combined with a strong emphasis on other forms of perception, including smelling, feeling, and touching. Laura Marks's notion of haptic visuality, already referred to in the introduction, becomes particularly relevant for *La niña santa*. In fact, one can think of few other films that demonstrate as forcefully Marks's claim that cinema is not just a medium of visual representation but a physical and multisensory embodiment of culture.

Martel's comment about the interrelatedness of the two films points to important continuities between them. Working again from her own script, Martel had Lita Stantic repeat as producer, now in collaboration with the Almodóvar brothers, Pedro and Agustín, a clear sign of the international stature her *ópera prima* gained her. Mercedes Morán stars again, this time as Helena, a beautiful but lonely divorcée. Both films share a similar setting—a remote, almost hermetic location in the province of Salta—and a focus on the interactions between middle-class adults and adolescent girls. Momi's quest for signs of wonder is continued here by Helena's daughter, Amalia, who seeks her own path to God. Yet despite these and other similarities, *La niña santa* is an altogether different film. What stands out right away is that, in contrast to the many interwoven strands of *La ciénaga*, Martel's second feature revolves around a single character, the titular holy girl, whose point of view the camera frequently assumes, and whose spiritual and sexual crisis forms the core of the narrative.

Together with her mother and her uncle Freddy (Alejandro Urdapilleta), Amalia (María Alché) lives in a hotel with thermal springs that has seen better days and where a medical convention is taking place. One of the participants is Dr. Jano (Carlos Belloso), who takes an interest in Helena, which the lonely divorcée openly welcomes, even though she is warned that he is married. Unbeknownst to Helena, Jano sexually molests her daughter: while they are listening to a concert in the street, the doctor rubs his groin against Amalia's buttocks. Amalia reacts with shock but also a hint of sexual excitement. Taking her lessons in Catholicism literally, she makes it her calling to "save" the perpetrator. She confides the incident only to her best friend, Josefina (Julieta Zylberberg), and begins to spy on Jano, even entering his hotel room when he's not there. Meanwhile, Helena, who suffers from tinnitus, incidentally Dr. Jano's specialty, agrees to take part in a doctor-patient role play, which is to serve as the closing event of the conference. The narrative takes an unexpected turn when Josefina, in an attempt to cover up having sex with her cousin, tells her mother of Amalia's molestation, who decides to report it. The film ends with the climax left hanging: while Amalia and Josefina peacefully drift in the thermal pool, Dr. Jano and Helena take the stage, just as, with his family in attendance, the doctor's transgression is about to be made public.

As in *La ciénaga*, Martel here employs a visual style that foregrounds the sensual and emotional components of human experience. The director frequently uses a shallow depth of field where characters move in and out of focus. Windows or doorways often frame the shots, highlighting the act of spying on or listening in on other people. Numerous close-ups, often so extreme that they are unsettling, focus on parts of the body or the face, particularly the ear; equally disorienting is Martel's habit of eschewing establishing shots or camera movements that allow spatial orientation. Again, off-screen space becomes very important. With the explanatory role of the visual weakened, the significance of sound, already so important in *La ciénaga*, further increases. The hotel, the main location for much of the film, is experienced as a labyrinth of rooms, hallways, lecture halls, and dining halls, their layout only imaginable because of the sound, which suggests proximity where none is shown. The hotel is also the source of numerous noises that punctuate conversations, including water dripping from pipes, murmurings and whisperings, and painful high-pitch sounds emanating from the hotel sound system. Against the backdrop of this cacophony emerges a densely layered story that unfolds in far less linear terms than the plot summary might suggest. As J. Hoberman aptly observed, *La niña santa* "is a movie as much choreographed as directed" (2005).

The opening scene of *La niña santa* skillfully announces its aesthetic registers and the film's central theme, the exploration of the relation between religion and sexuality. We open to a medium close-up of a group of girls listening to the voice of a young woman singing a religious hymn, which has already been heard during the credit sequence. As is often the case in Martel's films, diegetic sound precedes the image from which it emanates and the reaction this sound creates—the girls listening with a mixture of rapture and boredom—in turn precedes the representation of its origin, the teacher Inés. "Look at the extreme vileness that is singing like this to you today," Inés intones off-screen, her beautiful face, when shown moments later, a startling contrast to the self-loathing lyrics typi-

52 | **Lucrecia Martel**

cal of the Roman Catholic Church's repression of the body. Meanwhile, the camera moves across the faces of the students of her catechism class to single out Amalia and Josefina, who both observe the teacher with a blasé, inscrutable look. Fighting to hold back tears, Inés pauses for a moment and the room goes silent.[17] We can faintly hear nearby noises, soon to be identified as coming from the hotel lobby, where a group of doctors is checking in for a conference. When Inés haltingly starts singing again, Josefina sarcastically comments on Inés's emotional fragility as a lack of singing technique: "she is short of air, she doesn't know how to breathe." The snide remark mocks Inés's inner turmoil, but the meaning of the hymn's pleading, "what is it, Lord, you want of me?," is not lost on the girls, nor are the strong sexual overtones of the concluding line, "For I have given in to you." Indeed, the heightened experience of spirituality, mysticism and eroticism, embodied by Inés, will soon impact Amalia's own sexual awakening.

The hymn Inés sings is called "Vuestra soy"/"I Am Yours" and was written by Teresa de Ávila, a prominent Spanish mystic (Jagoe and Cant 2007, 178). In one of her visions, de Ávila describes being pierced by a seraph's lance and how suffering and bodily pain produced unparalleled spiritual experiences: "I saw in his hand a long spear of gold, and at the point there seemed to be a little fire. He appeared to me to be thrusting it at times into my heart, and to pierce my very entrails; when he drew it out, he seemed to draw them out also, and to leave me all on fire with a great love of God. The pain was so great, that it made me moan; and yet so surpassing was the sweetness of this excessive pain, that I could not wish to be rid of it."[18] It is allegedly this vision that inspired Bernini's famous sculpture *The Ecstasy of Saint Teresa*, widely considered a masterpiece of the High Roman Baroque for how it captures the orgasmic moment when sensual and spiritual pleasure meld. When Josefina gossips to Amalia about having seen Inés passionately kiss an older man and experiencing epilepsy-like fits, Amalia recognizes in her teacher's face this kind of fusion of the senses.

Inés concludes her lesson by telling her students about their "vocation": they must be ready to hear the call of God when it comes. It is a scene with many extreme close-ups, where the silhouette of a girl often blocks more than half the screen, emphasizing the acts of speaking and listening in an intimate setting. Soon thereafter a honking car summons

Inés, the off-screen sound suggesting the existence of a boyfriend and thus contradicting the image of a chaste young woman following a purely divine calling.[19] When the strange sound of the theremin is suddenly heard, the girls fall silent and eventually are drawn outside to the street.

The scene of the theremin concert introduces the film's main plot point: Dr. Jano's violation of Amalia. The central concern with proper and improper touching here reveals an ironic twist, because Jano's illicit contact happens while Amalia and the rest of the crowd are listening to an instrument that is played by *not* making physical contact. An early electronic instrument from the 1920s, the theremin produces its sound by sensing the movements of the player's hand and transforming them into audio signals.[20] As Jens Andermann has pointed out that "this spectacle of the invisible provides Dr. Jano with the condition of anonymity he exploits to impose himself on Amalia, confident that the young girl will not dare to leave her position of spectator to challenge him and reveal herself the victim of sexual aggression" (2012, 157). Yet what Dr. Jano cannot see is that Amalia's reaction of shock and shame is tinged with a bit of sexual curiosity. As she soon explains to Josefina, Jano's transgression has become "the call" Amalia has been told to wait for, and she will make it her mission to save the doctor—except that the divine vocation is fueled by raging hormones. When on a subsequent day Dr. Jano again attends a theremin performance—the melody played is the highly seductive "Habanera" aria from Georges Bizet's opera *Carmen*—Amalia purposefully positions herself in front of him; when he leans into her, she startles him by grabbing his hand and turning around to face him, forcing him into a hurried escape. (Already earlier, she had reversed the scenario by standing closely behind him in the hotel elevator and slightly touching his hand.) As many critics have noted, this return of the gaze—and the touch—is a form of female self-empowering that challenges not only Jano's dominance over Amalia but also a key element of mainstream narrative cinema, namely the objectification and fetishization of the female body.

Yet it would be too simple to explain Amalia's reaction to Jano's second frottage as mere desire to break male dominance (which was still the driving force for the heroine of *Rey Muerto*), since her face is nearly impossible to decipher—pouty and mischievous, she seems both repelled and fascinated by this predator. "There is something fascinating

Figure 8. Returning the gaze in *La niña santa*

about her gaze," Martel has explained of the face that won Alché the role during casting, "a space between her pupil and her lower eyelid, as in religious paintings. It's associated with adoration. You also see that type of look in nineteenth-century photographs of madwomen" (quoted in Taubin 2005, 174). The young actor maintains this inscrutable demeanor throughout the film, offering only the minutest reaction of eyes and mouth to keep us guessing at her real feelings.

It is ironic that Amalia finds her vocation at almost the same moment as her mother refuses a call of a different kind, namely to speak on the phone to her ex-husband, who wants to inform her that his new (and presumably much younger) wife is pregnant with twins. It is reasonable to speculate that it is this news that leads Helena to flirt more seriously with Jano, just when her daughter plans her own advances on the doctor. The parallel between daughter and mother is further underscored by the use of the theremin, which not only connects Jano and Amalia but provides the background music when Helena first dines with the doctor, this time played within the hotel but just out of view.

As these opening scenes indicate, in contrast to *La ciénaga*, *La niña santa* introduces its main characters, and the triangle they will form, in the film's first ten minutes. The first scene that Helena, Jano, and Amalia actually share is a beautifully composed sequence at the hotel's pool—here again a key location, as is the bed—that highlights the importance of vision

A Poetics of the Senses | 55

and sound. At this point, Amalia already knows who Jano is (she has seen his photo in the conference brochure) and begins spying on him. Resting near the pool, she observes him drifting on his back in the water below (Amalia will assume the same position in the film's last scene), a shot with extreme shallow depth of field that only gradually lets us distinguish the doctor. When he looks in Amalia's direction, she hides and begins to recite a psalm, the simultaneity of preying and praying perfectly capturing her paradoxical mission (Jubis 2009, 61). Several shots of Jano as seen from Amalia's perspective follow, each framed a bit tighter and with a particular focus on his eyeglasses and his ear. Then Helena disrobes and gets into the pool, but problems with her ear quickly make her get out of the water again. Helena's seductive body as well as her obvious discomfort are closely observed by Jano, who will later use her medical condition to get closer to her, making science serve desire. Helena returns to Amalia and admonishes her not to waste time on memorizing useless prayers. The scene concludes with a close-up of Amalia's ear.

On the level of the visual, the sequence contrasts Jano's gaze, already introduced when he first spied Helena upon entering the hotel, with Amalia's reversal of the male gaze and of the equally gendered roles of pursuer and pursued. She knows who he is, but he does not know her, nor is he even aware of her presence. While his gaze follows Helena quite openly, hers is discrete. If Jano first saw only Helena's bared back, literally making her a woman without a head, the camera equally cuts off Jano's head when Amalia spies on him in the pool. With its strange emphasis on ears, the scene furthermore highlights what Amalia and Helena are hearing (or not). Throughout this very quiet scene, we only discern the dripping of water, the murmur of other bathers, and a brief hissing sound when Helena experiences her discomfort. Against this subdued background noise, Amalia's distinctly "hears" her "call," which provides her with precise directions, as her vigorous praying indicates; in contrast, the noises that bother Helena are impossible for her to locate and have profoundly disorienting and debilitating consequences.

Helena's sense of confusion carries over into the immediately following scene: when at night Helena hears cries of "Mama! Mama!," she wakes up startled and looks for Amalia, only to realize that the words have come from the television, where Raúl de la Torre's film *Heroína* (1972) is playing—a rare instance of intertextual playfulness in Martel's

Figure 9. Rare moments of obvious intertextuality: Graciela Borges (Mecha) in *Heroína* and Mercedes Morán (Tali) in *La niña santa*

oeuvre. Made during the boom of psychoanalysis in Argentina, the film is about a woman, played by Graciela Borges, who, traumatized and suicidal after her brother dies, seeks psychiatric treatment.[21] Given the film's serious subject matter (and the fact that she falls asleep while watching it), Helena's verdict to call the film "beautiful" seems strange. In the brief scene on Helena's TV, we see Borges playing a distressed medical translator wearing headphones, an image pointing to the discomforting hearing test Helena will soon undergo at the hands of Dr. Jano.

Helena, Jano, and Amalia make up an oddly asymmetrical triangle of desire, given the diversity in age, marital status, and the widely disparaging knowledge they have about each other: only late into the film does Jano realize who Amalia is, and Helena will only learn about her daughter's violation at the very end. All three characters blur the line between being upright and dishonest. Most viewers will experience divided sympathies for Dr. Jano; he is seemingly a pedophile and eager to cheat on his wife, but he comes across as surprisingly sympathetic. As Geoffrey Macnab has put it, "if he is a predator, he is a strangely diffident and harassed one" (2005). An attractive but lonely woman on the wrong side of fifty, Helena is an equally complex figure; she willfully ignores Mirta's advice about Jano's marital status and openly flirts with him, her infatuation and self-absorption leading to a certain parental neglect (though not on the scale of Mecha and Gregorio). If Jano's reflection in the mirror when entering Helena's room points to his duplicity, Helena's mirror image indicates something different. She is contained in the image and repeatedly exhibited to a male gaze, but it is an exhibition in whose organization she takes an active part. We constantly see her posing in front of the mirror and asking others, including Jano, what she should wear. Unlike him, she gains her sense of identity by imagining what she looks like in the eye of the (male) other. But Helena also becomes aware of the extreme objectification this gaze may produce: During the hearing test, when she allows herself to be put on display in a small booth, she experiences obvious signs of unease, perhaps an indication that the sexual overtones of "playing doctor" have become too overt for her (she will soon voice the wish to withdraw from the concluding performance).

Just as Dr. Jano is not made to look like a monster, Amalia is not a helpless victim either. For Aguilar, the titular girl saint is holy without traces of irony (2008, 92), an unambiguous embodiment of what is good. Yet Amalia's behavior is hardly in accordance with her Catholic upbringing, as she clearly takes delight in turning the tables on Jano, enjoying the power she has over him. In one scene, she hides behind a plastic tarp while he is in the pool—one of many veil-like contraptions in the film—tapping her fingers against a metal frame to catch his attention and taking delight in his bewilderment. Amalia's carnal fantasies—she masturbates in her bed after having sneaked into Jano's room, and she passionately kisses Josefina—also indicate that it is not just love of one's neighbor that prompts her desire to save the doctor.

As a character who behaves as in a trancelike state, driven by voices only she can hear and taking pleasure in stalking her prey, Amalia easily fits the bill for protagonist of a horror film, a genre for which, as Deborah Martin has argued, "the child, and in particular the adolescent girl, has a special relevance" (2011, 60).[22] Indeed, the ingredients and conventions of this genre permeate all aspects of *La niña santa*. Chief among them is the theremin, which accompanies both Amalia's and Helena's first contact with Jano and which reappears numerous times during the film. For filmmakers of Martel's generation, the sound of this instrument is strongly associated with cheap horror films from Hollywood's classic period. Indeed, the name Dr. Jano itself sounds like straight out of Universal Studio's 1930s horror cycle. According to Roman religion and myth, Janus is the god of beginnings and transitions. He is usually depicted as having two faces, since he looks both to the future and to the past. This two-facedness is echoed by the moral ambiguity that surrounds the doctor in Martel's film, as well as his double attraction toward mother and daughter. Late in the film, Amalia observes Jano in his room with his image doubled by a mirror—one of many shots involving this device—as if to even further underscore his duplicity. Perhaps not coincidentally, it is in this scene that Jano declares to Amalia that he will explain everything to her mother, as if the decision to come clean will unite the two opposing sides of his personality.

Beyond the theremin music and the Jano figure, *La niña santa* contains numerous ingredients that are a staple of the genre.[23] The dilapidated hotel, which appears to have fallen out of time and space, recalls the Bates Motel of *Psycho* (a film also referenced in *La ciénaga*) and the Overlook Hotel of *The Shining* (Stanley Kubrick, 1980). Replacing the crumbling estate La Mandrágora, Hotel Termas is a famous spa where the Argentine upper crust and foreign dignitaries once stayed. As Joanna Page has written, "the hotel metonymically represents [. . .] the sharp decline of Argentina from the turn of the century, when it took its place among the richest countries of the world, to the economic ruin of the film's present" (2009, 184). Along similar lines, Cécile François has noted that the dark, labyrinth-like interiors of the hotel facilitate the emergence of erotic fantasies (2009, 4). The remoteness of the location is duplicated by the disconnected lives of the sibling owners, Helena and Freddy. While Helena vehemently blocks any news from her ex-husband, Freddy has lost complete touch with his former wife and children, leaving the two siblings in a shared seclusion of mutual dependency ripe for incest. (When Freddy locks himself out of his room, he wakes up his sister rather than asking the concierge, and then falls asleep in her bed.) At one point, Amalia even compares her mother's room to a grave, because it is so cold and dark. The feeling of death is carried over into a scene in which we watch Amalia's hand hovering just inches above her sleeping mother's body, as if, like a theremin player, she is trying to feel the vibrations of an inanimate object.

The most direct quote of a horror film, however, shows a group of girls inspecting the scene of a car accident outside the city. Filmed with a handheld-camera style evocative of *The Blair Witch Project* (Daniel Myrick and Eduardo Sánchez, 1999; see D. Martin, 2011, 62), we follow Amalia and Josefina as they chase each other through the dense underbrush, jokingly spooking each other out and getting genuinely frightened when sudden gunshots are heard. Wavering between the silly and the scary, this seems a gratuitous scene that the film could have well done without: It does not propel the narrative forward (surprisingly, almost all scenes in *La niña santa* do), and it is the only one that does not take place in the hotel or the city. Yet the scene claims an important space in *La niña santa* as well as in relation to the other two films that comprise the Salta trilogy. It has been prepared by an anecdote, told by one of the girls, according to which a truck driver comes upon the scene of a gruesome accident. He is stopped by a woman who pleads to rescue her child; only after the child has been saved does the driver realize that the dead mother holding the child is the woman who flagged him down. Reminiscent of the tales of Horacio Quiroga, the story of the accident also harks back to the supernatural tale of the rat/dog from *La ciénaga*. That film is also referenced by the sudden appearance of two boys with hunting rifles, the origin of the shots Amalia and Josefina heard in the woods, and whom one might well imagine to be "Martín and Joaquín, a bit taller but still waiting to have that perpetually procrastinated eye operation" (Jubis 2009, 67). What is more, when Josefina and Amalia finally escape the underbrush and run onto the country road, they are almost hit by an oncoming truck, thus anticipating the car accident of

La mujer sin cabeza. More than any other it is this sequence, then, that underscores the shared uncanny universe of Martel's Salta trilogy.

Yet despite the numerous references and allusions to the creepy and the disturbing, *La niña santa* is not a horror film in the strict sense. What Martel makes of a film that revolves around sexual violence, forbidden sex, and uncontrolled desire is very different from what a mainstream director in the United States would have done. *La niña santa* is neither a film about a pedophile gone berserk nor a feminist revenge fantasy, but a dryly comic drama. In contrast to *La ciénaga*, no blood flows and no one dies. Instead, Martel's interest in horror lies in the genre's general propensity to question our epistemological foundations. Horror unsettles our assumptions about what is right or wrong, or what is even real. "I love the dissolution of reality in horror film," Martel has commented. "The lack of certainty, and the lack of security. What are you seeing? What are you hearing?" (quoted in Wisniewski 2009).

Indeed, one can read *La niña santa* as an extended reply to the question of what happens when we can no longer rely on the certainties and hierarchies with which religion and medical science—two things that are closely linked for Martel (cf. J. Wood 2006, 168)—provide us. Martel's playful self-description as a "Catholic without God" (quoted in Matheou 2010b, 31) points to the challenge of filling a moral and epistemological void once we have acknowledged that God is dead: it now falls on humans to decide what is right or wrong, or real or unreal. In a post-Catholic predicament, the need for a guiding moral universe remains, but the responsibility to erect and maintain it now lies with us. Interpretation and intuition have to take the place of authority, which often leads to a blurring or disappearance of existing boundaries and hierarchies.

The burden of interpretation is an explicit topic of conversation at the medical conference. As Dr. Vesalio explains to Jano and Helena, the key question in their profession is "how can we interpret correctly what a patient wants to tell us?" But Vesalio is a hypocrite—he soon abandons the conference in a hurry, after his affair with a lab technician has become public—and the statement is made to convince Helena to participate in the role play with Jano, of whose attraction for the hotel owner he is well aware. Science, it turns out, is not without self-interest. And nor is religion. Just as the patient's description of his or her symptoms is necessarily the subject of an expert's interpretation, so is the meaning of holy scripture. During her catechism class, Inés is frustrated by her students who pose questions she cannot answer. To evade any dispute about exegesis, Inés disqualifies the photocopied texts the students bring to class because of their "dubious origin." Clearly, it remains the privilege of the priest (or the doctor) to decide what and how to interpret. Throughout the film, there are numerous instances in which the discrepancy between the teachings of the Roman Catholic Church and human practice becomes evident: The phone booth from which Jano calls his wife looks like a confessional, but what he shares with her is far from the truth. In Josefina's idiosyncratic view, anal intercourse does not count as premarital sex as her hymen is intact. To distract her mother, who has caught her in flagrante with her cousin, she gives away Amalia's secret and breaks her promise of silence. And as Amalia's reaction to her molestation shows, the church can safely rely on the silence of the victims. But the film's overall interest lies less in debunking Catholicism and all it stands for than in embracing the ambiguities and uncertainties that a post-Catholic world view must face. Seen in this light, the film's sensual overload and its visual and aural idiosyncrasies serve the purpose of questioning any modes of rational explanation and facile comprehension. Repeatedly, viewers catch themselves having jumped to wrong conclusions (we are led to believe, for example, that Freddy is Helena's lover before we realize that he is her brother). By making serious demands on our interpretative faculties, viewers are left in the same state of confusion and slight irritation that is experienced by the characters and their fraught negotiations of desire and repression.

The failure of rationalism is perhaps most evident in Martel's use of dialogue, which rarely ever serves the purpose of relaying information or advancing the plot. Characters continuously talk past each other, failing to listen or to understand. What remains unsaid is often more important than what is articulated, reinforcing the significance of Martel's handling of the off-screen. Nevertheless, her characters do talk a lot and what they say (or not) tells us volumes about them. As the director explained, "the dialogue is fundamental in my films, not because it serves to inform the spectator but because it seems to me to be an interesting place to mask or hide things" (quoted in James 2005, 20). The wicked humor of Martel's films, often overlooked particularly by foreign critics, frequently results from a comedy of errors caused by misunderstanding. A case in point is Dr. Jano's visit with Helena, right after having seen Amalia in his room, with the firm intention to confess his perturbed relation with the teenager. When he enters and ashamedly searches for words, Helena erroneously believes his insecurity to be proof of his affection for her. "I feel the same—it's madness," she exclaims as she embraces him. The kiss Amalia was trying to steal from Jano now Helena firmly places on his mouth, thus doubling Jano's illicit touches and moral dilemma. Soon thereafter, Jano's wife and daughter inform him about rumors that a scandal involving a hotel guest and "the girl by the pool" is about to be made public, completely unaware that their father/husband is the culprit. Within minutes, Jano's good intentions have been turned into his worst nightmare simply because of a failure of communication. In *La niña santa*, nothing is ever said or understood in time—and if it is, it will be subject to denial: After Helena has repeatedly refused to accept a phone call from her ex-husband, she complains to Freddy that she is upset about not being told in person about the twins, a highly neurotic gesture that seeks to displace blame onto others.

Perhaps no other single factor serves Martel's agenda of radically questioning boundaries and hierarchies better than the film's main location, the Hotel Termas, which, like La Mandrágora, is almost a character in the film. As Martel has explained, the hotel "has thermal waters and is therefore something between a hotel and a hospital. [. . .] It's a public space that also reproduces the private space of the home" (quoted in James 2005, 19).[24] Indeed, the blurring of the public and the private underwrites the film in fundamental ways. As an atypical nuclear family, mother, daughter, and brother-uncle constantly conflate the permanent and the transient in their roles as manager, resident, and guest. Amalia roams the entirety of the hotel as if all rooms were her own, eating in the dining room, swimming in the pool, or napping in the laundry room. On her expeditions, she frequently touches the hallway walls, the towels, or the chairs in the guest room, as if gathering information through touch, like an insect through its feelers. Repeatedly, she enters Dr. Jano's room when he is not there and even twice when he is. (When Jano first catches her in the room, he gives her money for a cab home, unaware that the hotel *is* her home.) At the same time, Amalia apparently has no room of her own, sharing a bed with her mother into which her uncle Freddy frequently intrudes. Helena, too, behaves like a guest, dining at the

Figure 10. Stolen kisses in *La niña santa* |

best table, ordering meals just prepared for her, and enjoying the pool and massages while never really lifting a finger (as all real work falls to Mirta).[25] Even though her room is constantly invaded by her brother as well as various employees and their offspring, none of these intrusions bother her; indeed, the concept of privacy as commonly understood does not apply to her or any family member and even rubs off on some of the hotel guests. Just consider Dr. Vesalio, who is placed in Dr. Jano's room without Jano's consent because of a shortage of rooms. Completely unaware that he may be an imposition, Vesalio uses Jano's shaving cream,

64 | **Lucrecia Martel**

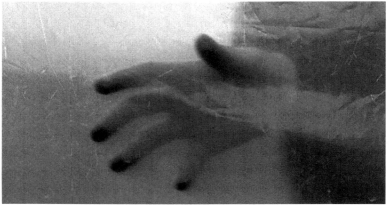

Figure 11. Amalia gathers information by touch in *La niña santa*

undresses in his room, invites in another colleague, and finally hands out presents to the female lab assistants with barely disguised intentions.[26]

The camera work does much to underscore the lack of privacy. Throughout the film, frames are often crowded with bodies and faces, depicting people crammed into tight spaces such as the elevator, the lecture hall, or the storefront during the theremin concert. A murmur of other voices and conversations can constantly be overheard, forming part of a soundscape that emphasizes indistinct proximity. The hotel thus becomes a densely layered contact zone where bodies and sounds mingle, and where gossip travels fast. Yet with this proximity comes also a certain fear of contagion. Indeed, "contact" and "contagion" are both derivatives of the Latin *contagio* (which in turn is related to *tangere*, touch), explaining the film's complex concern with hygiene and contamination. A chief symbol of this are the thermal waters, which have healing powers but which are also the reason for Helena's tinnitus, as water apparently damaged her ear when she was a diver. Similarly, shampoo, shaving cream, and air freshener are recurring objects with distinct connotations and smells that structure the film like leitmotifs. As Mirta explains, the shampoo is of low quality due to the hotel's budget constraints and to be used sparingly, but Helena offers it as a much appreciated gift to Josefina's mother. It's safe to assume that the air freshener, generously dispensed by the maids, is meant to disguise unpleasant odors caused by the hotel's ailing infrastructure; nobody ever asks for or refuses its application, which is anything but subtle. The origin of a more pleasant smell, Jano's shaving cream is coveted by Amalia, who dabs it on her blouse as an olfactory reminder of the doctor. Indeed, *La niña santa* is a film one can almost smell.[27]

Both the shampoo and the shaving cream serve the treatment of hair, which is yet another potent symbol of sensory conflation because, as Deborah Martin observes, it is both beautiful and polluting. As she points out, while part of the human body, hair is actually dead matter, straddling the divide between the animate and the inanimate (2011, 71). All characters devote considerable time to its care: Helena uses her carefully coiffed hairdo to attract Jano, and she massages Freddy's receding hairline. (Freddy's concern with hair loss makes him a close cousin to Gregorio in *La ciénaga*, who dyes his hair; their superficiality and vanity mark them as two of the many pathetic males that populate Martel's films.) Amalia lovingly strokes Josefina's long hair, which Josefina plans to donate for an effigy of the Virgin, much to her mother's dismay. Equally disconcerting for her are the head lice that may have infected her younger daughter and that require painstaking inspection. A source of attraction and disgust, hair represents a paradoxical form of sensuality that is symbolic for the entire film.

The interpretive challenges of Lucrecia Martel's films—their insistence on ambiguity, uncertainty, and the opaque—have repeatedly led critics to directly ask the director for clarification, but Martel has routinely avoided answering the kinds of questions her films so carefully and insistently leave open. If she provides commentary, it mostly revolves around her stylistic choices, particularly the look and the sound, as well as the circumstances surrounding the production of films. Yet at times she has offered up certain autobiographical aspects, particularly in regard to *La niña santa*. As such she has, for example, described the post-Catholic stance of the film as based on her own loss of faith (García and Rojas 2004, 13–14), and she has particularly emphasized her own proximity to the figures of Amalia and Josefina: "We were fourteen or fifteen years old. The world had the exact measure of our passions. The intensity of religious ideas and the discovery of sexual desire made us voracious. We were relentless in our secret plans. [. . .] We were alert, because we had a spiritual mission, even if we didn't know what it was. Every house, every hall, every room, every gesture, every word needed our vigilance. The world was monstrously beautiful. It was then that I met Dr. Jano" (Sartora 2004). Elsewhere Martel has reiterated parallels between the catechism class the girls attend and her own religious activism with a group called Acción Católica, as well as between Amalia's incident and her own experiences as teenager (J. Wood 2006, 168). Yet it would be wrong to read *La niña santa*, or any film of the Salta trilogy, as an autobiographical film in the strict sense of the term. In contrast to María Luisa Bemberg's *Miss Mary*, for example, Martel's intention is not to paint a more or less faithful portrait of her adolescence but to create a film that mimics the layers of experience of a young women growing up in the provinces. Just as all three films of the trilogy carefully avoid any direct references to the city and the province of Salta (there are no signs with names of towns, streets, no readable license plates, etc.), so, too, must we avoid drawing on the director's biography as master narrative explaining the meandering paths of her protagonists and their mixed emotions. The distinct personal memories that Martel reworks never coalesce into a coherent (autobiographical) narrative but remain insular moments, at pains to be absorbed into a greater whole. While Martel's idiosyncratic style shapes every frame, *La niña santa* is not a personal film.

If the film opens with a scene of adroitly listening and watching, the final scene is even more contemplative, as Josefina and Amalia idly drift in the turquoise waters of the hotel pool. With Josefina's betrayal, the fuse has been lit to blow up Dr. Jano's reputation, but the film cleverly refrains from showing the explosion. Instead, we watch the girls peacefully floating on their backs, the proverbial calm before a most ravaging storm. While *La ciénaga* closes just after the catastrophe of Luciano's death, *La niña santa* ends when the worst is yet to come. Viewers are left to imagine the fallout from the public scandal. Dr. Jano may not only lose his reputation but also his wife and children, while Helena might be shocked but also shaken out of her self-absorption. Whatever little hope there may have been for a shared future will quickly evaporate with the announcement. Amalia's reaction is even harder to fathom. What will she feel: embarrassment, because an incident has been revealed that she wanted to keep secret? Anger, because Josefina broke her promise? Relief, because the story is finally over? Disappointment, because Jano will be forever beyond reach? Or even the kind of pity that Martel has expressed (though obviously in hindsight) about her own Jano experience: "Those men who rub themselves up against kids in the streets are infantile; there's an innocence or even naivety about them" (quoted in James 2005, 20). Yet regardless of the outcome, *La niña santa* is a more hopeful film than the deeply pessimistic *La ciénaga*. The growing pains of its protagonist may leave some scars, but her assertiveness, independence, and sense of determination will serve her well on whatever path she chooses to follow. Unlike Momi or Verónica, Amalia will not become a copy of her mother.

Consolidating the success of her breakthrough film *La ciénaga*, *La niña santa* catapulted Martel into the upper echelon of international auteurs. Supported by a Cannes writers-in-residence program in Paris, the film was premiered at the Cannes Film Festival in 2004 and garnered considerable attention, which subsequently won Martel a spot on the festival's international jury. *La niña santa* was chosen by the *New York Times* as one of the ten best films of 2005. As that newspaper's leading critic, A. O. Scott, effused, "*The Holy Girl* is a film that defies categorization, but I'm tempted to call it a miracle" (2004). Writing in the *Los Angeles Times*, Kevin Thomas stated that the film "reveals the style, insight and confidence that are the marks of a major director" (May 13, 2005). But there were also critical voices, all of them taking the director to task for what they perceived as her mannerisms. Contrasting Martel's first two features, Kent Jones had much praise to offer but concluded on a more critical note, stating that both films "feel strangely disconnected from the rest of cinema [. . .] a little *too* self-contained and sealed-off from the rest of the universe" (2005, 24). Martin Tsai took issue with

68 | **Lucrecia Martel**

Figure 12. Amalia and Josefina idly drift while a storm brews indoors in *La niña santa*

Martel's penchant for creating uncertainty: "too much ambiguity is not a good thing" (2005, 56). And in Argentina, Diego Trerotola observed that "Lucrecia Martel seems almost trapped by her talent, which is beyond doubt" (2004, 9). Martel has repeatedly stated that she does not read reviews of her films, but her third feature, *La mujer sin cabeza*, seems almost an answer to these more critical opinions. Her most political film to date, and in her own words her "strongest movie about Salta" (quoted in Matheou 2010a, 312), here she revisits her main thematic and stylistic concerns and takes them in new and different directions.

Dazed and Deceitful: *La mujer sin cabeza*

> My films are completely political, but in this sense: to make a film, for me, is the desire to share this doubt about our reality. [. . .] To do cinema is a way to be a citizen.
>
> —Lucrecia Martel (quoted in Matheou, *Faber Book*)

A dusty country road in the Northeast. Three boisterous *campesino* boys and their dog, a German shepherd, are chasing each other along the embankment of a highway, their heedless play briefly interrupted by an oncoming bus, a sign of imminent danger reminiscent of a scene

A Poetics of the Senses | 69

from *La niña santa*. While one, named Aldo, climbs a rusty billboard another somersaults into a deep culvert, followed by a timid third boy. There's talk about a bicycle, but none is to be seen. We abruptly cut to a group of middle-class women gathering in a parking lot outside their social club. Amid screaming kids, they converse about cosmetics and the upcoming inauguration of a new pool; there are rumors that turtles have entered and contaminated the water because the pool has been built close to a veterinary clinic. Soon, the camera hones in on a blonde with large sunglasses, Vero (short for Verónica), who is being complimented on her new hair color, but Vero fears it will fade with the chlorine.

As is customary in the Salta trilogy, both scenes avoid establishing shots of any kind and the characters are joined in mid-conversation, rather than introduced. We catch snippets of the women's exchange of trivialities while the boys, for reasons unknown, hurl swear words at each other. We note the obvious contrast: whereas the playground of the dark-skinned boys is the arid and dangerous countryside, the women and children inhabit the sheltered world of the social club typical of the privileged white middle class. The backdrop of their conversation is the new pool—we see it in use toward the end of the film—while the boys play in the dry *arroyos*, or canals, which are there to contain the sudden flash floods that are frequent in this area. (Sudden changes in the weather also create the titular swamp in *La ciénaga*, which is actually dry terrain that turns into a form of quicksand during the rainy season.) Clean, safe water for the purpose of leisure is contrasted with treacherous, muddy waters that can catch people off-guard. This threat is implied for now but confirmed the next day, when we see a canal filled with rainwater, in which a boy allegedly drowned and which also wrecked the car of Vero's brother. The contrast in surroundings extends to the people who inhabit them: the women's insularity is conveyed through the close-ups of their faces, which are first seen reflected in a windshield while those of their children are pressed against the closed windows of the cars (as Luciano's was in *La ciénaga*). Their chatter revolves around health and safety while the boys engage in rituals of machismo. At the end of the second scene, Vero gets in her car and drives away. The two worlds are about to collide.

The next shot shows us the same country road, now seen from inside Vero's moving car. There are no traces of the boys and their dog. From the passenger seat, the camera patiently observes Vero as she is driving. When her cell phone rings, she briefly takes her eyes off the road to search her bag. Suddenly, a violent thump jolts the car, followed by another. Vero's head is jerked forward and her sunglasses fly to the floor. She stops the car. After a brief moment she reaches for the door handle but then decides not to get out. Instead, she picks up her glasses, starts the engine, and drives on. Throughout the scene, the upbeat pop song "Soleil, Soleil" is playing on the radio, performed by a band ironically called Middle of the Road. We cut to a shot through the rear window that shows the dead body of the German shepherd, seen earlier with the boys, sprawled on the ground. A ninety-second sequence shot of Vero follows, taken again from the passenger seat. Children's handprints are clearly visible on the car window next to her face. Finally, Vero decides to stop along the road and get out of the car. Thunder is heard and a hard rain starts to fall. From a fixed shot with the steering wheel in the foreground, we see Vero pacing back and forth, finally coming to a standstill so that her torso is visible through the windshield. Only the pelting of the rain on the car roof is heard. The screen goes black and the title credit appears.

The frame that concludes the stunning first three scenes, which occupy about ten minutes of screen time, indicates to viewers that the title of the film is to be taken literally: the collision we just witnessed will have a profound psychological impact on the protagonist, even though neither she nor the viewers can be sure exactly what, or who, has been hit.

Figure 13. The camera turns Vero into the titular headless woman in *La mujer sin cabeza*

A Poetics of the Senses | 71

Already in the short *Rey Muerto*, there is an incident in which a pickup truck runs over a bicyclist. Instead of helping the victim, the driver insults and kicks him, leaving the bloodied man to die in the road. The short scene at the beginning sets the mood for a film in which machismo and male violence reigns in an apparently lawless rural region. Here, by contrast, violence enters in very different ways. Instead of focusing on the collision itself, *La mujer sin cabeza* points its lens on the impact that doubt, uncertainty, and disavowal will have on Vero and those who surround her.

In interviews, Martel has stated that she considers *La mujer sin cabeza* "the strongest movie" she has made about her native city (quoted in Matheou 2010a, 312). Indeed, class difference, while never absent from her previous features, takes front and center here. The middle class's pact of silence regarding the possible victim, their complete disavowal, and their stealth and eagerness in covering up all traces can be seen as barely disguised reference to Argentine society during the dictatorship, when an estimated thirty thousand people were disappeared. It is an interpretation that Martel has sometimes endorsed and at others refuted, insisting that the ambiguity of *La mujer sin cabeza*, as well as her other films, resists clearly defined political messages.[28] When the film was premiered at Cannes, the critical reception was mixed, applause interspersed with catcalls. The irritation may have been caused by Martel's stubborn refusal to explain and to psychologize, choosing instead to paint the portrait of a woman in an altered state of mind. What is more, with this film she significantly extends her repertoire of visual and acousmatic storytelling, making her already opaque style reach new levels of density and complexity.

Viewers familiar with Lucrecia Martel's films will immediately notice that, apart from the heightened drama, there are important stylistic innovations. Most notable are the extended tracking shots that capture the before and after of Vero's collision, which are the longest in her filmography to date, and the use of Cinemascope. Given Martel's fondness for what she calls layering, it is surprising that she did not use this format earlier, as it lends itself perfectly to contrasting action that is at the center of the frame with that on the margins. As she explains, Cinemascope "is ideal for getting close to the body, and to the face. Also, of course, it gives you a lot of space around them to work with. You can put in many layers

Figure 14. Extreme shallow focus conveys Vero's lack of awareness in *La mujer sin cabeza*

of activity" (quoted in Matheou 2010a, 317). Indeed, the signature shot of *La mujer sin cabeza* consists of a close-up of Vero in extreme shallow focus, her blonde hair dominating the foreground of the frame, while behind her, and out of focus, various secondary characters, often the indigenous servants and maids, are barely distinguishable. It is a shot that not only captures the protagonist's self-absorption and confusion but also the mindset of her class vis-à-vis the social and racial order of society.

Following the collision, someone drives Vero to a hospital, where a nurse examines her and X-rays are taken. Visibly disoriented, Vero wanders off unnoticed and checks into a hotel, where a man, later revealed to be her husband's cousin, runs into her. They have sex together and spend the night. The next morning, Vero's phone rings; when she hears a male voice, she hangs up. Her lover takes her home, asking her if she wants to be dropped off at a corner or at the house. Instead of indicating what she prefers, she simply replies "fine." After she is home, her husband enters the house, carrying a dead deer, which he apparently just shot while hunting. When he looks for her, she locks herself in the bathroom before getting into the shower with her clothes on. Back in the kitchen, the maid tells Vero that she is expected at her clinic and orders her a taxi. After arriving there, she sits down in the waiting room until the receptionist finds her. When asked by her staff if they should ask her brother, also a dentist, to take her patients, Vero declines, but she leaves without attending to any patients.

A Poetics of the Senses | 73

We next see her at the house of her cousin Josefina, where her aunt Lala and Candita, her teenage niece, live. There are many people present, apparently all members of one religious group. In an upstairs bedroom, Aunt Lala is watching a grainy video of Vero's wedding. The aunt calls one of the visitors, Juan Manuel, "effeminate," which draws Vero's protest. It turns out that he is her lover from the hotel. Following yet another hard cut, we find ourselves in Josefina's car, who is driving her boys to the county club, passing the scene of the collision, which greatly disturbs Vero. At the club, Vero sees a boy lying motionless on the soccer pitch, which further aggravates her. She flees to the bathroom and for the first time breaks out in tears. The next day she tells her husband that she ran over a person. Alarmed, together with his cousin (Juan Manuel) and Vero's brother, he begins to make inquiries and cover any possible traces, and he has her car fixed in another city. In the meantime, Vero returns to domestic chores. She goes to a nursery to buy pots. It turns out that one of the boys working there has been missing since the day of Vero's collision. Later we learn that the body of a boy has been found in the rain-flooded culvert adjacent to the country road where Vero had her collision, apparently drowned. Soon thereafter, Vero changes her hair color from blonde to brown and joins a celebration of friends and family at the same hotel in which she spent the night after her collision. It seems that all is well again.

As this lengthy summary reveals, the film is not a narrative in any conventional sense. In lieu of motivated turning points, we follow a string of seemingly random scenes, which only in hindsight accrue meaning. The point of the film is not to show a woman's reaction to shock, but, as Amy Taubin has it, "the description of a condition of consciousness" (2009a, 23). Martel has commented on this condition as follows, "The accident comes in stages: there's the moment where Vero's perception is altered, and the strange way she feels in the following days; then the moment of confession; then how the family moves toward the 'nothing happened' position; and finally everything falls back into place" (quoted in Matheou 2010a, 309). While we are familiar with a sense of circularity and stagnation from Martel's previous films, the "return to normal," as it were, is more upsetting here, because Vero's crime of omission—the failure to get out of the car and inspect what happens—is neither punished nor, it seems, the cause for prolonged feelings of guilt.

74 | **Lucrecia Martel**

La mujer sin cabeza creates a form of contrast and suspense not found in the previous two features. The opening's intercutting of two separate scenes, which are then conjoined in the third, builds toward the initial climax, the collision. Equally new is the focus on a single person. While a whole ensemble populates *La ciénaga*, and a triangle dominates *La niña santa*, now we follow just one central character, the dentist Vero. Yet despite her centrality, we do not have access to her inner thoughts and feelings through point-of-view shots (as we did with Amalia) but see her through an impartial camera that observes her from close range as if seen by an invisible character in the film. A case in point is the depiction of the collision itself. As James Quandt has correctly pointed out, the shot of the dead dog "has been described as subjective, as being from Vero's point of view, but probably isn't" (2009, 95). Indeed, there is no indication that Vero turns her head to look backward or upward toward the rear-view mirror. This ambiguity, Quandt continues, has important consequences: "The film's central mystery rests on the ontological status of that one image" (2009, 95).

Many critics, among them Quintín and Daniel Quiros, have understood Vero to suffer from amnesia as a result of the collision, an interpretation that Martel refutes (Quintín 2008, 43; Quiros 2010, 251). According to the director, the protagonist's behavior reflects what happens "when you lose the link between things, and the link between a thing and what it means to you. [. . .] It's not about a woman who feels guilty; it's about a woman whose worlds are nearing collapse" (quoted in Wisnieswki 2009).[29] Yet the critics' confusion about the protagonist's state of mind is not accidental—the behavior of the headless woman is simply too erratic and too mysterious to allow for an unambiguous diagnosis. It is true that Vero recognizes certain people, which a person suffering from amnesia might not, but she does not know what her relation to them is. Every conversation she has is peppered with her non sequitur responses, everything she does contradicts the little she says. The difficulty of understanding her is amplified by the fact that the film does not follow a person to whom certain things are happening; rather, we are privy to Vero's perception and what she *thinks* is happening. Vero's head is the point of origin, but the camera is not *in* her head but close to it, impartial and mercilessly indifferent.[30] As Karen Backstein comments, "partly because of Vero's zombie-like persona in the wake of the hit-and-run, events both big and small feel as if they're of equal weight—or perhaps because after what she did, no other action can ever be important by comparison. Tensions within her family, including her husband's possible affair, her own sexual relationship with a relative, a niece's crush on her, and an aunt's growing dementia, fade in comparison and are not dwelt upon" (2009, 65).

But not just the sequence of events and their apparent lack of logic are confusing; every scene and every frame radiates with ambiguities, contradictions, and enigmas. Are the fingerprints on Vero's car window from the children playing in the parking lot of the club or from someone she ran over? Who is driving the car that takes her to the hospital? Why does she wear a bandage over her right eye when her head did not make contact with anything during the collision? If *La ciénaga* is a film that, in hindsight, reveals the many incidents that announced Luciano's accidental death, *La mujer sin cabeza* is one that revisits the scene of the collision over and over. Vero returns three times to the dusty country road, each visit becoming more disturbing, until she no longer wants to take that route. Metaphorically speaking, the collision leaves its traces in many shots. As Martel told Amy Taubin, "the accident is present in every scene in different forms: maybe there is somebody who is digging or something that is thrown on the floor. So I'm not spelling out the accident thing, but I have elements that evoke that" (2009b).

Perhaps the cruelest example of these traces is the scene in which Vero drives to a nursery to pick up some pots for her garden. It's a scene that seems rather mundane until we become aware of its sinister implications. At the nursery, Vero converses with the owner about which pots she'd like; incidentally, they are heavy and have been stocked on a high shelf, which the owner cannot reach without his young helper. But this particular helper has been missing from the job since the day of the collision. The tenuous connection between the two events becomes stronger when we realize that the owner's other helper, Changuila, is the same boy who also played in the canal, presumably the missing boy's brother. The car in which Vero plans to transport these pots might be the very car that is responsible for the absence of the helper, though by now, of course, stripped of any signs of the collision.

The ghosts of the collision are most strongly felt in a four-minute sequence near the film's halfway mark that indicates a crucial turning point. It begins with Vero sitting in her bathroom and telling her husband that she ran over a dog. When the maid enters the house, she lets Vero know that "the boy who washes cars" is here, the maid's and the boy's dark bodies captured, yet again, out of focus and in the background of a frame dominated by Vero's blonde hair. Vero consents to having her car washed, perhaps a purification of the material meant to attend her repeated physical cleansings. We cut to Vero sitting in Josefina's car, who is driving her kids to the club. When one boy throws the other's sneaker out of the window, Josefina has to stop. Incidentally, the shoe marks the very spot where Vero had the collision; the canal alongside the road is now filled with water. Another cut shows us Vero and Josefina at the club and walking on the perimeters of a soccer field, with a sprinkler spraying at full throttle. Gradually, the two women are engulfed in a yellowish haze, perhaps due to the mist, and ambient noises are replaced by an eerie piercing sound, followed by a loud thud and a dog's barking—the very sounds that accompanied the collision. Suddenly, Vero sees a boy lying motionless on the sandy pitch. It is all too much for her. She escapes into the bathroom and tries to rinse off, but the water has been cut off. When a worker tries to fix it but can't, she breaks out into tears. Hesitantly, he hugs her, his dark hand coming to rest on her back. It is the only moment of tenderness and compassion of this kind in the entire film. He leaves and returns with a bottle of water, which he dabs over her head, quickly reestablishing the roles of master and servant. Vero puts her sunglasses back on—as after the collision, the gesture marks her regained self-composure—and disappears with a brief, "Good afternoon." The next day, she tells her husband while they are in the supermarket checkout line that it was a person she ran over.

Bookended by two bathroom scenes, this sequence is by far the most ominous and terror-inducing in the entire film, leading Vero to dramatically change the account of what happened on the road. The four individual scenes are tied together by the various forms of water present in each, which include the bathroom and the boy who wants to wash the car, the canal filled to the brim, the sprinkler and its haze, and the bottled water poured over Vero's head. María Delgado's comment that Vero lives "as if suspended in a fish tank" (2010) finds its most literal embodiment in this sequence. The motionless boy on the dusty soccer field will be the most concrete reference to the corpse we never see. As

A Poetics of the Senses | 77

elsewhere in the film, the sensations created by sound challenge what we see, the former both anticipating and contradicting the latter.

Like the scene of the actual collision, this prolonged sequence draws much of its impact from the restrained yet powerful performance by María Onetto. In interviews, Martel has explained that she originally wanted to cast Mercedes Morán again (Wain 2006), but when Morán was unavailable Martel quickly became convinced that Onetto, an accomplished television and theater actor, was the perfect choice.[31] This was Onetto's first leading role in a movie, the slim, tall body and light facial features certainly making her casting more attractive. From interviews with Martel it becomes clear that the professional actor brought the same attributes to the role as the teenage María Alché did for Amalia: "I had the feeling throughout that I would never really get to know her [Onetto]," she has remarked. "Which was, of course, fascinating for me. [. . .] When she's fully engaged, she is completely in the character's skin. The character is all she cares about. I find that extremely fascinating" (quoted in Magary 2008).

Indeed, the film depends almost entirely on Onetto's performance, not only because Vero is in virtually every scene but also because, due to Martel's refusal to psychologize, so much depends on the actor's ability to convey through nonverbal means the confusion and transformation Vero undergoes. A case in point is the long tracking shot that depicts the initial collision. This ninety-second shot, taken from a fixed camera in the passenger seat, records Vero's brief distraction, the impact of the collision, and her subsequent reaction. Only the minutest signs of distress and concern register on Vero's face, the brief thought of stepping out of the car quickly overcome by her resolve to drive on—never has a crime of omission been depicted with such minimalist acting, making its chilling implications even more horrendous. For the remainder of the film, there will be hardly a scene without Onetto in it, the above-mentioned signature shot of the blonde woman in the foreground against out-of-focus, dark bodies in the background repeated time and again.

Vero's blonde shock of hair also serves as a motif for the film poster, which was designed by Juan Gatti, famous for the numerous posters he created for Pedro Almodóvar. As Mariano Kairuz comments on the poster, "the black and white curls against a furious red hypnotize even more because they stand out in the muffled universe of Argentinean movie posters" (2008, 55). The curls are indeed a labyrinth that induces vertigo much as Kim Novak's carefully coiffed bun disoriented Jimmy Stewart's character in Alfred Hitchcock's *Vertigo*. In Spain, Martel's film was released as *La mujer rubia/The Blonde Woman*, making the poster indeed apropos.

Throughout the film, Vero's hair and its color are a constant topic of conversation and object to be fetishized, beginning with the parking lot scene prior to the collision and ending with the exclusive family reunion in the hotel. Unlike in *La niña santa*, where hair is both an object of adoration and disgust, here it is exclusively to be admired, touched, smelled, and washed—whether it be the "lavado Chino" (lit. Chinese hair-washing, which amounts to dabbing the hair with splashes of water from a cup) in Josefina's house or the many times Vero washes her hair in the shower. The most memorable comment is certainly Josefina's, who says it's "brave" to choose that particular color (i.e., platinum blonde), which, given Vero's overall cowardice, is profoundly ironic.

A final comment on Vero's hair is provided by the elderly Aunt Lala, who lives with her daughter, Josefina, and her grandchild, Candita. While Vero is the sole protagonist of the film, the three are important secondary characters. The men, as often in Martel's films, look and act alike, not so much individuals as interchangeable representatives of a certain way of thinking. Josefina, in contrast, is an important soundboard for Vero, while teenage Candita openly displays her deep affection for Vero—an unabashed form of cruising that hardly merits a comment from either her mother or her aunt. In Martel's universe, this kind of same-sex, same-family desire is not considered worthy of comment. This self-imposed silence, which also rules Vero's house, is broken by Aunt Lala, whose unfiltered opinions give voice to a truth most others like to repress. Like Mecha, Aunt Lala is a matriarch confined to her bed, where she dwells "in a sort of lucid senile dementia" (Sartora 2010, 64). "Both in *La ciénaga* and *La mujer sin cabeza* there are women incapacitated through sickness or old age who, from their bedsides and propped up by high wooden backrests, vestiges of the degraded 19th century European royalty, preside over a space in the process of disintegration," comments Marcos Vieytes (2009, 129). These matriarchs are played, respectively, by Graciela Borges and María Vaner—they star together in Raúl de la Torre's *Heroína/Heroine* (1972), which Helena watches in

Figure 15. Cruising along: Candita in open pursuit of Vero in *La mujer sin cabeza*

La niña santa—who both rose to stardom during the 1960s, when they often played middle-class women who struggle to define their role in Argentine society.

Aunt Lala's psychological derangement is, like Vero's, difficult to pinpoint. She suffers from a form of dementia but has very lucid moments—among all people surrounding Vero, Aunt Lala is the only one to notice any change in her when she says, "That voice doesn't sound like yours"—and to Lala belong some of the film's most poignant lines. When she is first introduced, we see her watching a home video of Vero's wedding, on which she comments by saying, "You were so beautiful. Why let yourself go?" For Daniel Quiros, this line reveals "an obsession by the women of Vero's class with appearances, particularly that of women [. . .] which implies an invisibility of Vero as a person" (2010, 253). While there is certainly some truth to this, I would argue that the issue here is not Vero's invisibility, which can hardly be upheld in comparison to the truly invisible indigenous people. Rather, the aunt's remark serves as corrective to the many fake compliments Vero's hair color attracts, pointing to the superficiality of the moneyed middle class.

Even more fascinating is Aunt Lala's observation about ghosts: "The house is filled with them," she notes. "Don't look at them, and they'll go away." Is this a veiled comment directed at Vero, who is trying hard to repress the possibility of a dead body on the road? A mere acknowledgment of the supernatural, which belittles the Catholicism that rules Josefina's house (she also claims that one woman in the video must already have been dead when the wedding took place)? Or a racial slur about the indigenous maid sitting next to her on the bed and operating the remote control? No matter what we make of these comments, Aunt Lala clearly introduces a new type into Martel's universe—a type that is indeed unique to her hometown, as the director has explained: "This character is inspired by what happens to many women in Salta who, until the age of forty-five, experience enormous social pressure that includes the family, married life, etc. Yet once they reach that age, it is as if they rebel and turn into adulterers or alcoholics, and once they pass sixty they turn into the family's 'crazy aunt,' which in the end turns out to be the most lucid" (García and Rojas 2008, 10).

Critics have argued that with *La mujer sin cabeza* Martel worked for the first time more squarely within the confines of a genre, yet there has been some dispute which genre exactly that is. For Matheou, the film is "a hit-and-run drama" (2010a, 306), but it is doubtful whether the presence of one key plot element constitutes a genre of its own.[32] As in her previous films, there are again strong elements of horror—just note the title, the many eerie and indeterminable sounds, Vero's zombielike behavior, and the presence of ghosts, which include not only the ones seen by Aunt Lala but also the ghostlike existence of the "invisible" indigenous people, who usually appear blurred in the background or at the margins of Martel's widescreen cinematography. The film's main locations are equally disquieting. Vero's house harbors numerous mysteries: why are there children's clothes when her daughters have grown up and moved away? And what lies buried in her garden?

The hospital, too, looks far more sinister than the one in *La ciénaga*, evoking a prison with its dark corridors and the handcuffed woman held in custody, a premonition of Vero's possible future. And as in *La niña santa*, the hotel is a location full of secrets, but now even more enigmatic and impersonal: Why does Vero come here after the collision? Does her lover know she's there? And why is there no record of her stay? Even creepier is the final scene there, when her return to the status quo, as it were, is celebrated behind frosted glass to the tune of "Mammy Blue." The scene reminds Sergio Wolf of the end of Roman Polanski's *Rosemary's Baby*: "The sinister forces regroup to form a circle that encloses Vero, which she in turn welcomes, demonstrating the impossibility of escape" (2008, 44). For Leonardo M. D'Espósito, too, Martel's film

A Poetics of the Senses | 81

evokes other horror films, particularly David Cronenberg's *The Dead Zone* (1983), which deals with a man who, after suffering a car crash, awakes from a coma with the ability to see the future and must now save his country from a despotic president (2008a, 106). D'Espósito also asserts that the film is "an authentic Argentine horror film. Or to be more precise: the first film about Argentine terror" (2008b, 51), alluding to the film's political implications.

In interviews, Martel has asserted that *La mujer sin cabeza* is based on her own nightmares, with the significant twist that she dreams of being the perpetrator, not the victim. In one, she fantasizes about killing a man with a stick and hiding his head on a kitchen shelf; in another, she finds a black hand in her purse, which presumably belongs to the maid. "Many people have these dreams where they are chased by someone who wants to kill them, it's very common. But in my case, I am the chaser. And the killer" (quoted in Matheou 2010a, 308).[33] Elsewhere, she has cited as an important inspiration the B horror flick *Carnival of Souls* (Herk Harvey, 1962), in which a woman dies in a car crash but continues her life as a living dead.[34]

Despite these references, Martel has asserted elsewhere that the thriller, rather than horror, has been her main model—perhaps not a contradiction given that the two genres are close cousins. For many critics, too, this is the dominating genre (Delgado 2010). Vero's house, in which the blinds are always drawn, is a space of shuttered twilight reminiscent of film noir, as is the film's insistence on moral ambiguity. Martel herself has explained that Vero's hairstyle was inspired by Alfred Hitchcock's *Vertigo* (quoted in Wisniewski 2013), in which Kim Novak's character changes her hair color as part of an elaborate scheme to cover up a murder. Like Vero, Novak's character has trouble remembering things and wanders about as if in a trance, even if in that case it is a carefully created ruse. As in most Hitchcock films, in *La mujer sin cabeza*, too, a good amount of time is spent looking for clues and evidence and for ways to cover up a crime—with the significant twist that neither the protagonist nor those protecting her can be sure whether or not this crime has even been committed. And in contrast to most US thrillers, the film ends without resolving the central mystery—a rebuffing of the audience that Hitchcock, at least in this manner, would have never approved of.

Ultimately, then, *La mujer sin cabeza* follows *La niña santa* and *La ciénaga* in alluding to conventions from various genres without committing to a single one. Cecilia Sosa summarizes: "The film could be classified as a Latin American thriller, an existentialist reflection, a murder mystery, a social satire, or even as a middle-aged woman's psychodrama. It winks at all these genres but does not conform to any of them" (2009, 253). Most critics agree that it is this mixing that attributes to the film's power. James Quandt, one of Martel's most eloquent champions, insists that the film is part "trance film, ghost story and political allegory" (2009, 95), while Matheou notes that it is a film "that crawls under your skin and stays there, elusive and troubling" (2010a, 306).

Whatever genre conventions one may ultimately consider dominant, the highly topical film brims over with political references. As in the other films of the Salta trilogy, class is again defined strictly along racial lines, but in relation to *La mujer sin cabeza*, Martel has spoken of a caste system, thus even further emphasizing the impermeable lines that separate the indigenous poor from the white middle class (D'Espósito 2008c, 40; O'Hehir 2008). Yes, the members of different classes interact, they surround each other, but they ultimately do not inhabit the same space. We see this in the bleak hospital, where the poor wait in long lines for treatment while Vero is attended right away. When Vero offers a *campesina* a ride home, she has to ask for directions back into town, as the area is completely unfamiliar for her. Just how out of place she is becomes evident when we realize that Vero has unwittingly stopped at the home of the dead boy, whose brother, Changuila, is seen comforting the grieving mother.

This division between classes is also upheld in Vero's own home, where two maids, a gardener, and a masseuse attend to her. Conversations are short and to the point, conveying bits of information, orders, or requests. As noted, throughout the film the servants are literally in the shadows, the background, or simply out of focus; we see them filtered through windows, glass doors, or water, while the camera holds firmly on Vero. However, the racial slurs uttered by Mecha in *La ciénaga* or Josefina's mother in *La niña santa* are absent in this film; one wonders if this is due to Vero's particular state of mind, which seemingly renders her incapable of aggression, or whether some form of quasi-apartheid has been reached where racism doesn't even have to be voiced anymore. What is perhaps most striking is that relations of class, race, and power are never directly articulated, even though they determine everything. They are accepted as natural and God-given and cannot be questioned or changed. The fatal collision has the potential to challenge this divide, because, in this brief moment, the classes come into violent contact. Yet surprisingly, Vero is never suspected or confronted by anyone. Apart from her mental crisis, there is no fallout. In this almost feudal society, patriarchy still persists. Once Vero has told her husband that she has killed someone, he astutely orders the servants to leave the room and sets out to systematically erase any traces by calling in favors from the well-connected.

Many critics have read the film as an allegory about Argentina during the dictatorship: the dead indigenous boy recalls the willfully disappeared, his act of killing disavowed by those who, like Vero's family, look away, pretending that nothing has happened ("no pasó nada" is a much-repeated phrase by the men) but nevertheless covering up evidence, just in case. Theirs is a chilling demonstration of the power the privileged have to control the flow of information. Such a reading is sustained by the film's many references to the 1970s, including the clothes, the men's sideburns, and the music on the radio—escapist tunes such as "Soleil, Soleil" and "Mammy Blue," which Martel calls "the soundtrack of the dictatorship" (quoted in Enriquez 2008; Taubin 2009b).[35]

Yet while Vero's guilt of omission is symptomatic for a society in denial, this form of denial has not stopped with the end of the dictatorship. In other words, to read *La mujer sin cabeza* as a specific comment on the Dirty War is too restrictive if we imply that with the end of that period all forms of behavior fostered by the dictatorship have ceased to exist as well. In contrast to her other films, Martel has been very insistent about the political implications of *La mujer sin cabeza*: "The social mechanism of silence that was present during the dictatorship is still alive. It is still present in the way poverty is denied. Nonetheless the methods are increasingly sophisticated and because of that more accepted." And she adds, "to me, what is most striking about the dictatorship is not the crimes of the assassins—by which I do not mean to say that they are not terrible—but the complicity of society, which is what most affects us today, because it continues to work like this. The neoliberalism of the 1990s would not have been able to succeed if the civic structures had not been undone. [. . .] The dictatorship bears fruit in the 1990s [La dictadura cobra sentido en los noventa]" (quoted in D'Espósito 2008c, 41).

One very concrete result of the neoliberal agenda of the Menem regime is the greater prosperity for some middle-class families, which in turn has led to a sharp increase in car registrations in Salta and a concomitant rise in car crashes. While nightmares may have shaped the origin of Martel's script, so, too, has a true story. In 1995, María Victoria Mon, a teenager from a wealthy Salta family, struck fourteen-year-old Juan Pablo Acuña while driving home from a dance, killing him. In order to divert suspicion, she reported the car stolen, but the truth eventually came out. According to the local press, the trial was dubious, with the defense lawyers exerting undue pressure on the judge and district attorney. In the end, Mon received a suspended jail sentence of two years and four months and some charity work.[36] The light sentence seems to prove that power relations have largely remained unchanged during the last decades in this part of the country.

The end of *La mujer sin cabeza* can be seen as a provocation and a challenge to viewers, even more so than with Martel's other films. While there remain doubts about who was the victim of the collision, there are no doubts about Vero's guilt of omission. When she allows her husband and her family to act on her behalf without making any attempt to stop them, this omission turns into a cover-up that cements her culpability. While Jubis claims that at the end of the film, "Vero's consciousness has developed as a consequence of the accident and its repercussions" (2006, 96), I contend that no such development occurs. Vero's brown hair is a clear indication that whatever happened during her blonde phase has been flushed down the bathroom sink along with the remnants of that color. I concur with critics who read the film as a call to break the silence, a call addressed not solely to the Argentine middle class but to all of us, as Amy Taubin has aptly stated: "We are all, to one degree or another, headless women. I would not leave a dog or a child to die alone on the road, but the suffering I turn my back on every day is beyond measure" (2009a, 23). We will recall that the last words in *La ciénaga* were Momi's lament about the apparition of the virgin, "I didn't see anything." The first words we hear in this film also refer to the eyes: "Close them, close them," somebody commands. *La mujer sin cabeza* is an extended reflection on what happens when we do.

A Poetics of the Senses | 85

When Pedro Almodóvar introduced *La mujer sin cabeza* at the New York Film Festival in October 2009, he explained: "The movie doesn't end tonight for you. This is a movie that remains in your head and your mind. [. . .] It will accompany you."[37] Indeed, even more so than Martel's previous films, this is a work that keeps hold over viewers because it not only steadfastly refuses to answer the very question it poses at the beginning—who or what did Vero kill?—but also because it carefully accumulates evidence as to why the real issue is not finding an answer to that question. As Karen Backstein notes, the film is "a moral mystery of incredible richness that merits repeated viewings" (2009, 65). The crucial term here is "repeated," which the film may not just merit but in fact require. The considerable demands it makes on viewers implies that it is less than perfect for the festival circuit, where attendants watch several films per day, often with little time to process them. The fact that there were catcalls during one of the 2008 press screenings in Cannes may hence be attributed to the film's stubborn refusal to reveal its meaning at first sight; even though the protagonist returns to normal, as it were, as viewers we are far from closure when the curtain closes—a good thing for Almodóvar, but a bad thing, perhaps, if you have to turn around and churn out a review. One of the critics who was underwhelmed in France was Amy Taubin: "In truth, I did not fully appreciate *The Headless Woman* until I looked at it on DVD in my own time, rolling backward and forward over certain crucial scenes, finding out for myself what its protagonist refuses to face" (2009a, 22).

Critics who were less patient include Adriana Mora, who writes that the film "loses sight of the rhythm of the narrative [. . .] and it lacks the provocative elements of her earlier works" (2008, 111). A more devastating critique came from the renowned Quintín, who rather than criticizing its opaqueness found fault with how conventional it ultimately is: "As disquieting as the plot and the ambience of Martel's film may be, *The Headless Woman* is ultimately very reassuring in its conception of life and art" (2008, 43). A very different take on the Cannes catcalls is that of Jens Andermann, who asserts that the critical sentiment was not just directed toward Martel but to the New Argentine Cinema in general: "The reserved if not openly hostile reception of Lucrecia Martel's *La mujer sin cabeza* [. . .] was only the most obvious symptom of [a] recent sea-change in Argentine cinema's critical fortunes" (2012, xii). For Andrew O'Hehir, in turn, the negative voices at Cannes have yet another reason. In his aptly titled defense of the film, "Why the Cannes Boo-Birds Are Wrong (as Usual)," he writes that the negative press about having made an incoherent movie is somewhat ironic: "A bunch of journalists from around the world, assembled in an elite resort town, can't understand a story about the invisibility of class privilege. (Properly speaking, that's not even irony. It's just a striking illustration of the film's point)" (2008).

In hindsight, it has become clear that the critical voices heard at Cannes (as well as those of Mora and Quintín) are indeed in the minority. Martel chalks it up to the usual shenanigans of how the festival circuit works. "Since *La ciénaga* came out and did well, I have not stopped thinking when it would be my turn. Because I've seen it many times with others. It was waiting for me" (quoted in Enriquez, 2008). Elsewhere, she has added, "it's a kind of Cannes tradition, to boo a film. Now I'm in the club" (quoted in Matheou 2010a, 307). But in Europe, the United States, and Argentina, where the whistles of Cannes had actually led to a delayed opening date, there was overwhelming praise. In *Sight and Sound*, Maria Delgado writes that Martel's latest film is "ultimately the most enigmatic, accomplished and rewarding" (2010), while John Margary sees *La mujer sin cabeza* as "a creeping beauty, but a beauty all the same" (2008). Josefina Sartora contends that the film "has confirmed Martel as the most intelligent, original and subtle director in contemporary Argentine cinema" (2010, 67), while Jens Andermann calls it "arguably [Martel's] finest, most complex and politically devastating film" (2012, xii). For James Quandt it is simply "one of the great films of the decade" (2009, 97).[38]

With the completion of *La mujer sin cabeza*, it became clear that the so-called Salta trilogy is very much of one piece. While the director's increasing repertoire of visual, aural, and narrative strategies is at the service of various thematic emphases, all three films share a focus on female protagonists of the provincial middle class and their experience of the repressive and exclusionary systems of power, gender, race, and social standing. Sexual desire, often in connection to incest, is a constant force that challenges traditional notions of the family and privacy. The coherence of Martel's moral universe is signaled not only by the pervasive sense of stagnation and degeneration but also by the repeated

A Poetics of the Senses | 87

use of key locations such as the swimming pool, the hotel, the hospital, and the family bedroom. Martel's much-touted meticulous attention to detail becomes further evident in the many small and seemingly random incidents and objects that set the three films in dialogue with each other. For example, although a miracle may or may not have occurred in *La ciénaga*, one does occur in *La niña santa*, when a naked man survives a death plunge. Even props recur: the same ladder from which Luciano falls to his death leans against a wall in the Hotel Termas. In that hotel we witness a scene (completely unmotivated by the narrative) in which several girls spray some boys with a hose, reminiscent of the exuberant dam scene in *La ciénaga*. In all three films, ice cubes clink in wineglasses while the presence of hunters reminds us of the frontier mentality of the province capital.

It would be easy to add to this list. What this form of intra- and inter-filmic dialogue proves, on the micro level, is the same that the thematic and stylistic continuities prove on the macro level—namely, that Martel's Salta is a world of artifice, a filmic representation that is the result of careful planning and skilled execution. "The city of birth is always an invention," she has stated (quoted in Panozzo 2008b, 15). For her, this process of denaturalization is not just postmodern playfulness but an aesthetics with political implications, reminiscent of Brechtian defamiliarization: "This idea that the 'reality' we live in is not natural—the meaning of relationships, the emotions, the desire, the economics, everything. We made it, we can change it" (quoted in Matheou 2010a, 313).

While Martel herself initially rejected speaking about a trilogy, with the conclusion of *La mujer sin cabeza*, which is based on an idea she had first developed at the same time as *La ciénaga*, she conceded that the term may be appropriate after all: "Even though I never thought of my three films as a trilogy, I do note that with *La mujer sin cabeza* it is as if a circle has closed" (quoted in García and Rojas 2008, 10). At the time of the film's French premiere, she began talking in interviews about her then latest project, which indeed signaled a radical departure—the adaptation of the graphic novel *El Eternauta* (lit. sailor of eternity), written by Héctor Germán Oesterheld and drawn by Francisco Solano López, which tells of an invasion of Buenos Aires by extraterrestrials and the resistance of a handful of survivors.

88 | **Lucrecia Martel**

Leaving Salta: Recent Shorts and a Lost Film

> YouTube has become for me an intermediate space between wakeful-
> ness and sleep. [. . .] Immersing yourself in that magma is unavoid-
> able—it gives me back my faith in humanity, it makes me more humble
> as well, and reassures me about death. The YouTube autoplay system
> combined with the word you use to start the search is my favorite psy-
> chopharmaceutical.
> —Lucrecia Martel (in "Voyage of Time")

In 2008, Lucrecia Martel was approached by Oscar Kramer, of Kramer y Sigman Productions (K&S), to work on a film adaption of Héctor Germán Oesterheld's science-fiction graphic novel, *El Eternauta* (Daniel Merolla, 2008). The novel is an icon of Latin American comics, and one of the signature Argentine narratives of the second half of the twentieth century, and still enjoys a cult following, partly because of its originality and daring, and partly because of the tragic death of Oesterheld, who in 1977 was disappeared by the military junta, together with his four daughters. Martel's enthusiastic embrace of the project is a clear signal of her decision to change the direction of her work after *La mujer sin cabeza*; even though the project was abandoned in 2009, it points forward to her adaptation of Antonio di Benedetto's novel *Zama*.

The nine-year span between the release of *La mujer sin cabeza* and the premiere of *Zama* is a complex and conflicted period in Martel's career that only in hindsight reveals larger thematic, stylistic, and political continuities as well as decisive ruptures and new departures. After considering the graphic novel and its appeal to Martel, I discuss three shorts made during this interim as three distinct experiments in how to leave behind the world of Salta, before turning to Antonio Di Benedetto's novel *Zama*. In contrast to Martel's early shorts, these later ones are readily accessible on YouTube, and the director clearly considers them part of her oeuvre. Indeed, while Martel has no presence in the social media networks (at least not under her real name), and has publicly called Facebook "a disaster" (Diz and Lerer 2017), she has repeatedly stressed the significance of YouTube. The platform has provided her not only with inspiration and has helped her in her research for *Zama*, but it has become a medium that far exceeds the possibilities of cinema (as indicated in the epigraph to this section). When during the postpro-

A Poetics of the Senses | 89

duction of *Zama* Martel fell ill and serious doubts arose whether or not she could complete the film, she even considered making the footage available online, so that YouTube users could create their own film out of the fragments posted there, as she told us during our Venice conversation. (Whether or not her producers would have gone along with the plan is, luckily, a moot point.) Martel's latest work to date, the music video *Fantasmas* (2018), featuring Julieta Laso, exists only on YouTube, perhaps an indication of what her future trajectory might look like.

El Eternauta (published in English as *The Eternaut*) was first published in a hundred weekly installments between 1957 and 1959, in the journal *Hora Cero Semanal*, with text by Oesterheld and drawings by Francisco Solano López. An immediate success, it tells the story of Juan Salvo and his small circle of friends whose peaceful game of cards is interrupted on some fated evening by a mysterious snowfall, a highly unusual event in Buenos Aires. The group quickly realizes that these are no ordinary snowflakes but "una nevada mortal" (a lethal snowfall) that spells instantaneous death. In due time they learn that Buenos Aires, and indeed the whole planet, is under attack by an alien invasion and the group must find ways to survive in a devastated landscape and to possibly defeat the unknown enemy.

Oesterheld's neologism "eternauta" references the Greek Argonauts as well as the Soviet cosmonauts, combining the timeless heroism and sense of adventure of Greek mythology with the 1950s atomic age and space race. Among the novel's most striking characteristics are its portrayal of the alien enemy, the role of technology, and the presence of a collective hero. Although the alien invaders—beetle-like creatures called *cascarudos*, elephantine beasts called *gurbos* (roundies), and the humanoid species *manos* (featuring hands with many more fingers than humans)—are initially introduced as antagonists to the human race, the humans eventually realize that these creatures are controlled by a greater, more sinister, and unknown other called *los ellos* (the them). As Juan Sasturain has commented, the unnamed *ellos* take on a metaphysical dimension, becoming "almost a metaphor of the evil incarnate in the thirst for power and the universal will to oppress" (2010, 162).

As in many sci-fi stories, there is a strong emphasis on technology, but in *El Eternauta* it plays a unique, twofold role as it is used both to destroy and defend the human race. Following North American and

European conventions, the alien invaders have a superior command of technology, which they use to enslave the human race and cause mass destruction. On the other hand, however, it is their own resourceful mastering of technology that enables Juan Salvo and his friends to withstand the radiation and defend themselves. Rather than being trained specialists and scientists (Professor Favalli being the only exception), they are electronics enthusiasts who know how to use their hands; as one critic put it, they are "Argentines who could put a spaceship together with two screws and a piece of wire" (Miguel Briante quoted in Page 2010, 48). This ease with technology by everyday people clearly undermines hierarchies of class and education. Along the same lines, one of the most alluded to characteristics of *El Eternauta* is its introduction of a collective as the true hero of the novel. Despite Juan's role as the protagonist, survival is only possible through collective efforts, and decisive actions are carried out by a range of characters rather than a sole individual. "Now that I think about it," Oesterheld explained in his foreword to the reprint, "it occurs to me that the reason why I remember *El Eternauta* with great pleasure is because there is no central character. The real hero is a collective hero, a human group. I see it now, it wasn't a conscious decision back then, but my intimate conviction is that the only valid hero is a hero 'in the group,' not an individual hero, a lonely hero" (quoted in Isabelinho, 2014, 41). The collective is also important because *El Eternauta* is not only a story of human versus aliens but also a drama among human survivors, who turn on one another to fight for limited resources. Against the law of the jungle, which pits survivors against themselves, the integrity and dignity of the group surrounding Juan is a strong conveyor of humanistic ideals that have ensured the novel's appeal and relevance over the decades.

While the comic is clearly a product of the 1950s cold war, when popular culture brimmed with alien invasions that provided ready metaphors for more concrete enemies and political threats, *El Eternauta* transcended accepted conventions on many levels when it was first published. It avoided promoting the kind of superheroes that were the trademark of Marvel Comics, featuring instead a group whose friendship transcends class barriers and who must work as a team; indeed, even the military becomes an ally, in contrast to the many European and North American versions, where the army is an entity not to be trusted or is in cahoots with the invaders. Most importantly, perhaps: *El Eternauta* is unmistakably Argentine. Arguably its single most endearing feature for contemporary readers was its faithful and detailed depiction of many recognizable Buenos Aires landmarks, of its architecture and street life, including political slogans spray-painted on walls, creating a verisimilitude that offered an important local grounding vis-à-vis the supernatural invasion. Told from an Argentine perspective—another first for a science-fiction comic in this country—it proudly showed that the forces rallying in Buenos Aires were major players in thwarting a global threat.

Lastly, what elevates *El Eternauta* above most other contemporary graphic novels is its modernist frame narrative. The comic opens with a *guionista*, or writer of comics (who clearly resembles Oesterheld), being visited late at night in his study by a man in strange clothing who slowly materializes in the seat facing him. The stranger, who we later learn is Juan Salvo, explains his fate to be "traveling in time, navigating eternity, my desolate, lonely condition as pilgrim of the centuries," and he is hoping to rest for a bit before he continues on his endless odyssey (Oesterheld 2016, 3). The Eternaut then proceeds to tell the bewildered yet enraptured writer his story, which ends in tragedy. Just when Juan and his family seem to have reached safety, his panicked mishandling of an enemy spaceship separates them into different time zones, condemning him to eternally search for his wife and daughter. Yet at the end of the novel there awaits an unexpected twist: When the Eternaut learns from the writer that the year is 1959, he realizes that the invasion has not yet happened and runs to his house to be reunited with his family. The writer follows him and discovers him mysteriously changed into contemporary clothes and surrounded by his family, with no memory of having ever spoken to him. For a moment the writer wonders whether he dreamed the whole story, just when Salvo's buddies show up for a game of cards—the very routine that only four years later will be interrupted by an alien invasion. Suddenly, what looked like a mere adventure story has turned into prophecy, burdening the writer with the creation of a cautionary tale that must alter the path of history to avoid the coming catastrophe.

When *El Eternauta* was first published in the late 1950s, its domestic and later also international success was primarily due to Oesterheld and

Solano López's creative rewriting of the established conventions of the graphic novel for a Latin American readership. In 1960, Oesterheld returned to the material to publish a remake, this time with drawings by the Italian Alberto Breccia. While this altered version follows the original closely, it features a strong anti-imperialist rhetoric. In this new version, the Western superpowers (i.e., the United States) have struck a deal with the aliens to surrender Latin America in order to save their own territory. Furthermore, Breccia's artwork differed significantly from that of López, replacing his meticulous attention to detail with more abstract collages. Readers were not happy with the changes, and the remake was widely considered an artistic disaster (Trillo 2013, 8).

When in 1975 the original version was republished in a single volume of 350 pages, it became an unexpected success, prompting Oesterheld to think of a real sequel. Teaming up again with Solano López, they created *El Eternauta II*, with Oesterheld himself now featuring in the story as a full-fletched character. At this point in his life, Oesterheld had become politically radicalized and had joined the Montoneros, a leftist urban guerilla group, and he used the comic as a thinly veiled mouthpiece to warn of an impending totalitarianism. The new Eternaut had changed, too. Juan Salvo had mutated and now possessed superhuman strength, was capable of mind reading, and he could even predict the future, approximating the very kind of superheroes the original had stayed away from. The sequel suffered also from the fact that it was written under great time pressure; there are frequent ruptures in the narrative, and events are at times extremely condensed. Critics bemoaned that this new version was schematic and lacked the imagination and unpredictability of the original. "The first part is a tale that explores and illuminates reality; the second part is a fable that interprets it," Sasturain lamented. "The 'bourgeois' Oesterheld writes better than the politically 'engaged'" (2010, 179).

To be sure, the original version was a cultural icon long before the publication of the remake, the sequel, and Oesterheld's disappearance by the Junta. Yet after the end of the military regime, Oesterheld assumed the figure of a martyr. In hindsight we realize that *El Eternauta* is a work of speculative fiction whose imaginations seem to have come true. As Adam Rosenblatt has noted, "it is full of strangely prescient metaphors for Argentina's experience under military dictatorship: the spasm of the unforeseen and indiscriminate violence that begins the alien invasion, the weak pockets of resistance, and the 'gland of terror' that *los ellos* insert into subjugated species in order to keep them obedient. [. . .] As he joined the long list of Argentina's disappeared, Oesterheld came to resemble his creation Juan Salvo, dislocated in time and space from a family that nevertheless shared in his tragic fate" (83f). Over the years, Oesterheld's own biography has become inextricably linked with the story of the Eternaut, in the process completely eclipsing Solano López's contribution, so much so that we think of the novel today as entirely the sole creation of the writer rather than a collaboration.

It is easy to see that Martel's interest in this novel was a radical departure from the Salta trilogy: it would have been her first film based on the writings of another author, initiated by a producer, not herself; it would have been her first genre film; the first not set in her native Salta; and it would have been her first film featuring a male protagonist—a whole series of changes, many of which would eventually come true with *Zama*. Martel worked on the project for eighteen months, writing an entire outline and completing about 80 percent of the script. In

Figure 16. Juan Salvo, hero and savior of the graphic novel *El Eternauta*

interviews she explained that she wanted to develop *El Eternauta* from a humanist perspective: her version of the film was to take place in a modern-time Argentina, and her main focus was to use the city as a setting for a plot that looked at the enemy from within—that is, a world where the enemy were humans themselves who resembled zombielike robots (a figure of particular prominence also in the Salta trilogy). While her interpretation wanted to respect the structure of the graphic novel, it would have transformed the identity of the alien enemy. In this regard it is fitting that in Martel's version the military does not aid Juan Salvo and his group; to think of the military in such positive terms is difficult for Argentines of Martel's generation, who grew up during the dictatorship. Most importantly, the alien invaders were to be more human than the humans themselves. "The invaders wanted to create a green world, an organic world, so-to-speak," she explained to fellow directors Christoph Hochhäusler and Nicolas Wackerbarth, "but in order to do that, they had to 'extract' the humans," which is to say that they would become resources to be harvested for the aliens' own survival.[39]

A particularly intriguing challenge was the handling of sound—what does a city sound like when there are no more birds, no more cars, and only utter silence? As Martel commented at the time, "I know that I'll be able to pull it off only when I understand—personally, emotionally—to see my city, the city I live in, being destroyed" (quoted in Magary 2008). Even though the development of the project had advanced quite a bit, and Martel had already presented the script to the producers, they canceled the production without a rehearsed reading of the script. It was widely reported that conceptual differences between the director and the producers ultimately proved irreconcilable (Macovsky 2009). While rumors about other directors taking on the project have not ceased since then, Martel's *El Eternauta* must now count as a lost film in the history of world cinema.

In the aftermath of what constituted a major rupture in her career, Martel made three shorts, which, while independent, stand-alone works, can be seen as exercises in envisioning otherworldly scenarios that break away from the Salta trilogy and that offer glimpses of what *El Eternauta* might have looked like. At the same time, these three shorts also already point toward her adaptation of *Zama*, not least because for Martel there exists a strong affinity between the treatment of time

A Poetics of the Senses | 95

and space in Oesterheld's science fiction adventure and Di Benedetto's reinvention of the past.

The only short of these three to truly evoke a sense of science fiction is *Muta* (2011), the second of what were by then eight shorts made by various directors for the ongoing series, *Women's Tales*, commissioned by fashion designer Miu Miu. In this cryptic and surreal tale, we watch an all-female cast of fashion models invade an abandoned steamship on a river through a porthole, as if hatching from a cocoon, only to soon disappear again, leaving behind some of their clothes and accessories, which then take on a life of their own. The title translates as "it, or she, mutates" and the models indeed seem to be strange form of mutants, wearing futuristic gas masks that resemble the eyes of gigantic bugs, while moving around like robots and spinning silky thread like spiders. (Among them is María Alché, the protagonist of *La niña santa*, who has since then become Martel's close friend, confidante, and collaborator.) Essentially mute, they communicate only by looks, small gestures, hisses, the snapping of fingers, and fantasy language. They clearly are other-worldly intruders who make the foreign environment safe by spraying disinfectant (recalling the hotel maids in *La niña santa*). While they all possess the exterior attributes of professional models—they are tall, slim, long-legged, and with long, thick hair—we never see their eyes, which are hidden behind huge sunglasses (some of which feature the owlish shape Martel herself favors). Martel's idiosyncratic use of sound—the batting of false eyelashes, for example, causes a loud rattling noise—creates a disquieting and ominous atmosphere, coupled with electronically enhanced sounds of insects, offset somewhat by the absurd premise and the sheer beauty of the camerawork. Repeatedly, an animated object moves inside a leather purse, but no one opens the purse to see what is in it. No men are witness to the ship's take-over; we only briefly spy a male hand that emerges from the water to grab the railing, yet no one offers any help, and it plunges into the river again. As mysteriously as the invaders appeared, they depart, as if melding into other spaces. The final shot is of masses of insects buzzing around lights in the nighttime sky, perhaps the ultimate mutation.

While the robotic, insect-like creatures recall the menagerie of alien invaders from *El Eternauta*, the location of the shoot, revealed in a short making-of featurette to have taken place on the Paraná River,

96 | **Lucrecia Martel**

near Asunción, already points to the setting of Di Benedetto's *Zama*. Martel's adaptation of that novel contains startling underwater close-ups of fish, which accompany the title sequence. These fish are the titular protagonists of *Pescados/Fishes* (2010). If *Muta* is puzzling, perhaps even more enigmatic is this four-minute experimental short, which largely consists of close-ups of gaping Japanese koi carp accompanied by the electronic music and sound effects of Argentine singer-songwriter Juana Molina. Yet another intriguing exercise in exploring the contrast between image and sound, *Pescados* is exemplary for Martel's more recent thematic and stylistic predilections. The film opens with a shot of a heavy thunderstorm as seen through the windshield of a driving car. After fading to black, spherical music with strange sound effects sets in. We cut to a close-up of a multitude of colorful carps swimming in a densely populated pond, their big gaping mouths breaking through the surface as if to breathe. Soon we can make out voices, their inaudible words seemingly synchronized to the opening and closing of a pale fish's big mouth—it is as if the animal wants to speak to us. A subtitle appears, apparently a translation of what the fish wants to communicate: "We were all rolling along on the road . . . we all were a car . . . wheels . . . plastic, lights, we were a car." Other fish with different voices squeeze to the center of the frame, jockeying to make themselves heard. More subtitles appear—"rolling, rolling, horns and lights . . ."—but none match the actual sounds we hear. Among the few words we can make out on the audio track are "autos," "yo lo vi" (I saw him), and "vamos" (let's go), yet only the latter appears as a subtitle.[40] A brief insert shot of heavy truck traffic, speeding through the dense rain, momentarily startles us before we cut back to the fish, still clamoring toward the lens of the camera as if in a feeding frenzy. "A dormir, a dormir . . . Vamos, señores . . . Vamos" (to bed, to bed, let's go, gentlemen, let's go) the final subtitles declare, and all the fish swim away. We fade to an out-of-focus shot of the now-dark streets; blurred streetlights and traffic signs fly by as we descend into the night. A constant rumble is heard, but we can't be sure if it is the thunderstorm or the underwater bubbling of the disappearing fish.

What to make of a film like this? Why do the fish speak of cars and roads, and to whom? Are they dreaming of being cars? And why are the atmospheric images of the rainy highway paired with those of ornamental fish telling us "there were no dogs"?

Like *Muta*, *Pescados* intrigues by being both ominous and enigmatic, but it also adds an absurdist tone that foreshadows *Zama*. Like the models, the fish seem to communicate in ways that are just beyond human comprehension. While the film's ambiguity is unsettling, its beauty is enthralling, particularly Molina's soundtrack, which combines guitar, synthesizer and a whispery voice, dubbed over minimalist melodies, to create loops and patterns that evoke a sense of delirium. *Muta* and *Pescados* are both films that float into other worlds, away from the heightened realism of the Salta trilogy, toward new artistic terrains. Playing with conventions, be it from horror, science fiction, or the surreal, these shorts develop a hypnotic power by striking a careful balance between the utterly strange and the vaguely familiar.

The Paraná River, which provides the setting for *Muta*, already provided the backdrop for Martel's 2006 *La ciudad que huye*/The City That Runs Away, a short documentary that investigates the rise of gated communities in Tigre, a city just north of Buenos Aires, on the Paraná delta. The increase of *countries*, as these communities are called, is a direct result of the arrival of a neoliberal economy in Argentina, which saw the privatization of many industries, including transportation, water, air travel, communications, and ultimately urban development. Driven by fears of crime and an increased desire for security, these communities operate on the logic of exclusion and class division. As Martel explained, what concerned her in this made-for-television piece is how "the exaltation of private space" comes at "the degradation of public space" (quoted in Panozzo 2008b, 16). The short, the only one in which she briefly appears herself, is dominated by images of private-security guards (apparently shot clandestinely), and of walls and billboards that both advertise and hide the new communities from sight. In one shot the director points out how flowers, hedges, and trees have been planted so as to disguise, even render invisible, the concrete borders beyond.

If *La ciudad que huye* is Martel's short that is most reminiscent of investigative journalism and undercover reportage, a different political impetus informs the highly intriguing *Nueva Argirópolis*/New Argiropolis (2010), Martel's third short made after *La mujer sin cabeza*. Commissioned by the Argentine Ministry of Culture for the official 2010 bicentennial celebration of the May Revolution, *Nueva Argirópolis* is one of twenty-five eight-minute shorts that form the compilation

98 | **Lucrecia Martel**

film 25 *miradas: 200 minutos* (25 vistas: 200 minutes). The prompt for each filmmaker was to contribute a meditation on the foundation of Argentina, and on what national identity means today.[41] In this film the Paraná is not just front and center but in a sense also its protagonist. Martel's title alludes to "Argirópolis" (from Greek "silver city"), an 1850 visionary text by Domingo Faustino Sarmiento, president of Argentina from 1868 to 1874, in which he proposed building a city on the island of Martín García, at the confluence of the Paraná and Uruguay Rivers, to house the capital of the (yet to be founded) Confederated States of Plata, comprised of Argentina, Paraguay, and Uruguay. Shot in the Chaco region (where parts of *Zama* were also filmed), the highly elliptical and elusive film focuses on the Paraná as a contested terrain: here groups of indigenous people come into conflict with state authorities who, suspecting them of drug trafficking, pick them up in their makeshift boats; students learn about the course and color of the river, and about islands formed by moving sediment that are inhabited by nobody; and a native elder urges her people via YouTube to mobilize and resist the forces of the state.[42]

In a short piece in the Buenos Aires daily *Página/12*, Martel spoke of her contribution as "lightly inspired" by Sarmiento's text. "We liked the pretense of founding a space that would be a new social order," she explained. "Its genre would be science fiction, I think. Faraway islands, unknown languages. Fragments of a founding movement" (2010).[43] Commissioned by the Ministry of Culture, the official purpose of the shorts presumably was to showcase the splendor and diversity of the Argentine nation; Martel's film, by contrast, highlights how the indigenous populations have been marginalized and ignored by that same nation. A key concern in Sarmiento's "Argirópolis" was the navigability of rivers, which for the author was instrumental to economic and political progress of the nation and the eradication of barbarism (which implied killing off the Indian population). In a vignette of cryptic allusions, *Nueva Argirópolis* points to what this way of thinking has spelled for today's indigenous people. In her insightful analysis of the short, Deborah Martin argues that the film "takes the terms of Sarmiento's text and inhabits them subversively, redeploying them in ways that work against their original aims" (2016b, 459).[44] A key example for this redeployment of meaning is the YouTube video, in which the elder explains to her

A Poetics of the Senses | 99

viewers, "we ought to be wiped out by now, after everything this nation has done [. . .] Let's go on the rafts. *Let us see noble equality enthroned. We are invisible.*" The line in italics, taken verbatim from the national anthem, is a reappropriation that serves as a "form or subversive mimicry, a re-signification of the hegemonic ideas and sentiments of national foundation" (2016b, 456, original emphasis). Translated by a young girl, the YouTube video becomes an important means of internet activism and self-empowerment; the video is given a further, self-reflexive twist by virtue of the fact that Martel's short itself now streams on YouTube (after *25 miradas: 200 minutos* had a limited run in movie theaters across the country).

While the Ministry of Culture was looking for new vistas (*miradas*), Martel was interested in what remains hidden from view, or excluded from dominant discourses. Yet again, what is heard becomes more important than what is seen. Chief among what is heard are several indigenous languages—one unidentified men lists Guaraní, Wichí, Mocobí, Toba, and Ilarrá among them—that are not understood by state officials. The interrogation of the captured boat people, for example, fails since the officials do not understand their language. Throughout the film, native speakers provide *partial* translations to the monolingual *criollos*, carefully controlling what information gets relayed. In a post-screening discussion of *Zama* at New York's Lincoln Center with Esther Allen, Martel specifically referenced this aspect of *Nueva Argirópolis*: "I wanted to capture all the languages that are spoken in Argentina, because no one thinks of them as Argentine languages. In 200 years since independence from the Spanish rule we have done nothing for the indigenous communities, they are the poorest of the poor. And the poorest of the poor speak two languages, but that means nothing to the rest of the population" (Allen 2018b). As I show in more detail below, the handling of subtitles in *Zama* contributes much to its reenvisioning of a colonial past.

The systemic disadvantage and discrimination experienced by indigenous populations is also the subject of Martel's twelve-minute short, *Leguas/Leagues*, one of eleven stand-alone shorts that form the omnibus film, *El aula vacía/The Empty Classroom* (2015). Assembled under the creative direction of Mexican actor and producer Gael García Bernal, the project brings together eleven directors from seven countries to address the crisis of school education across Latin America, where on average more than 50 percent of the students never finish high school. While many of the ten shorts focus particularly on the insufficient education available for rural populations, Martel turns her lens on indigenous youths in Argentina's Northwest, because, as the closing caption informs viewers, "indigenous populations have the highest high school dropout rate in Argentina." The film begins and ends with teenage Erick as he's being harassed by local landowners who accuse him and his family of grazing their cows on what they consider their land. As an elder family instructs the youngsters in the indigenous community, it is due to faulty measurements, the titular leagues, that the whites have claimed lands that do not belong to them, thus evoking the long history of theft and broken treaties that are common in the colonial Americas. Revisiting the landscape and topoi of the Salta trilogy, including dense-wooded hills, on which a dead cow decomposes, the short turns the indigenous community into the protagonists that in the trilogy only populate the margins.

Contested territories also lie at the heart of Martel's most recent project, currently in preproduction, *Chocobar*, a documentary about Javier Chocobar, an indigenous Argentinian activist murdered in 2009 over a land dispute. According to Tom Grater, the Argentina–United States coproduction will chronicle his murder "and the removal of his

Figure 17. Fighting land dispute in *Leguas*

community from their ancestral land in Argentina. The film unravels the 500 years of actions that led to this shooting, both with a gun and a camera, and contextualizes it within the system of land tenure that emerged across Latin America" (2018). There seems to be a natural connection between this documentary and *Zama*, as that film scrutinizes colonialism just shortly before the wars of independence, envisioning a past that could have been while also pointing toward how the colonial heritage continues to play out in the present

Since the Paraná River plays such a central role in Martel's shorts, it is perhaps fitting (or simply a clever form of self-stylization) that it was on this river that Martel first read Antonio Di Benedetto's novel *Zama*. "I owe the particular circumstances under which I read *Zama* to *El Eternauta*," Martel told Brazilian filmmaker Kleber Mendonça Filho. "The script ends with the survivors fleeing on boats toward the north on the Paraná River [an ending that changes the more pessimistic outlook of the novel]. To a place where, allegedly, no deadly snow has fallen. And together with my friend María Alché, I thought of an escape like the survivors, and we disembarked. We took a wooden sailboat, which was very inadequate for this adventure, and sailed on the Paraná toward Asunción. We never made it there. During this trip, in January of 2010, I read *Zama*. I had escaped *El Eternauta*, but I had entered *Zama*" (Mendonça Filho 2017). Asunción is, of course, also the city where Di Benedetto's Zama is posted (even though the name is not specifically mentioned in the novel), a place the author had never visited when he wrote the story. Indeed, like Martel, he was very much an artist closely connected to the region he grew up in—in his case, Mendoza—where he spent much of his life working as a journalist, far from the literary hub of Buenos Aires.

This commitment to his hometown and to life in the province is an important reason Di Benedetto never acquired the fame of his compatriots Jorge Luis Borges and Julio Cortázar, even though the former spoke highly of his work. In contrast to Borges, who was a truly cosmopolitan writer and deeply read in both the Western and Eastern canons, Di Benedetto was more of a regionalist—not in the sense of reveling in the folkloric or local color but in evoking a sense of place, its flora and fauna, its people, and their customs and languages. He prepared for writing *Zama* by immersing himself in all aspects of life in Paraguay

102 | **Lucrecia Martel**

around 1790, studying everything from religion, medicine, indigenous tribes and their languages, and colonial society to water tables, minerals, plants, herbs, architecture, and maps of Asunción—only to discard all of these sources at the time of writing. "I separated myself from the historical Paraguay and from history; my novel is not a historical novel and was never meant to be" (quoted in Lorenz 1970, 194; see also Néspolo 2004, 251–64). As a result, *Zama* is not a re-creation of the past but the construction of a vision of a past—a move that Martel's film amplifies even further.

Roughly of the same generation as Cortázar, Mario Vargas Llosa, and Gabriel García Márquez, Di Benedetto wrote in a terse, clipped style, typical of a newspaper writer, which set him at odds with the rhetorical flourish of the boom writers that put Latin American literature on the global map. As a result, Di Benedetto's stories and novels did not fit the mold of the boom writers, and they were out of print for a long time. Only in the late 1990s did new Spanish-language editions of his major works lead to a certain critical renaissance, and an English translation of *Zama* did not appear until 2016 (after being held back because of delays with Martel's film). Only now, some sixty years after its initial publication, is *Zama* finally getting the broad recognition it deserves.

The controlled prose of Di Benedetto, with its avowal of commentary and omniscience and its distant observing, recalls "the cool efficient manner of film treatments" (Kunkel 2017, 72). And indeed, from early in his career, Di Benedetto had a strong interest in cinema. Something of a film buff, he reviewed films for various papers in Mendoza, he attended the 1966 Academy Awards in Los Angeles and film festivals in Berlin and Cannes, and he wrote two screenplays, *Álamos talados*/Felled Poplars (1960) and *El juicio de Dios*/The Judgment of God (1979). His novel *Los suicidas*/The Suicides (1969) became the basis for Juan Villegas's 2005 film of the same title, and his stories were adapted for the screen for *Chiquilines*/Childish Ones (Mario A. Mittelman, 1991) and *Aballay*/Six Shooters (Fernando Spiner, 2010). Ironically, none of the films based on his work were a critical success. It is notable that, prior to Martel, no adaptation of *Zama* existed, his most famous work and the one its author considered his most accomplished.

Di Benedetto's life was marked by hardship. He was among the first to be imprisoned when the military junta came to power in 1976.

It was long believed that this occurred possibly because of a personal vendetta of a jealous rival, or because he was mistaken for someone else, though more current research shows that it was most likely his defense of freedom of the press.[45] During his eighteen months in various secret prisons, he was tortured and on four occasions he was subjected to mock executions, a horrible fate he shared with his literary role model, Dostoyevsky. In interviews Di Benedetto has stated that not knowing why he was imprisoned was the biggest punishment of all. Due to the intervention of an international alliance led by Nobel laureate Heinrich Böll, who had read *Zama* in German translation, he was released in 1977. He immediately moved to Europe, where he lived in exile in Paris and then Madrid; when he returned to Argentina, in 1984, he was a broken man who died lonely and impoverished in Buenos Aires two years later.

One gets a sense of Di Benedetto's dire existence, as well an astute appreciation of his prose, by reading Roberto Bolaño's short story "Sensini." Its narrator, a struggling young writer and fervent admirer (a thinly disguised Bolaño), strikes up a correspondence with the title character, who is clearly modeled after Di Benedetto, with whom Bolaño exchanged many letters when both lived in exile in Spain. In the course of the story it is revealed that Sensini lives hand to mouth in a rundown apartment in Madrid, supplementing his meager income by entering short-story competitions for modest prize moneys. His masterpiece *Zama*, here renamed *Ugarte*, was dismissed by critics, the narrator tells us, as "Kafka in the colonies" (Bolaño 2006, 3). Elsewhere, he remembers a short story by Sensini, a tale about a man who moves to the countryside, as "a claustrophobic story [. . .] set in a world where vast geographical spaces could suddenly shrink to the dimensions of a coffin"—certainly an apt description of the relation between nature and subjectivity in *Zama* (2). That novel he characterizes in turn as "a cold book, written with neurosurgical precision" (5). Only three years old when *Zama* was first published, Bolaño shares Di Benedetto's fate of having been largely ignored by the literary establishment during his lifetime; when he published "Sensini," in 1997, he did not know that belated fame was about to catch up with him, making him a world-renowned author just before he died at age fifty in 2003.

In hindsight, *Zama* reads like a cruel allegory of Di Benedetto's life. Like his eponymous protagonist, the writer waited in vain for his ship to come in. When he wrote *Zama*, the dictatorship was still some twenty years away, but the novel's sense of dread and foreboding, of lack of direction and futility, reads like a description of life under tyranny. In interviews he has stated that he felt as if his torturers had read the novel, thereby suggesting that they used it as a manual to inflict maximum pain on him.

It is perhaps no coincidence that Di Benedetto and Héctor Gérman Oesterheld, the two writers who so fascinate Martel, were both victims of the military junta, although for different reasons. Both are representatives of a literature of resistance, and both *Zama* and *El Eternauta* revolve around a male protagonist lost in time and space. While we will never know what her adaptation of the graphic would have looked like, we do get an inkling by watching *Zama*.

The Myopia of Colonialism: *Zama*

> Let's imagine a world where just a few films are produced, but it's necessary to see them several times.
>
> —Lucrecia Martel (in Sachs, "Interview")

Much anticipated by audiences and critics, *Zama*, Lucrecia Martel's last feature to date, premiered in August 2017 at the Venice Film Festival. Delayed several times by a fraught production, for which some thirty producers combined efforts, and the director's life-threatening illness, the film has been showered with praise following its premiere and subsequent festival screenings at Toronto, New York, Rio de Janeiro, London, and Madrid. It also enjoyed a warm welcome in Martel's native Argentina, with an unexpectedly strong performance at the box office in a market where domestic features always struggle for screen time in cinemas inundated with Hollywood blockbusters (Battle 2017a). *Zama* was the country's official submission to the Academy Awards for the best foreign film, and with twelve nominations also led the pack for the 2018 domestic Cóndor de Plata competition, ultimately winning in eight categories, making it by far the most decorated film that year.[46] It also won four awards in the 2018 Premios Fénix, which recognizes film productions from Latin America, Spain, and Portugal.[47]

While formally and politically consistent with her previous work, *Zama* clearly marks a new direction in Martel's oeuvre. Her most expensive production to date, it is also her first literary adaptation, her first period piece, the first to be shot digitally and using a 16:9 ratio, the first to be set outside her native Salta, the first featuring a male protagonist, and the first without a swimming pool.[48] It's a leap forward that does not so much capture a world through a heightened realism, which marked the Salta trilogy, but thoroughly reinvent it.

Set on the outer frontiers of the Spanish Empire during the last decade of the eighteenth century, *Zama* pushes traditional notions of a colonial adventure tale to its parodic limits. Based on Argentine writer Antonio Di Benedetto's 1956 novel of the same title, the film follows the plight of Don Diego de Zama (Daniel Giménez Cacho), a creole (defined as a Spaniard born in the Americas and considered in Spain to be a second-class citizen) who serves as magistrate for the Spanish Vice-royalty of Río de la Plata. Resentful of his demotion to the provinces, he yearns for a transfer to the city of Lerma, where his wife and family live, and where he hopes to escape the deadening routine of his assignment. As the viewer slowly realizes, however, Zama's frustration is the result of his repeatedly denied desires: political, monetary, and sexual. He woos the Spanish noble woman Luciana Piñares de Luenga (Lola Dueñas), neglected by her husband, but realizes too late that she only toys with him; some time later, he has a son with an indigenous woman, in the false hopes that this will speed up his promotion, and swiftly neglects both. Toward those under his command he is arrogant and unjust, while failing to demonstrate enough submission toward those he serves. As time passes, one governor succeeds another, while Zama only becomes ever more destitute and miserable. In a last-ditch effort to gain the favor of his superiors, he finally volunteers for a mission to hunt down the dangerous criminal Vicuña Porto (Matheus Nachtergaele). This foray leads him deep into native territory, where his sense of displacement and personal undoing only escalates.

Zama provides a startling portrayal of the conceits of empire and the paradoxes it breeds, carefully eschewing genre-driven formulas and relying on fantasy and imagination, sometimes to an outrageous degree, to reenvision the colonial past. As someone who lacks complete control over his fate during his increasingly stagnant post in the province, Zama is no typical colonial hero, nor is his story a typical historical epic. Born in the New World but serving the Old, Zama suffers as much from geographical uprooting as from his self-perception as a second-class citizen, constantly wavering between frustration and expectation. Only at the end, with his hands amputated and barely alive, does he seem able to reconcile the discrepancy between what he wants to be and what he is. Miraculously rescued by a band of unseen strangers, and traveling barely conscious in a dugout canoe, Zama is asked by an indigenous boy if he wants to live, and ever so barely Zama nods—a sign, Martel has commented, that he will survive this ordeal because he has finally accepted the fate that has been handed to him.[49]

In its basic outline, Martel's film follows Di Benedetto's novel, but both novel and film are far more elliptical than this summary suggests. Crucial for Di Benedetto was the task of reproducing in the reader the disorientation his protagonist experiences, a sensation amplified even further in Martel's film. While the novel is also set in an unnamed city on a large river, details such as street names make it clearly identifiable as Asunción (today's capital of Paraguay), whereas the film carefully avoids concrete geographical markers. The novel's distinct three-part structure, indicated by the headings "1790," "1794," and "1799," delineates a set timeline that the film intentionally blurs and indeed collapses. We notice that in Martel's film Zama's physical state is slowly deteriorating, and the passing of time is indicated by the fact that he has dealings with three different governors, but viewers are left to their own devices to establish any clear temporal markers, reproducing in them Zama's declining grip on reality. Particularly the novel's third and final part, set in 1799, has a distinct symbolism that the film erases. The date alone signals that with the new century a new world order would arise—as indeed it did, with both Paraguay and Argentina gaining independence in 1811 and 1816, respectively. In hindsight, Zama's obstinacy and self-hatred can be seen as part of the fuel that lit the fire of the colonies' struggle for self-rule, even if the novel itself hardly invites such a straightforward interpretation.

The opening sequence of the film paints Martel's departure from previous practices in bold strokes. After the credits listing the many producers have rolled by (actually eliciting chuckles from viewers during the Venice premiere I attended), the screen goes black and we hear a menacing rattle, as if from a snake on high alert—the first of many threatening or disorienting sounds with which this film brims (later in the film it is shown to be created by the shaking of dried twigs). The first image is of Zama standing on a sandy shore with a tricornered hat and a sword, imperiously overlooking a wide river while in the background a group of indigenous children fetches water. The sound of lapping waves mixes with those of insects and birds. As Zama climbs the dunes, he hears faint giggling and, following the noise, discovers a group of naked women on the beach. We cut to a close-up of several Guaraní women taking a mud bath, in their midst Luciana and her black slave, Malemba (Mariana Nunes). Zama settles down to listen to them but is found out and called a *mirón* (voyeur). Malemba dashes toward a fleeing Zama and grabs his ankle; cornered, he slaps her hard twice and rushes away.

If the first scenes establish Zama as a violent man with delusions of grandeur who spies on women, the following scene hardly portrays him in a kinder light. Wearing an ill-fitting wig, symbolic of how thinly the veneer of civilization has worn in the wilderness, Zama oversees, with smug detachment, the torture of a native prisoner who refuses to confess to a crime that remains unexplained. Impatient with the lack of progress, the governor takes Zama aside and explains that the prisoner needs to talk. "To free oneself of one's position," he reminds his magistrate, "one must first take care of it." It is the first indication that Zama is dissatisfied with his posting. Seemingly contradicting this order, Zama's assistant, Ventura Prieto (Juan Minujín), has the prisoner untied and tells him he is free to go, whereupon the man runs headlong into a wall and collapses. Lying on the floor, he mumbles: "There's a fish that spends its life swimming to and fro. Fighting water that seeks to cast it upon dry land. Because the water rejects it. The water doesn't want it." As this tale begins, we cut to a low angle close-up of the bewildered faces of Prieto and Zama, listening in disbelief.

Suddenly the title "Zama" flashes onto the screen, projected over murky brown waters, and a catfish with long barbels closely swims past the camera's lens (the first of several animals to gaze directly at the viewer). The prisoner's fantastic story, now illustrated by images of real fish, continues as a voice-over: "These long-suffering fish, so attached to the element that repels them, devote all their energies to remaining in place. You'll never find them in the central part of the river, but always near the banks." The sequence is accompanied by the song "Luces en el Puerto" (Lights in the harbor), performed by Los Indios Tabajara, a group of North Brazilian faux Indians who during the 1950s became famous for their kitschy music as well as their exaggerated folkloric outfits. The song's Hawaiian theme evokes images that contrast strangely with the muddy water and the grotesque-looking fish, creating a sense of slight parody that pervades the entire film. While the shots of the catfish may be reminiscent of Martel's short *Pescados*, nothing in her oeuvre has prepared viewers for a title sequence that features underwater photography, anachronistic non-diegetic music, and a surreal voice-over tale—a most startling contrast to the sketch of white male entitlement and colonial hubris that precedes it. Indeed, this contrapuntal tension spills over into the next brief scene, in which Zama, now with his back turned toward the viewer, looks at the river again, at the bottom of which the just-described species supposedly lives, leaving us to wonder if he, and we, should believe in the existence of this fantastic creature.

Disregarding the title sequence, the opening five minutes of *Zama* present a series of three seemingly unrelated short scenes that turn out to be united by a narrative thread and strikingly similar visual compositions and soundscape. In each of them, Zama figures in the foreground, predominantly in a pensive or observing position, while black or indigenous figures move around in the background. They are played by nonprofessional actors, or what in most productions would be labeled extras, a term that proves inappropriate here as they assume increasing significance as the story develops. In the opening shot, Zama's commanding posture is already undercut by the children's joyful play, his grandstanding a means of accentuating his mere hubris. The children are actually commenting on a dead monkey in the water, an important image from the novel (to which I return), but this exchange is lost on Zama (and the vast majority of viewers, as their Guaraní is not subtitled). We later come to realize that this visit to the river might well be part of his daily routine, anxiously awaiting the ship that carries news from his wife, or the letter from the king with the much hoped-for promotion. (The beginning of the second part of the film is also marked by Zama overlooking the river, this time with a boat arriving in the background, while the final part is announced by Zama sitting at the river's edge, now looking rather disheveled, as he signs on with the third governor for a trip into the heart of darkness.)

In the first scene, Zama is in the foreground of the frame, immobile as a statue, while the viewers' attention is directed to the children's

A Poetics of the Senses | 109

movement in the background. This formal approach literally decenters Zama, creating a dialectical tension between him and other figures in the frame that is consistent throughout almost the entire film. It notably differs from the extremely shallow focus in *La mujer sin cabeza*, which blurred the servants in the background, serving as a metaphor for the invisibility of the native population in the eyes of the white middle class, and thus highlighting their schizophrenic position as being at once present and absent. Here, by contrast, the extreme depth of field forces viewers to follow the action in the background, becoming increasingly mindful that Zama, who is present in almost every scene of the film, is unaware of what's happening around him.

When in the following scene Zama settles down on the dune above the bathers, the viewers' eye is again directed toward the background, where the women smear themselves with mud. Again, it is this part of the frame that matters: the mud conceals the pigmentation, erasing the markers of class and race between whites, *indios*, and blacks, and thus the hierarchies through which colonial rule operates. Unusual for a Spaniard, Luciana is learning the Guaraní terms for spider and wasp, showing an interest in the culture of the other that neither Zama nor any other of the colonial rulers seem to share. Just as Zama's positioning at the river is twice repeated in the film, the spider wasp is also referred to twice more, first when Luciana has a tête-à-tête with Prieto (with Zama again spying on her), and then in the third act, when the commander of the search party suffers from an infection due to a bite from this insect. Such minor plot elements, together with numerous auditory and visuals clues, are repeated and modified throughout the film, creating an intricately layered narrative that reveals itself only after repeated viewings.

The scene in the dunes is also remarkable for the brief female nudity and assault against a woman, both rarely seen in Martel's films. In this she remains faithful to the novel but significantly reduces its graphic violence, as she does throughout the film, sparing viewers the novel's rape scene, Zama's slaying of dogs, or a woman being trampled to death by horses (in our interview, Martel discusses the rationale for these changes). When Zama slaps Malemba, his body blocks hers from view, thus obscuring both her nakedness and the impact of his blows. In confronting the *mirón*, Malemba rejects the role of woman as the passive object of male desire, clearly a more direct response than the

110 | **Lucrecia Martel**

playful but ambivalent subversion of the voyeur position we see in *La niña santa*. Martel has pointed out that Zama is actually more listening than watching, because the voices of the women remind him of his absent wife (Allen 2018b). Throughout the film, one senses the director's sympathies for a protagonist who, for most viewers, will be difficult to like.

Malemba's reaction to Zama's behavior is a sign of courage and agency. That she is the only servant with a backstory further underscores her importance for the narrative. As Luciana reveals to Zama, Malemba ran away from an abusive tobacco farmer but was caught and cruelly punished by her captors, who skinned her feet and rubbed a poisonous plant on her soles, resulting in a permanent limp. Her muteness must be seen as an act of protest—or an aftershock of the trauma inflicted on her—because, as Luciana explains, "she has her tongue."

As the opening scenes already indicate, *Zama* consists mostly of short vignettes, all of which center around the protagonist, making the film far more episodic than any of Martel's previous ones. The narrative moves at a slow pace, conveying the stagnation in the backwaters of the viceroyalty, only to be propelled forward by significant ellipses that challenge the viewer to fill in the gaps. Yet "the film's sluggish rhythm," Jessica King aptly notes, "belies a surfeit of incident: every scene is steamy with background activity, the air thick with hidden motivations and unspoken crosscurrents" (2017). The cinematography underscores this hidden activity. The extreme depth of field reveals an overabundance of details, and there are frequent tableau-like arrangements in which the camera remains still while the people move within the frame, crowding each other out. Various animals that enter official spaces, or furniture of forgotten splendor that stand around in a yard—objects that are conspicuously out of place—amplify this struggle over space. In one memorable scene, a llama walks into the governor's office and, to surreal effect, gazes directly at a petrified Zama just as he is informed that Prieto is being "punished" by receiving the posting in Lerma that Zama had hoped for.

The frequent use of off-screen space and decentered compositions heighten a state of confusion that reproduces in viewers the anguish and incomprehension that plague the protagonist. Equally confounding are the sets. Doors and windows, rather than providing access, often keep

Figure 18. Hands that reach out of nowhere in *Zama*

events out of sight; one constantly senses that important events are occurring off camera. Much of the story takes place not in grandiose buildings but ramshackle huts that contrast sharply with the gaudy regalia of the Spanish functionaries. Tight frames and a highly selective focus that often eliminates important parts of the body from view capture the puzzling architecture and floor plans of the huts.

In one memorable sequence, Zama and Ventura Prieto attend a formal event in Doña Luciana's house, where upon entering they are announced by a servant with a faux Castilian accent. Then Zama moves into an adjacent room, which turns out to be a barn with a horse, while the next room over serves as a brothel. While a black man has his skin painted, Zama is informed that "the mulattas are here," and a man immediately strips naked. The incongruity of these adjacent spaces, divided merely by lattice, both puzzles and amuses.

If the configuration of spaces has viewers scrambling, consider Martel's trademark use of idiosyncratic soundscapes, elevated to new heights in *Zama*. As in her previous films, sound often precedes the image, underscoring the director's belief in the primacy of hearing over seeing, but she has added new layers. As Martel has commented, the sounds we hear are predominantly those of crickets, frogs, and birds of the Chaco region, but even though they are real, "the spectator connects [these sounds] to a digital or electronic environment" (Martel quoted in Moseguí 2018). Rarely do sounds illustrate or amplify what is already seen, and their origin and nature mostly remains mysterious. Only now and then is their nature revealed: for example, when after a sudden loud bang a small plume of smoke appears, implying that the sound was a gunshot. At other times, the dialogue becomes barely audible, as if someone has turned down the volume, making it another element of an inscrutable or cryptic soundscape. And then there's the Shepard tone, an anxiety-producing sound that we hear at several key moments, often when Zama is realizing that his ambitions are coming to naught, or when he doubts the reality of what he is perceiving. This auditory illusion creates the impression of a continuously swelling sound when in fact the pitch is stuck in a repeating loop—an aural correlate to the optical illusions of M. C. Escher. Lastly, there is easy-listening non-diegetic music that, after the title sequence, is used several times as a contrapuntal and parodic element, its jarring anachronism further heightening the film's sense of an imagined past.

The complexity of the sound is matched by the rich diversity of languages. There are a number of different inflections of Spanish: while a royal *castellano* is spoken by Luciana and the governors, Zama speaks in a more neutral and nonspecific Latin American diction, while some have an accent from Corrientes and other northern provinces, and the character referred to as the Oriental talks like a *porteño*. Then there's Portuguese, spoken by most of the men in the search party, and

A Poetics of the Senses | 113

Portugnol, a mixture of Spanish and Portuguese typical of the border regions of Brazil, Argentina, and Paraguay. Most important, there are various indigenous languages, none of them subtitled. As Lucrecia Martel explained in conversation with Brazilian director Kleber Mendonça Filho, "an old woman speaks Pilagá in the scene with the blind Indians; the bird people speak Qom; and various people speak Guaraní, but in its most Mesopotamian version. [. . .] The multiple languages are not a political affirmation in favor of cultural minorities. I simply wanted to capture the beauty of a diverse world" (2017).[50]

And then there is *Zama*'s striking color scheme. While muted colors such as a washed-out pink, the ochre of the sandy riverbanks, and an array of blue hues dominate for the first hour of the film, bright greens and reds make for a striking contrast during the final third. The stunning, almost blinding cut from a bleached-out riverbank to the bright green fauna of the Chaco region, which marks the beginning of the final section of the film, rivals Stanley Kubrick's famous cut from stone age to space age in *2001: A Space Odyssey* (1968). The look of Zama changes as well, though more gradually. While he is never seen without his mauve velvet jacket and brown vest in the first hour of the film, he looks more and more disheveled as time passes. By the time Zama signs on for the search for Vicuña Porto, he is sporting a long gray beard, dirty clothes, and a gaucho hat. Sitting astride a diminutive horse, this once

Figure 19. The bright green of the Chaco in *Zama*

proud-looking magistrate now oddly resembles Don Quixote, setting out to tilt at his own windmills.

The aesthetic choices that drove Martel's adaptation take on a clearer shape through a closer look at the film's 1956 source novel by Antonio Di Benedetto, only now considered a masterpiece of Latin American literature. As already noted, Di Benedetto had many affinities to the cinema, and the novel's abbreviated, clipped style resembles a script. At the same time, *Zama* has long been considered an unfilmable novel, both because of its idiosyncratic distortion of time and place, conveyed through the interior monologue of an unreliable and highly unsympathetic narrator, and the novel's sad track record of aborted efforts in bringing it to the screen (a point I return to below). "The curious thing about this adaptation of the novel," remarked the renowned Argentine critic Quintín, not always a supporter of Martel, "is that it is very faithful and at the same time completely distinct" (2017). Martel herself has described her process as follows: "For me, it was important to stay true to what I perceived in the novel. I don't know if that's the actual novel, but it's what the novel provoked in me, and to that I was absolutely faithful. It's not interpretation, it's not adaptation, it's not translation [but] infection. [. . .] It's the best way to describe what a book does to you. It's like a disease" (quoted in Marchini Camia, 2018a, 45).[51] The result of this infection is an entirely independent, stand-alone work that neatly complements, comments on, and expands Di Benedetto's novel.

One of the biggest challenges in adapting the novel was its first-person narrative. Early on in the process, Martel decided that there would be no voice-over. Instead, she opted for a plethora of off-screen sounds, which apart from the natural audio track include inscrutable noises, indistinguishable voices, and fragments of dialogue. Zama's voice is never heard in the many scenes with off-screen dialogue by others. Even though Zama is the central character, the story is not told from his perspective. Instead, the film describes the universe of his experience and memories; we witness Zama's reactions as events unfold around him. Frequently shown listening to others, he is a strikingly taciturn protagonist, with few lines of dialogue, some of which are later repeated by other characters, as if someone else had authored them. And whereas a first-person narration always gives the protagonists a certain intentionality and the ability to reflect on what is going on around them, Martel's main character, by contrast, is often surrounded by people who seem to know more than he does.

While the film has no voice-over, a notable early scene comes close, when the Oriental and his son are disembarking their ship. During their voyage on the river, the captain explains, he has told the son about Don Diego de Zama. When we first see the boy, he is sitting on a chair, which a black slave carries on his back, forcing Zama to look up to him. Turning away from Zama, the boy whispers, "The magistrate Don Diego de Zama. A god who was born old and can't die. His loneliness is atrocious." Confused by these lines, Zama asks, "Are you talking to me?" As the boy is being transported away, he stares at Zama and for the first time we hear the Shepard tone. Then we hear the boy's voice again, but he is not moving his lips, making us wonder whether he is actually speaking or whether this is Zama's imagination. "El doctor Don Diego de Zama," the boy's voice continues, "vigorous, in charge. The pacifier of Indians." Then we see the boy's lips move again as he continues, "He who did justice without drawing his sword." Inexplicably, the boy holds Zama's sword in his hand (later, Porto will also steal Zama's sword and finally use it to cut off his hands). Baffled, Zama looks for his sword, but the camera does not reveal whether it is still on him or not. The boy concludes: "Zama the *corregidor*. A *corregidor* with the spirit of justice. A man of law. A judge. A man without fear." Almost the entire scene is shot with a handheld camera (rare in this film), adding a visual instability to the blurring of authorial voice-over and Zama's imagination. This surreal scene is the only one where Zama's backstory is hinted at; tellingly, its mise-en-scène calls into question the truthfulness of what it conveys, namely that Zama was once a powerful, effective, and respected servant of the Crown.

As Don Diego de Zama, Daniel Giménez Cacho gives a weary, bone-dry performance. "Cacho plays every indignity kicked his way with wonderful stoicism simmering with slow-boiling frustration," comments critic Dan Schindel (2017). As the central character, and the only one present in almost every scene of a highly episodic narrative that has most secondary characters enter and exit, it falls on this actor to hold the film together (and without whom, as Martel has repeatedly noted, she would not have made the film). When Giménez Cacho first read the script, he was appalled by the character, as Selva Almada notes: "What a

Figure 20. The mysterious boy looks down on the hero in *Zama*

gray and boring guy! How can you make a film with someone like this?" (2017, 87).[52] This negative assessment of Zama is aptly fleshed out by J. M. Coetzee, who in an enthusiastic review of the novel describes its protagonist as "vain, maladroit, narcissistic, and morbidly suspicious; he is prone to excesses of lust and fits of violence, and endowed with an endless capacity for self-deception" (2017). Martel's film, however, turns Zama into a more sympathetic character, eliminating many scenes in which his violent or misogynist streak comes out—a necessary change, as Martel explains in the interview included here, for the story to work. Instead of being despicable, Cacho's Zama goes about his work and life with a mixture of contempt, boredom, and incompetence. While he is still a figure full of brittle vanity, resentment, and anger, his plight is portrayed in such a way that it also elicits our compassion.

Martel cast Lola Dueñas—primarily known for her performances in films by Pedro Almodóvar—as Luciana because of her comedic background, and indeed her scenes with Zama are among the funniest of the film. Her quick wit and sarcasm provide a contrast to the brooding, introverted hero.[53] Hers is a particularly dry sense of humor; when Zama is waxing nostalgically about fur-clad princesses in snowy Russia, she curtly observes, "Europe is best remembered by those who were never there," hitting the nail of Zama's identity crisis on the head (as well as the identity of present-day Argentina's, as Martel explained to José Teodoro: "*that* is Argentina!" [2017, original emphasis]). Equally offhand are Luciana's comments about Malemba's plans for marriage: "She bought her freedom and already wants to lose it." Indeed, Luciana and Malemba are more than master and servant; their fight for independence makes them kindred spirits. While Malemba flees an abusive master and bravely confronts the eavesdropping Zama, the Spanish noble woman despises all men's desire for her body, including her husband's, but has affairs with whom she pleases. (In the novel, she confesses to Zama to have been coerced into an arranged marriage with her husband at age eleven.)

Describing her transition from adapting *El Eternauta* to adapting *Zama*, Martel has stressed the parallels between the genres of science fiction and colonial adventure, and between envisioning a future and a past. *Zama* carefully avoids the convention of Argentine historical dramas: "These films tend to be solemn and serious," Martel has lamented. "All of the characters are heroes; all the problems are tremendous. The entire dialogue is solemn" (quoted in Lazic 2018). Her Zama, by contrast, is not a typical hero, and his is not a heroic story. There are no grandiose battles, no elaborate sets, no special effects. As cinematographer Ruy Poças further explained during the Venice press conference, it was a conscious decision not to show any candle light or open fires, nor shadows on people's faces to convey emotions—tricks of the trade he and Martel considered "too easy."[54] Equally absent are references to the Catholic faith or the church, as Martel wanted to envision a life where the church's presence and domination is not ubiquitous. The single exception is a priest, who after the death of the Oriental is primarily concerned with what will happen to his estate, not to his soul.

Like Martel, Di Benedetto was not interested in following established patterns of representing life in the colony. The novel does not adhere to the conventions of historical novels in the tradition of a Walter Scott or James Fenimore Cooper: there are no references to real places, events, or figures, and Di Benedetto's use of symbolism and descriptions of nature border on the surreal. The renowned Argentine writer Juan José Saer, an early advocate of Di Benedetto, called *Zama* "a refutation of the idea of a historical novel. [. . .] It is not a reconstruction of a certain past but the *construction* of a vision of the past" (1997, 48, original emphasis).[55] Nevertheless, the novel contains numerous indirect references to real events of the time. Foremost among them are the reforms by King Carlos III, who replaced creoles—or *americanos*, as they are called in the novel—in the higher administration with people hailing from the Iberian Peninsula. This creates an insurmountable obstacle to Zama's ambition—a demotion that is briefly referred to in the film, but since its reasons remain unexplained, one is tempted to see it as the result of personal mistakes. Another important fact concerns the recently abandoned system of forced labor (*encomiendas*) through which the Spanish crown granted the conquistadors control over indigenous people and the land they owned, turning them into de facto slaves. In a scene that captures like no other Zama's racism, we see him presiding over a case where landowners, the descendants of pioneers who settled the land and chased off or killed the Indians who lived there, now find themselves without workers, and claim an *encomienda* of "forty tame Indians." Defending this now-antiquated system, Zama rules in their favor even though there is no appropriate paperwork. Disgusted with Zama's flattery of those in power, Prieto sarcastically comments, "I am astonished by the number of Americans who want to pass for Spaniards instead of being what they are."

Apart from these references to important historical events, many details in the novel convey a sense of a real place and time. Di Benedetto has stated that he consulted numerous sources describing the flora, fauna, geography, and history of a region he never visited himself, only to discard all of them to rely instead entirely on his imagination (Lorenz 1970). Nevertheless, there is ample evidence of the author's meticulous research.[56] A similar point can be made about Martel's film. Even though it is certainly correct to insist that her *Zama* is also primarily a product of the imagination, she, like Di Benedetto before her, read widely about the region's geography, particularly its rivers, its wildlife, and its indigenous communities before writing her script. As her most important source, the director cites Félix de Azara's *Voyage dans l'Amerique meridionale depuis 1781 jusqu'en 1801*, published in Paris in 1809. Following the 1777 Treaty of Ildefonso, in which the Spanish and Portuguese Empires agreed to divvy up the South American continent between them, Azara (1746–1821), a Spanish military officer, naturalist, geographer, and engineer, was sent to Paraguay to negotiate border disputes between

A Poetics of the Senses | 119

the two empires. Yet since the Portuguese intentionally delayed the process, Azara, like Zama, spent the next two decades there basically idle in a similar state of stagnation. (And much like Zama's vain hope for a transfer, Azara's request to return to Spain was unanswered, because unbeknownst to him his letters were held back by officials who feared that news of their delay tactics would reach the Iberian Peninsula.) To pass the time, Azara created a map of the region, which involved extended journeys throughout the vast expanse of the Viceroyalty of La Plata, during which he also observed its wildlife, plants, climate, and indigenous populations. Today, his *Voyage* ranks among the most accurate and detailed accounts of the region dating from the last two decades of the eighteenth century, much praised by Darwin and other naturalists and cartographers.

Unlike Zama, then, Azara was able to turn his frustration into something very useful. Among the many details he recorded, there are quite a few that seem to have found a place in Martel's film. Both the director and the explorer share a fascination with rivers, whose sheer magnitude, Azara repeatedly points out, exceeds by far anything found in Europe. Particularly the Paraná, so crucial for Martel's oeuvre, is described vividly. This river, he notes, "is of such immense proportions as if one hundred of the biggest European rivers had been united. Once it has taken in the Uruguay River, it is called La Plata, undoubtedly one of the biggest rivers in the world, which by itself contains as much water as all rivers of Europe combined" (26).[57]

Paraguay is a land of wonder for Azara, where decapitated turtles still manage to escape their hunter (in the film, this image is preserved through that of a box apparently moving by itself across the floor), and where wild beasts like the jaguar, the capybara, and the armadillo roam. (The llama, which enjoys its own scene in Martel's film, is notably absent in Azara's taxonomy.) The most startling example to have made it directly into the film is Azara's account of a wasp that kills a spider and skillfully buries the dead insect in its nest, where it provides the food supply for its freshly hatched offspring. Renamed a spider wasp, this insect is referred to three times in Martel's film, while infected wounds, caused by insect bites or worms, also occupy Azara quite a bit.

While oblique references to the history of the viceroyalty dot the film's first sections, they are completely abandoned in the third act, which also strays most from the novel's plot, tone, and outlook. If the earlier sections explored the increasingly blurred borders between Zama's reality and imagination, here the film truly becomes a frontier story of geographical, cultural, and psychological displacement. In this third part, Martel's ambitious envisioning of the past reaches its peak.

Zama's decision to join the search party for the infamous bandit Vicuña Porto is a last-ditch effort to achieve the desired promotion, a move that leads him into an altogether different and unexpected direction, even farther away from Lerma, from civilization itself, and into the blank spots on the map where he literally falls out of history. Making his first physical appearance in this final part, Porto has actually been present throughout the story (unlike in the novel, where he first appears in the third part). From the very beginning, reports about his death alternate with rumors about his heinous crimes. When the Oriental asks on his arrival whether an armed escort is needed, as he has heard about a certain Vicuña, he is told, "he was killed a thousand times." Zama's landlord, too, fears for the safety of his three daughters, as Porto is said to enter houses at night and violate the women, but Zama calms him: "he has been executed." Soon thereafter, Prieto will mock Zama by claiming that Porto was "almost executed" by his superior. Apparent physical evidence of this death is later offered by Porto's shriveled ears (another veiled allusion to the primacy of sound), which the second governor wins in a game of dice and proudly wears around his neck as a trophy. Soon thereafter, however, it becomes clear that this trophy is alive and well. In the scene in which Zama signs on with the third governor, Porto is one of the figures in the background who constitute the search party. Zama, like the viewer, is blind to him, which perfectly fits Porto's legend and plan.

For Martel, Vicuña Porto is not so much a real figure as a placeholder: "In situations of instability the government, or any other form of authority, needs an extreme evil to keep the public united" (quoted in Moseguí 2018). His fluid identity is suggested by his name, which alludes to an animal native to the Andes and an exquisite wine from northern Portugal, a combination of the Iberian and the South American that signals a cultural and linguistic crossover. He is the only character who speaks both Spanish and Portuguese and who knows the languages and customs of the various indigenous tribes of the region. He is a diminutive figure

A Poetics of the Senses | 121

with somewhat childlike features, his appearance belying his mythical proportions, and his fluid identity is the opposite of Zama's fixation with his status and standing. "The Vicuña Porto they talk about doesn't exist," he explains to Zama. "It's not me. It's no one. It's a name. Understand? My name is Gaspar Toledo."

As much as Porto seems a phantasm, the entire third part of the film is steeped in the fantastic and the absurd. Consider the first encounter with an indigenous tribe, which occurs at night, when dozens of blind men and women quietly pass the soldiers lying in their hammocks. "Nighttime is safer for the blind," explains Porto, adding that they walk fast so as to not reveal to their children that they cannot see. The next day, two Guanáes warriors wearing feather masks approach them and claim their horse. They are "fantasized," a man in the search party explains, only to add "disguised" when he notices Zama's lack of comprehension. Soon thereafter the men are taken prisoners by another tribe and are subjected to what appears to be a rite of initiation in a steam bath, where they are smeared with red paint, which mixes with blood and bruises. In tight close-ups, indistinguishable body parts crowd the frame, while we hear the sound of iron gates opening and closing. Any sense of time and place has been completely suspended by now. When the men find themselves released, we wonder if their rite of initiation was but a fever dream, a hallucination of some kind, were it not for the red paint on Porto's torso. Soon thereafter, Porto's men cut apart a large fish that resembles a stingray, hundreds of miles upriver from the ocean. Porto is in command now but spares Zama's life. "Bury your arms in the sand and you may live," Porto confides to him. Shortly before this verdict is spoken, a horse looks directly into the camera, breaking the fourth wall.

In this final part, the indigenous populations rule (and Porto and his men only survive because of his skills as translator). Their assuming control must be seen as the culmination of a revolt that has long been simmering, often displaying small gestures that reveal that their submission was never complete. Throughout the film, slaves and indigenous servants observe in judgmental silence as the whites give orders. The dark-skinned *mescla* (mixed-raced) granddaughter of the colonial landowners follows the court proceeding regarding the *encomienda* in stern silence, possibly the sign of some traumatic experience as she "was

122 | **Lucrecia Martel**

held captive by the Indians" (recalling the Natalie Wood character in *The Searchers* [John Ford, 1956]), but more likely because she is aghast at her grandparents' request and Zama's ruling. The camera pairs her profile with that of a dog, as if both belonged to a different order than the whites. To pay his respect, Zama kisses the plaintiff and his wife after the hearing, but ignores the granddaughter, as if she were not a member of the family. Full of stoic pride, a slave stands pressed against the wall of Luciana's private quarters as he operates a hand-cranked fan, his silence a startling contrast to the contraption's creaking sound. On a small desk sit bells of three sizes, each one apparently commanding a different servant, and Luciana uses them even when the servant is in the same room. A more overt rebellion is the dark-skinned prisoner's attempt at self-mutilation in the interrogation scene, to which Zama turns his back. It thus escapes him that the fish's "to and fro," which the prisoner so lyrically describes, is symbolic of his own stagnation. Throughout, the film conveys the impression that the servants and slaves know more than the masters they serve. The incommensurability of their status is

Figure 21. A strange dress code: the incongruity of slavery in *Zama*

A Poetics of the Senses | 123

perhaps most poignantly expressed by the outfit of a black slave, which consists of a velvet frock and white wig matched with a loincloth and bare feet. With deadpan humor, he delivers to Zama the message that "el gobernador dice que se vaya" (the governor says you must go), only to deflate the hope for a transfer by adding, after a second, "to his office."

It is worth pausing here for a moment to look at Martel's own relation to indigenous groups and how she has worked with them on the set. In the film, several Qom women smoke fat cigars, possibly an inside joke suggesting a certain solidarity with the director who acquired that habit at age nine. Martel's work with these actors is at the center of Selva Almada's book *El mono en el remolino: Notas del rodaje de "Zama" de Lucrecia Martel* (2017; The monkey in the whirlpool: notes from the shooting of Lucrecia Martel's *Zama*), which records in a very impressionistic way the location shooting of Martel's film and everything that surrounds it. The renowned Argentine writer visited the film set in Formosa at the invitation of Martel and her three young producers at Rei Cine, and while there kept a notebook in which she gathered impressions and short sketches of Martel at work.

The book's title alludes to the description of a decaying monkey cited at the beginning of this essay, which for Almada is a key image for understanding the novel ("El nuevo libro," 2017). Almada focuses primarily on the director's interactions, during casting and shooting, with the nonprofessional actors who are members of the indigenous Qom community and who came to trust and respect Martel. Almada describes their precarious living conditions, which are marked by extreme poverty, a low life expectancy, a high teenage pregnancy rate, and the widespread use of drugs. Their language is no longer taught to children, and there are no more shamans, notes Almada, which means that the Qom have been condemned to oblivion. Of Martel, Almada observes: "She delicately and carefully moves within an arc of love and respect. She resembles a nineteenth-century explorer. Or a rare bird from the twenty-first century" (2017, 25–26). This last image of the *rara avis* is a reference not likely lost on a Latin American audience, comparing Martel to Sor Juana Inés de la Cruz, the Mexican nun and poet celebrated as a Baroque genius of the colony for the breadth of her knowledge, her imagination, and her brilliance.

As noted earlier, *Zama* has long been considered an unfilmable novel, not only because of its elusive modernism but also because of the several failed attempts to bring it to the screen. (We briefly discuss the apparent curse that hung over the book in our interview with Martel.) In a speech given in 1970 at the University of Cuyo in Mendoza, Di Benedetto stated that, after he had been approached by Román Viñoly and Alfredo Mathé, a current adaptation by Nicolás Sarquís was now "much advanced" (2016a, 469f). As it turned out, this assessment was overly optimistic, but in 1984, after both Di Benedetto and Sarquís had returned from exile in Spain, the director took up the project again, only to fail completely. After a series of disagreements between the main actor, the Spaniard Mario Pardo, and the mostly Paraguayan crew and extras, Pardo abandoned the project (Fietta Jarques, 1984). In a profile of Selva Almada, Mariano Vespa notes that Di Benedetto had been unhappy with the casting because the "actor did not fit the image the author had of his main character, which resembled his own, namely short and with a potbelly" (2017). Vespa also adds that Sarquís had promised Di Benedetto that he would make a film that would not be inferior to Werner Herzog's *Fitzcarraldo*. That an Argentine filmmaker working in 1984 would try to measure up to Herzog's 1982 film is perhaps understandable, given the temporal proximity of the projects and Herzog's fame at the time. Yet the comparison is deeply ironic, as Herzog's project was mired in problems, not the least of which was actor Klaus Kinski's threat to walk off the set (according to legend, Herzog held him back at gunpoint).

Both *Fitzcarraldo* and Herzog's earlier *Aguirre, der Zorn Gottes/ Aguirre, the Wrath of God* (1972) are frequently mentioned in reviews of *Zama*, mostly as a compliment to Martel. Given the German director's deliberate reenvisioning of a colonial past, the respective protagonists' crazed states of mind, the two films' extremely challenging location shooting, and their extraordinary cinematography, the reference may be obvious. And Martel's insistence that "you can only *invent* the past," as she told us in conversation in Venice, comes close to what Herzog defines as ecstatic truth in his so-called Minnesota declaration: "There are deeper strata of truth in cinema, and there is such a thing as poetic, ecstatic truth. It is mysterious and elusive, and can be reached only through fabrication and imagination and stylization" (Herzog quoted in Ames 2012, ix).[58]

Yet a closer look at this comparison also serves to highlight what is unique about Martel and her film. Leaving aside Herzog's obvious disregard for nature, animals, and the indigenous actors who worked on *Fitzcarraldo* (which Martel has openly criticized) as well as his propensity for personal myth making, Herzog's films are set in Peru in 1560 and the 1890s and are therefore neither historically, politically, nor even geographically close to what was happening in the Viceroyalty of Río de La Plata circa 1800. Both adopt the perspective of their male white protagonists, something *Zama* consistently defies; even though Aguirre and Fitzcarraldo both fail in their endeavors, they are celebrated as tragic heroes, whereas Zama eventually becomes a humbled man, transformed by his experience. While *Aguirre* may fathom the follies of colonialism— the hubris of the conquistadors and their lust for gold and power, and the hypocrisy of the Roman Catholic Church—both this production and *Fitzcarraldo* cannot escape a mindset that pits man against nature, civilization against wilderness, and the white European against the natives. Both films are thus part of a long tradition of Western representations of colonialism that Martel consciously wanted to leave behind, if for no other reason than that it is essentially not a Latin American perspective. "You only address colonialism with solemn seriousness if you don't experience it daily," she observed. "But in Argentina, in Latin America, we still live under colonialism" (quoted in Lazic 2018).

Martel's postcolonial rewriting of history is clearly more radical than Herzog's, but it also goes further than other recent Latin American films that challenge established ways of representing the colonial past. These include the Brazilian films *Joaquim* (Marcelo Gomes, 2017), and *Vazante* (Daniela Thomas, 2017), Niles Atallah's *Rey/King* (Chile, 2017), the Colombian *El abrazo de la serpiente/The Embrace of the Serpent* (Ciro Guerra, 2015) and even *Jauja* by Martel's compatriot Lisandro Alonso (2014). Martel's virtuoso style makes the past entirely her own. It's a reckoning that shifts the perspective (including that of Di Benedetto's novel) from a male antihero to highlight the perspective of women and to imagine an indigenous population that is not entirely suppressed or silenced by the colonizers.

Zama is a frontier story that revisits the genre in an absurdist key. Set during the final decades of Spanish rule in Latin America, the film highlights the signs of decay and disorder that are everywhere. The veneer of civilization has worn ever so thin; when the noblewoman Luciana laughs, we see her blackened teeth. She laments the lack of entertainment in this backwater, then claps and laughs as if to generate her own amusement. While the first governor upholds a certain decorum, the second governor, overweight, bare-chested, and sweating profusely, works at a desk littered with food and booze. The head of a Kafkaesque bureaucracy, he operates through mindless rules and brutal violence and has no qualms about confiscating Zama's few precious possessions. "The gears of empire are oiled with blood," Dan Schindel aptly observes, "but they're maintained by schlubs" (2017). When the long-awaited merchant from downriver arrives, he brings fine brandy—and the plague. His son, the only fair-skinned child we ever see, dies with him: there is no hope for this caste. By contrast, healthy indigenous children abound, and we sense the future will be theirs.

Usually a male-centered narrative, this frontier story features female characters that are more complex than their male counterparts, often occupying the center of the frame as they seem to be more aware of what is happening around them. The indigenous characters, too, play a far greater role in this story. While still lurking at the margins in the first part, they gain greater prominence in the second, when Zama has a son with a Qom woman, Emilia, and the film devotes screen time exclusively to her and her family. By the time the third governor comes around, that governor speaks an indigenous language, a clear sign that the natives can no longer be ignored. In this final act, defiance will turn into rebellion, silent protest into full agency and assault. Carefully avoiding a paternalistic view on the natives, which would pretend to speak 'on their behalf,' Martel alters our perceptions to let different voices and representations emerge. As a result, *Zama* is an elaborate fantasy about a richness that is lost. The film creates a foreign world that we cannot easily relate to, in which blind people seem to see and a mute woman can actually speak. *Zama* reimagines a continent that no longer exists—still undefined, fluid, incommensurable, and immense. Most importantly, the film carefully avoids the creation of a false universalism that underlies almost all mainstream productions, regardless of country of origin. In the final scene of the film (not found in the novel) Zama moves toward a destination unknown, ready to meet his destiny. He has learned Porto's lesson—a name means nothing. He does not expect anything anymore, no letter, no pay, no transfer. In an absurdist twist, when his ship finally comes in, it turns out to be a dugout. As the music of Los Indios Tabajaras sets in again, Zama slowly drifts away from history.

Notes

1. The original reads: "Quiero lo opuesto a la comida chatarra, donde tenés que masticar rápido porque si apelás a la lentitud te das cuenta de que es una mierda." Unless otherwise noted, all translations from the Spanish are my own.

2. *Las Naves* is clearly modeled on the German journal *Revolver*, edited by filmmakers Christoph Hochhäusler and Benjamin Heisenberg, both key members of the Berlin School. For the elective affinities between the journals and indeed the Berlin School and the New Argentine Cinema, see Gemünden 2018.

3. "A veces, raras veces, en un fragmento de diálogo, en una coincidencia de sonidos, en una imagen incomprehensiblemente familiar, se asoma el artificio de la realidad.

"Toda nuestra potencia y el misterio del fin están en esas rajaduras.

"El cine me permite buscarlas y a veces, rara veces, encontrarlas.

"Pero duran muy poco y me las olvido."

4. "Uno está condenado a una forma de percibir . . . y el cine lo que te permite a eso es distorsionarlo un poco, y en esa distorsión para mí, con suerte, entre el que hizo la película y los espectadores, puede haber un cierto tipo de revelación . . . una pequeña revelación, no una gran verdad" (quoted in Sabat n.d.).

5. It is worth pointing out that the Alfred Bauer Prize is *not* given for best first feature, as is noted in most writings on *La ciénaga*, and that winning it was hence a much greater achievement, as the film successfully competed with those of many established and veteran filmmakers.

6. Pedro Amodóvar effused about her style: "It is difficult to talk about the films of Lucrecia Martel but it is an enormous pleasure to see and hear them, at least for me. An original creator, with an unfiltered look [vista inédita] and an incredible ability to place the camera and fill the screen with sounds" (2008, 8). On the Latin American activities of his production company El Deseo, which he runs with his brother Agustín, see D'Lugo 2013.

7. Some footage from these films is included in the 2015 Criterion Collection DVD of *La ciénaga*.

8. In a 1995 interview with *El amante*, Martel has called Subiela and Solanas "dinosaurs" and accused them of being "timid, fearful and taking recourse to

false metaphors instead of showing us the things the way they are" (quoted in Quintín and Bernades 1995, 24).

9. Lucrecia Martel, interviewed by Silvia Spitta and the author, Venice, September 2, 2017. A shorter version of this interview was published as Gemünden and Spitta 2018.

10. In response to my request for access to her early shorts and TV productions, Martel e-mailed: "Esas películas son malísimas. Cuando usted quiera voy a conversar con sus estudiantes, pero les ahorremos el mal trago de ver esos materiales. Muchas gracias por todo. Afectuosamente, L.M." (September 4, 2013). [These films are atrocious. I would be happy to converse with your students, but let's save them from the bad experience of watching these films. Thanks for everything. Warmly, L.M.].

11. The Spanish original reads: "Febrero en el noreste argentino. Sol que parte la tierra y lluvias tropicales. En el monte algunas tierras se anegan. Esas ciénagas son trampas mortales para los animales de huella profunda. En cambio, son hervideros de alimañas felices. Esta historia no trata de ciénagas, sino de la ciudad de La Ciénaga y alrededores. A 90 km está el pueblo 'Rey Muerto' y cerca de ahí la finca 'La Mandrágora.' La mandrágora es un planta que se utilizó como sedante, antes del éter y la morfina, cuando era necesario que una persona soporte algo doloroso como una amputación. En esta historia es el nombre de una finca donde se cosechan pimientos rojos, y donde pasa el verano Mecha, una mujer cincuentona que tiene cuatro hijos y un marido que se tiñe el pelo. Pero esto es algo para olvidar rápido con un par de tragos. Aunque, como dice, Tali, el alcohol entra por una puerta y no se va por la otra. Tali es la prima de Mecha. También tiene cuatro hijos, un marido amante de la casa, la caza, y los hijos. Vive en 'La Ciénaga,' en una casa sin pileta. Dos accidentes reunirán a estas dos familias en el campo, donde tratarán de sobrevivir a un verano demonio." www.litastantic.com.ar. Accessed 05/25/12.

12. In Quintín 2000, Martel also mentions a second important influence, Leonardo Favio's *Nazareno Cruz y el lobo/Nazareno Cruz and the Wolf* (1975).

13. Martel has insisted that "when I film dialogue, it has to be exactly as I wrote it in the script" (quoted in Romero 2005, 153).

14. As Martel has explained elsewhere: "I have written *La ciénaga* following the thread of many women's conversations, with my mother, my grandmother and other women in my family. Their words are irrational, literary, still foreign to psychoanalysis. People living in the province tend to relate long, elaborated and often absurd anecdotes fishing for compassion. Their way of telling stories implies a great effort, often crowned with success, that allows them to overcome their worries by expressing them with words" (quoted in Martín Morán 2003, 235).

15. As Martel told Haden Guest: "My grandmother told us Horacio Quiroga stories, but she never told us that these were inventions of another writer. I thought they were actual events, things that happened in my house" (2009). Quiroga's story "La gallina degollada"/"The Decapitated Chicken" (1917) features a young girl

who climbs a high wall and dies in the attempt; unlike Luciano, who falls when the ladder gives way, the girl is cruelly dragged to her death by her four idiot brothers.

16. Aguilar contends that the scene of Luciano's death is one of very few that resorts to "a somewhat artificial rhetoric" (2008, 42), a criticism that is hard to uphold if one considers how carefully it is integrated into the other narrative strands.

17. Aguilar asserts that Inés cries because she feels guilty about being "passionately in love with a man who initiates her into the world of sex" (2008, 87), an interpretation that assumes as certain what the film choses to leave open to speculation.

18. *The Life of St. Teresa of Jesus*, by Teresa of Ávila, chap. 29, para. 17: http://www.gutenberg.org/files/8120/8120-h/8120-h.htm#l29.0 Accessed 03/03/15.

19. As Jagoe and Cant point out, the camera never shows us Inés's body, thus denying the existence of her bodily needs (2007, 180).

20. As Aguillar has noted, rather than hire an actor, Martel hired a professional theremin player, Manuel Schaller, to play the instrument (2008, 97). This insistence on realism where none is needed—for how can we judge a realistic performance of the instrument when the musician does not even touch it—further underscores the ironic dimensions of the concert, as well as the importance of the instrument's sound for the entire film.

21. María Vaner, whom Martel would go on to cast as Aunt Lala in *La mujer sin cabeza*, has a supporting role in the film.

22. D. Martin cites *Rosemary's Baby* (Roman Polansky, 1968), *The Exorcist* (William Friedkin, 1973) and *The Shining* (Stanley Kubrick, 1980) as examples of films featuring a possessed or telepathic child.

23. Among the many commentators who have focused on the horror aspects in Martel's films, see particularly Amanda Holmes (2011), Deborah Martin (2011, 2016a, 2016b), and Cécile François (2009).

24. During filming, crew and cast were housed in the hotel, creating among the filmmakers the same mixed sensation of being a guest in the hotel while also working there. After filming concluded, the hotel underwent a complete renovation, the need for which is voiced several times during the film, making the Hotel Termas of the film a relic that no longer exists.

25. The figure of Mirta is another perfect embodiment of the erasure of the boundaries. Effectively managing the hotel in lieu of Helena, she is considered *casi familia*—almost like family—with a strong emphasis on *almost*. A voice of reason, she repeatedly councils Helena and is left to accept the unwanted phone calls, even though her advice, once sought, is always ignored. Ultimately, she is treated like an exploited employee, a form of abuse that Mirta in turn passes on to her own daughter, a physical therapist who doubles as cook.

26. Amanda Holmes has argued that the blurring of boundaries "creates new categories for the gendered dominance of spatial spheres" (2011, 138), because

the hotel is really ruled by Mirta, a woman. Yet this comment overlooks that a clear gender divide remains between the chamber maids (nameless and almost entirely invisible), hotel staff, and lab technicians, all of which are women, and the exclusively male conference attendants. Again, it is Vesalio who most ruthlessly exploits this divide.

27. The only film that can claim to have provided real smells is John Water's satire *Polyester* (1981), for which moviegoers were given an Odorama card, which they were prompted to scratch and sniff at key moments during the film.

28. I concur with Joanna Page, who argues that such an allegorical reading "may occlude a more radical understanding of the film's politics" (2013, 71).

29. In interviews, Martel has given as an inspiration for Vero Julianne Moore's performance in Todd Haynes's *Safe* (1995), where the actor plays an affluent housewife who becomes sensitive to common toxins in the environment and suffers a severe mental crisis.

30. Martel comments: "This is not a film about what the protagonist is objectively seeing; we do not follow a character to whom certain things are happening; rather, what we see is the perception of this character and what she thinks is happening. The entire construction of the film has its point of origin in the head of the woman without head" (García and Rojas 2008, 9).

31. More recently, María Onetto has played a related character in *Relatos Salvajes/Wild Tales* (Damián Szifrón, 2014), where she portrays the mother of a teenager who kills a man in a hit-and-run accident, which her husband tries to cover up by bribing the gardener to take the blame.

32. There are, however, a number of films that revolve around accidents with fatal consequences that make for productive comparisons with *La mujer sin cabeza*. These include *Muerte de un ciclista/Death of a Cyclist* (Juan Antonio Bardem, 1955); *Wolfsburg* (Christian Petzold, 2003); *Reservation Road* (Terry George, 2007); *Üç Maymun/Three Monkeys* (Nuri Bilge Ceylan, 2008); *Gnade/Mercy* (Matthias Glasner, 2012); *Pozitia copilului/Child's Pose* (Calin Peter Netzer, 2013); *Everything Will Be Fine* (Wim Wenders, 2015) and, as noted, one of the episodes in *Relatos salvajes/Wild Tales* (Damián Szifrón, 2014). When asked by an audience member at the 2009 UCLA screening, Martel commented that she was not familiar with Petzold's film and that Bardem's film was very different from hers as the conflict is within the same class.

33. As Martel has noted, "For *The Headless Woman*, I wrote a terror audition scene for the lead character in which she was in a public place and had the feeling that she'd walked by a corpse that was alive" (quoted in Oumano 2011, 70).

34. Harvey's film also served as inspiration for Christian Petzold's *Yella* (2007), a film that both stylistically and thematically entertains many points of contact with Martel's.

35. A number of critics have discussed *La mujer sin cabeza* in the wider context of the substantial cycle of films about the disappeared. Cecilia Sosa compares

Martel's film to Albertina Carri's *Los rubios/The Blonds* (2003), an idiosyncratic and highly original portrait of the director's parents, who were disappeared during the dictatorship (2009, 252). Other relevant titles include *Garage Olimpo/Junta* (Marco Bechis, 1999), *Historias cotidianas* (Andrés Habberger, 2001), *Papá Iván* (María Inés Roqué, 2004), *Buenos Aires, 1977* (Adrían Caetano, 2006), *Cordero de Dios/Lamb of God* (Lucía Cedrón, 2008), and *Un muro de silencio/A Wall of Silence* (1993) by Martel's producer Lita Stantic, the wife of a disappeared person. Yet Martel's approach is far more subtle and ambiguous than in most of the above-cited films, which predominantly see it as their goal to raise awareness about lacunae in the nation's history. As Chris Wisniewski observes, Martel's film indicts a historically specific form of willed forgetting "without engaging in the kind of overt metaphor-making of a movie like Patricio Guzmán's *Nostalgia for the Light*" (2013), which is about Chile under Pinochet.

36. "Mon fue condenada a dos años y cuatro meses de prisión en suspenso," *La Nación*, December 3, 1996, http://www.lanacion.com.ar/170344-mon-fue-condenada-a-dos-anos-y-cuatro-meses-de-prision-en-suspenso, accessed 05/05/15.

37. "The Headless Woman @ NYFF—Introduced by Pedro Almodóvar," Film Society of Lincoln Center, YouTube video, posted October 6, 2008, https://www.youtube.com/watch?v=PXGjeKoLMto.

38. Like other critics, Quandt puts Martel on a par with European auteurs ranging from Bergman and Buñuel to Michelángelo Antonioni: "The film shares with Antonioni a modernist concern with the tenuousness of perception, its central conundrum reminiscent of *Blow-Up*'s, its traumatized heroine, like Monica Vitti in *Red Desert*, anxiously wandering a once-familiar world whose features have become unfixed" (2009, 96).

39. Audio recording of full interview of Martel by Christoph Hochhäusler and Nicolas Wackerbarth, Berlin, July 8, 2018, and supplied to me by the interviewers. See also the shorter, published version of the interview, Hochhäusler and Wackerbarth 2018.

40. The full list of subtitles in *Pescados* reads: "We were rolling along on the road . . . We were all a car . . . Wheels . . . plastic, lights, we were a car . . . Dream, come! Come! Let's go, fish . . . time to sleep. I hear the horns from last night. We all hear it. Rolling, rolling . . . horns and lights. Rolling, rolling, rolling . . . rolling, rolling and lights . . . There were no dogs. We were a car. Sleep! Highways . . . tonight we run. To bed, to bed. Let's go, señores . . . Let's go." (Rodabamos por la ruta . . . Todos éramos un auto . . . Ruedas . . . plastico, faros, éramos un auto . . . Sueño, ven! Ven! Vamos pescados . . . hora de dormir. Escucho las bocinas desde anoche. Todos escuchamos. Rodar, rodar . . . bocinas y faros. Rodar, rodar, rodar . . . rodar, rodar y faros . . . No había perros. Éramos un auto. Duerman! Carreteras . . . esa noche a correr. A dormir, a dormir . . . Vamos, señores . . . Vamos.)

41. For an overview of the entire project, see Marcela Barbaro, "25 miradas 200 minutos—Los cortos del Bicentenario," El Espectador Imaginario, 2010, http://

www.elespectadorimaginario.com/pages/noviembre-2010/criticas/25-miradas-200-minutos.php, accessed 10/10/2014. Other directors included Albertina Carri, Lucía Puenzo, Pablo Trapero, Sandra Gugliotta, Daniel Burman, and Leonardo Favio.

42. A short scene in the film shows a group of people walking through the dunes near the river, a location that could be taken straight out of *Zama*.

43. "Nos gustaba la pretensión de fundar un espacio que sea un nuevo orden social. Ciencia ficción sería el género, me parece. Las islas lejanas, los idiomas desconocidos. Fragmentos de un movimiento de fundación."

44. The remarks that follow are indebted to D. Martin's reading of the film (2016a, 2016b).

45. In his enthusiastic review of the English translation of *Zama*, J. M. Coetzee has stated that Di Benedetto was imprisoned "in retaliation for his activities as editor of *Los Andes*, where he had authorized the publication of reports on the activities of right-wing death squads" (2017).

46. See *La Nación*, March 12, 2018, and *Diario de cultura*, August 14, 2018.

47. See "Premios Fénix 2018: 'Pájaros de verano,' 'El Ángel' y 'Zama,' entre las principales ganadoras," *Otros Cines*, November 8, 2018, https://www.otroscines.com/nota?idnota=13991, accessed 11-09-18.

48. At $3.5 million, *Zama* cost twice as much as Martel's last feature in her trilogy, the budget made possible only by an elaborate international coproduction of some thirty partners, including Vânia Catani, Rei Cine, Pedro and Agustín Almodóvar, Gael García Bernal, Danny Glover, and Joslyn Barnes.

49. In an interview with Carlota Moseguí, Martel has explained that this positive ending of her film is based on her understanding of the novel: "I am sure that Antonio Di Benedetto ended the novel with a Zama who will survive. There is no open end. Zama stays alive, and lives better than before because he has stopped hoping [*ha dejado de esperar*]" (2018b).

50. *Zama* is one of very few high-profile films from Latin America that feature extensive dialogue in a native language, subtitled or not. About 50 percent of the dialogue in Claudia Llosa's *La teta asustada/The Milk of Sorrow*, a Peruvian drama about a traumatized woman from the Andes relocated in Lima, is in Quechua. The winner of the Berlin Golden Bear in 2009, Llosa's film was the first internationally successful Latin American film to do so. That same year, Bolivian director Juan Carlos Valdivia premiered *Zona Sur/Southern District*, revolving around the shifting power relations between a well-to-do white middle-class family in an upper-class neighborhood of La Paz and their Aymara servants. When the film was first screened in Bolivia, Valdivia chose not to have the Aymara dialogue subtitled, a blatant gesture to make the *criollo* middle class, which makes up the vast majority of filmgoers in that country, aware of the fact that almost none of them understand an indigenous language spoken by roughly 42 percent of the population. Another Peruvian film shot almost entirely in Quechua is *Retablo* (Alvaro Delgado Aparicio, 2017), about

a troubled father-son relationship. The plot of the 2016 Paraguay-Argentina coproduction *Guaraní* (Luis Zorraquín) revolves largely around the efforts of its protagonist, the elderly fisherman Atilio, to pass on indigenous traditions and the Guaraní language to his about-to-be born grandson. Largely shot on and around the Paraná River at the border of Argentina and Paraguay, the film is a moving portrait of generational conflict that generates its drama through its protagonist's unwillingness (though not inability) to communicate in Spanish.

51. Martel has used *toxin* to describe the infectious nature of literature: "What we call masterpieces of literature manages to weave a very particular toxin into their letters, one that sickens, maddens, and then transforms humans into better animals" (2017).

52. Giménez Cacho has explained that, "had it not been a project with Lucrecia Martel, I would not have accepted the part" (2018).

53. Lola Dueñas explained that *she* approached Martel about working with her. Press conference, Venice Film Festival, September 1, 2017; from the author's personal recording of the conference. See also Almada 2017, 69.

54. Press conference, Venice Film Festival, September 1, 2017.

55. Saer had devoted a short essay to *Zama* back in 1973. He dedicated it to Nicolás Sarquis, who had adapted one of his short stories in his first feature, *Palo y hueso* (1967; *Stick and Bone*), based on a script cowritten by Saer and Sarquis.

56. For a detailed study of the sources on which Di Benedetto drew, see Filer 1982 and Néspolo 2004.

57. Underscoring the significance of the Paraná, Martel has commented: "The river is something that dominates in *Zama*. The rhythm of the protagonist's behavior comes out of the structure of a river. Latin American rivers are enormous, carrying a lot of sediment (that's why they are brown). Imagine you fall into the water—if you resist the current, you'll surely drown. However, if you let yourself be carried, it's more likely that you'll survive. This image is repeated many times in *Zama*" (quoted in Moseguí 2018).

58. This declaration was first shared with the public in a conversation between Herzog and the film critic Roger Ebert in Minneapolis in 1999. Reprinted in Ames 2012, ix.

Interviews with Lucrecia Martel |

David Oubiña, "The Cinema as Loving Intent: Interview with Lucrecia Martel" (2009)

DAVID OUBIÑA: *La Ciénaga* appeared a bit on the sides of the New Argentine Cinema.[1] It is included in the term, because the film is part of the same generation and because of its conflictive relation to several dominant films of the preceding cinema, but at the same time its production circumstances differ from films like *Mundo grúa/Crane World, La Libertad/Freedom,* or *Bolivia.* Which relation can you establish between your films and the others of the new cinema?

---

1. This interview was originally published as "Entrevista a Lucrecia Martel: El cine como intención amorosa" in David Oubiña's *Estudio crítico sobre "La ciénaga": Entrevista a Lucrecia Martel* (Buenos Aires: Picnic, 2009), 67–81. Translated and abbreviated by Gerd Gemünden. Reprinted here with permission of Aldo Paparella and David Oubiña.

LUCRECIA MARTEL: It seems that belonging to this category of a new cinema is present in all these films—not so much in terms of aesthetics but in the intent to mobilize a different form of what one recognizes as the real, which I connect to an attitude toward language. In *Mundo grúa*, for example, Pablo Trapero works with a certain manner of speech that situates the characters within the frame of reference to which they belong. The neighborhood of Palermo [in Buenos Aires] in Rejtman's films is a different example. In both cases there is a significant geographic affinity to the new realism each of these directors is trying to create. The generation of filmmakers that began in the 1990s with audiovisual storytelling was trying to establish a new realism by attacking the neutral Spanish or the *porteño* [the dialect of Buenos Aires] used in the 1980s. And therefore a new manner of speech emerged. And this is where I notice the proximity of *La ciénaga* to the new cinema. Because even though I worked with actors from various regions of the country, the lines of dialogue are written in the grammar of the North. They clearly have this expressive imprint. I see the search of this new cinema originating in a skepticism toward language, and every one of the filmmakers made their own journey toward believing again in the word. And in this way I do feel myself to be part of this new cinema.

DO: Often critics strained to read these new films as representing a strong break with the cinema that came before. What position does *La ciénaga* take up with regard to the films of the 1980s, and also to the whole tradition of Argentine cinema in depicting regional customs, or what is called *costumbrismo*?

LM: I am not too aware of that. I feel closer to oral traditions of storytelling than to the traditions of Argentine cinema. I paid attention to the tale, to the modes of speaking, to conversations. We do not know enough about the prevalence of oral traditions. Perhaps you acquire an awareness of this when you travel to countries that do not have this tradition; then you get the feeling that you do belong to a culture in which oral traditions are fundamental in establishing a surface of reality. In Salta this is very clear. For me this is so strong that I notice that this is not more widely appreciated, including by critics. It is clear in *La ciénaga*, and also, in a different form, in *La niña santa*, that the entire structure of the films corresponds to the drift of the conversations of my mother. I see that very distinctly, and I could enumerate the commonplaces of this form of storytelling. The death of Luciano, which is signaled a number of times, is something that is typical of oral traditions: when you tell an event that has already happened, you see foreshadowing that dates back to birth, as if this person had been condemned from the beginning. Faced with the terrible or the unexpected, there's always the desire that seeks to make it part of a plan. It seems to me that this is the structure of orality. In *La niña santa*, in contrast, we have more of a tale or a fable; thus the distance from reality is greater. In both films, I worked with accumulation and recollection, but in the latter film the desire for plot is much greater.

DO: *La ciénaga* seems to unfold according to a circular structure. Everything points to Mecha ending up like her mother, and José will probably become a good-for-nothing like his father, as if everyone was condemned to repetition. What was your idea—did you want to emphasize the onset of awareness, or the repetition, or both?

LM: Something that distressed me a lot during my adolescence was the sensation that my life was a carbon copy of other familiar lives. In my high school it was easy to see how repetition was applauded. For me this was terribly stifling—to the point that when I once had a little accident, I thought "well, this scar will be a marker that only belongs to me. It's mine only." Yet one day, when my grandmother's sister visited in Salta, I noticed a similar scar on her. Perhaps it wasn't even that similar, but I felt again this feeling of distress of having my life being a repetition. And each time my choices led me away from repetition (or what I perceived to be a repetition), I felt immensely happy. The end of *La ciénaga* signals that things will repeat, but the film also opens a little crack that may or may not widen. The film probably contains a lot of the traumatic elements of life in the province (*laughs*).

DO: The death of Luciano was one of the most controversial aspects of the film. Many viewers felt it was a forced ending, and also a low blow—they felt betrayed. Did you have doubts about this ending?

LM: It actually surprises me that the ending caught viewers by surprise. I had some doubts about the preceding scene, but not with Luciano's death. One always has a certain messianic impulse, and I had thought that the moment after the death should have stronger signs of break with repetition; but then I thought if there is to be any possibility of a rupture, it needs to be gentle and small.

DO: Death itself remains outside the frame, and the subsequent shots show the empty spaces of the house in a respectful and reserved manner, as if the camera did not want to see that. How does one film death?

LM: Having to tell a five-year-old, "now you're dead," is horrible. I remember how hard it was for me to explain to Seba [Sebastián Montagna, the child who plays the role] what he had to do. I told him, "in this scene we are pretending to be dead." What is important here, and not only in this scene but in the entire film, is that there's a certain emotion that emanates from death. And more than death itself it is the absolute loss of a certain dimension of the future. A dead person means that all he could imagine about the world will now never happen. An entire part of the universe is lost forever. It is this absence that interests me. Death suddenly sweeps away everything, and that is truly horrible. That's why we are inclined to move away from death. Death stuns you because of everything it does away with. The grace of movement that the dead person has lost is something so terrible that you cannot dwell on it. In a film where nothing happens, suddenly something happens that all of us recognize as awful. I am terrified by death.

DO: How did you decide on the mise-en-scène? Do you do storyboards or floor plans? Do you have a detailed technical guide?

LM: I had to do a storyboard, because one of the Cuatro Cabeza producers, Diego Guebel, asked me for it. It was completely useless. I did it quickly, a chore I had to do because they asked for it; it was an absurd task for me. Surely, parts of this storyboard could have helped me figure out the mise-en-scène, but I actually didn't even bring it to Salta. I had not even the slightest idea how to film any of the scenes before I arrived on location. In some cases, I may have had a vague idea or some image in mind, but we generally decided during filming. It depends on the light or what you rehearsed with the actors, and what that had looked like. I have always done it like this, and I continue like this to this day. I decide the position of the cameras when we do the walkthrough with the actors; I define the image on the set. What I do *not* decide there, because I have mapped that very carefully already, is the sound. I imagine what the soundscape is—what do you hear? What do you not see? That already gives me a very good sense of all the many things that will be off-camera.

138 | **Lucrecia Martel**

DO: The majority of directors tend to use sound merely as a point of reference. In *La ciénaga*, however, sound is truly an expressive force. And it is because of this that the image, for example, becomes something ominous. What were your criteria when working on the soundscape?

LM: For me, the beginnings of the narrative are found in orality. And I don't mean orality in the sense that some guy sits down and begins telling a story, but a situation in which something gets told. When your grandmother comes to tell you a story (and you are in bed with your brothers and sisters, all scattered about), perhaps you don't see the person who's talking, and there are your siblings playing around you—but her telling of the story invades the scene and orients your gaze. The sound guides you.

DO: What guided your choices with respect to the music? Why is there no music except what we hear on the tape recorder and during the carnival?

LM: In order to use music in a film, you need to know something about music. I get lost in the complexity of music. Therefore, I can only use it as this confusing noise that appears at a party or comes out of the radio. But I would not use music to help underpin the narrative.

DO: In your castings, you mixed professional actors with nonprofessionals, and you worked with a lot of children, which further complicates matters. How did you direct these actors?

LM: In 1997, I tried to put together a cast with only people from Salta, which proved impossible. I could not find anyone to play the roles of the older women, so I had to abandon that idea. But it did not cost me that much to abandon this idea, because I realized that the space I wanted to tell about was not called Salta; hence I felt no obligation to use only actors from the region. And from there on out, the space was configured accordingly, and in *La niña santa* I no longer had this problem, and I don't have it in the film I am currently preparing, *La mujer sin cabeza*. There's no folkloristic intent to describe a region, absolutely none. It is clearly a composite, and among the elements that make up this composite is the fact that the actors are from different places. As far as directing actors is concerned, I have no previous experience from theater or from acting, but I found a way of speaking with each person, and of creating a certain trust. This allows you to find out what you can and cannot say to another person, and what will, or will not, distort the acting and the lines they speak. With the children, my strategy was not to give them the screenplay, so that the written word does not overburden them. Professional actors can free themselves from the weight of the written word, but an inexperienced actor can be so impacted from reading the script that it ruins the possibility of a good interpretation. I do a form of warm-up so that in the end two or three words of dialogue come out, which is all I need. It's a longer route to get to what was in the script in the first place.

DO: There are no crane shots or traveling shots in the film—was that an aesthetic choice or a constraint of the production?

LM: Since it was my first film and I had a lot of actors, I decided to simplify certain technical aspects. That's at least what I told myself, but then I realized that it actually did not interest me. Now I see it as a limitation that I imposed on myself. In the new film there are scenes where a person is running, so I'll have to get up to speed on technological advances. But as Godard said, I sincerely believe that a traveling shot is an ethical decision. It makes me feel very uncomfortable, including in films that I like very much. My relation in regard to the image is very clear in my mind: since the overall structure of a scene is very much determined by the sound, the camera movement is already very restricted. But beyond that I also have the impression that the more intensely the gaze rests on one thing, the less we see. It's like a scientific trick—the closer you get, the less you understand. Maybe this phenomenon has to do with the optical construction of a camera. The quieter you are, there more mysteries there are. For me there is a lot of mystery in fixed shots. You stay in one place, and just by remaining so for a prolonged period, things appear and unfold naturally.

DO: Between your films there are points of contact and differences, but one can clearly track certain obsessions, certain stylistic elements, a certain way of representing things. What relation do you see between *La ciénaga* and *Rey Muerto* and *La ciénaga* and *La niña santa*?

LM: Obviously, the geography is the same. It would be very easy to sketch a map: at kilometer 84 is Rey Muerto, here is La Ciénaga, etc. And that helps me a lot to think about transitions, which is to say, not to include them. Perhaps I have done this in a clumsy way, but I do believe that this is what we all ultimately do with our city of birth. My hometown is never shown; it is an emotional fabric woven out of frag-

140 | **Lucrecia Martel**

ments of space, sounds, and people, and it really does not resemble at all what a documentary about this place would look like. Beyond this shared universe, the level on which *La niña santa* is situated detaches itself from the level of *reality* on which *La ciénaga* operates, and probably also *La mujer sin cabeza*. Because *La niña santa* is a story about these people that live in La Ciénaga. It's not something that happens to one of the characters, but something the people from there tell. There's a lesser degree of reality than in the other two films. *Rey Muerto*, in contrast, is obviously my little film school project, and even though it belongs to the same space, I see it as distinct from my other films. For me, it was a real cerebral approach to making a Western, like the ones we used to make with my siblings, when I got my first video camera. These were kitschy things inspired by *Keoma* [a 1976 Italian Spaghetti Western directed by Enzo G. Castellari], or the films of Franco Nero. I have four brothers, and it was much easier engaging them in a Western than in a more intimate film.

Gerd Gemünden and Silvia Spitta, "'I Was Not Afraid': Interview with Lucrecia Martel" (2017)

GERD GEMÜNDEN & SILVIA SPITTA: The first reviews of *Zama* have come out—are you happy about the overwhelmingly positive reception?[2]

LUCRECIA MARTEL: This is my first film release during the era of social media (I am not on Twitter or Facebook), and I am stunned by the speed of the process and how quickly everyone either praises or condemns. After the premiere, I was relieved to see how people from many different cultures appreciated different aspects of the film, how they picked up on distinct parts or subtleties.

I always trust that the spectator is smarter than what the market believes. This film is not made with an eye toward the market. The market has a reaction time of a few months; this film needs ten years. Let's not forget that *Zama* the novel needed fifty years to be recognized.

G&S: With this film, you have broken new ground in many ways. One

---

2. This interview was conducted on August 31, 2017, in Venice and originally published in *Film Quarterly* 71.4 (summer 2018): 33–40. It is reprinted here with permission of the University of California Press.

striking difference is that this is your first film with a male protagonist. Did that change your approach to how you tell the story?

LM: Not really. I would not say it's a feminist film, but more so than the others. Particularly in Latin America, men are brought up to achieve things, while women are much more prepared for failure, [and consequently] to have to do other things. I think that the lesson of *Zama* is a lesson that we women learned long ago. This is a transference of wisdom that we could make to the world of men. Because if you're not prepared for failure, the frustration and violence are enormous. In Argentina, every sixteen hours, a woman dies at the hands of her [male] partner or ex-partner or some family member. When a country is economically in shambles and the prospect of being provided for is diminished or has disappeared, the only territory over which you [as a man] can exert control is your wife or partner. If she falls out of love or falls for another man, the inferno begins.

G&S: Your protagonist Zama experiences this lack of control over one's own fate. In Spanish, the verb *esperar* means both to wait and to hope. The novel builds on this double meaning: Zama waits and hopes and waits and hopes, ultimately in vain. At the very end of the film, you give this lack of hope a more positive spin, in that Zama tells the bandit Vicuña Porto, "I will do you the favor that no one did me and tell you that there is no hope." Can you comment on this change that you made to the novel?

LM: The notion that there is no hope is very anti-Catholic. Catholicism always tells us to endure poverty, pain, and suffering, because there will be a reward in the afterlife. It was important for me to counteract this belief, so we created a film without any references to Catholicism. You will notice that there is not a single crucifix in the film—not on the wall, not on the furniture, not around people's necks. I wanted to create a world without Catholicism, even if that is historically incorrect: to imagine that the power of the church was not that homogeneous, that the world was more diverse. Because power is never *that* powerful. History tells us that the submission of the indigenous people was absolute, and that is impossible, because submission is never absolute. Not even in the concentration camps was despair absolute, that is, not even in the worst of places. This is why we included many small gestures of irreverence on the part of the black and indigenous characters in the film. The only thing that will save humanity is to avoid complete homogeneity. Homogeneity is the end of every organism; life is that which is diverse, diversity is the ABC of life.

G&S: The nonprofessional actors play a very significant role in this film. Who are they, where are they from, and how did you cast them?

LM: The black actors are from Senegal and Haiti, many of them recent immigrants to Argentina. The natives are Guaraní, Qom-lek, and Pilagá, and working with them was very interesting, because everything was an invention—their haircuts, the clothes, the feathers, the colors. Initially they assumed that they should play themselves, but I explained to them that they should act as if they were somebody else, somebody fictitious, and they really enjoyed that. The interaction with indigenous communities is always difficult. These are very poor people who are always in need and thus always asking for something, which makes you feel uncomfortable. And because of this guilt, your relation with them is always somewhat paternalistic. But we found that one way of establishing a certain form of equality was by asking them to talk about their dreams. And it turns out that we all have the same kind of dreams. In dreams, there is never a lack of money, an *indio* can fly, a white person can fly. We all have the same abilities and powers—it seemed important to remember that.

G&S: How did you communicate? Did you have a translator?

LM: I had a translator for the ones who spoke very little Spanish.

G&S: There's a whole cacophony of languages in the film, much of it not subtitled. Can you describe how you conceived and constructed the different languages heard in the film?

LM: Even though it's a period piece, we did not want the Spanish to sound entirely old, only slightly so. It had to sound like today's Spanish and not be too solemn, that was very important for me. In Mexico, they invented a "neutral" language to export *telenovelas* and commercials to the rest of Latin America. They made an analysis of the most-used words. Should a refrigerator be called *heladera* or *nevera*? They chose *nevera*, because it is used in more countries. To that invention, we added the different dialects of the regions of Argentina, plus Portuguese and the mixture of Spanish and Portuguese, or *Portugnol*, which is a phenomenon of the border. Those red-painted natives you see are supposed to be Guaycuru, but they speak Qom. The Guaycuru language, spoken by the natives who attacked in the eighteenth century, is extinct.

Interviews | 143

Nothing of what you hear is real, it is completely anachronistic, no one spoke in that manner at the time. I wanted to capture the beauty of a diverse world. The film also needed a strong Latin American presence. We did not want it to be an Argentinean film, and the most logical coproducer was Brazil, both because of the significance of the Brazilian film industry and the subject matter of the film.

G&S: There are many changes from the novel. One of them is that the protagonist in the film is much more likeable than that of Zama in the novel. Why did you make this change?

LM: If you have an unlikeable main character, you would need to make the film much longer so as to explain the character in more detail. What I carried over from the novel, however, is the somewhat ridiculous or absurd tone. The film is not a serious depiction of the past but pure invention. We aimed for a tone that was not too serious, sometimes even slightly parodic. And we omitted many of the violent scenes, particularly the violence against women. I do not care to watch that, nor to film it, because the camera can become complicit in the violence. Nor did I want to show the blood when Zama's hands are amputated. It is enough to hint at it.

G&S: Prior to *Zama* you worked on an adaptation of *El Eternauta* (Sailor of eternity), an Argentine science fiction comic from the late 1950s by Héctor Germán Oesterheld, on which you spend almost two years before the project had to be abandoned. Did anything from this project carry over into *Zama*?

LM: Since *El Eternauta* is a science fiction comic, we thought a lot about time and how we are always ready to imagine the future. But what happens when you apply that freedom of the imagination to thinking about the past? So we kept the same arbitrariness that you have in science fiction to our recreation of the past and we turned the past into pure invention, pure fiction. This was ultimately a very liberating and entertaining process. You can only invent the past, you cannot re-create it.

For the film, it was important to invent a coherent universe and not repeat what the history books tell us. History is the history of those who won. You have to find other ways of representing the past, to introduce a political element. But we also used common sense. In a lot of period films set in Latin America, you see soldiers walking around in leather boots, which are completely useless if you're knee deep in water, as we frequently were.

G&S: This is also the first time you shot digitally. Was that a conscious change as well?

LM: It would be very difficult, in fact nearly impossible, to shoot analogue nowadays. And whether digital or analogue—it's really the same to me. What matters is not the medium, but the depth of the work. There is a certain nostalgia for analogue film, and I think it often reflects a mediocre way of thinking about the image. Things are changing, and we have to accept that this technology is more affordable and that it allows us to do what we want to do. And we need to master it.

G&S: Your cinematographer was Ruy Poças, who made several films with Miguel Gomes. What was the look you were trying to create with him?

LM: We wanted to create a look that is different from the many other, mostly European, period films about Latin America. For example, there is no candlelight, no open fire, because you have that in every film. There's also no play of light and shadows on the faces of the characters. That's just too easy. We wanted to create the impression that time has stopped.

G&S: Can you say something about the music, which sounds somewhat anachronistic?

LM: The music you hear is by Los Indios Tabajaras, two brothers from an indigenous community in Northeast Brazil. They dressed up in fantasy costumes and feathers, a bit like Yma Sumac in Peru but less scandalous. Their music is from the 1950s, hence the type of music Di Benedetto might have listened to, as he was writing the novel. Los Indios Tabajaras are the sort of Latin American musicians who want to make it in Hollywood by exaggerating the stereotypes. There is a pretentiousness here, which for me is something very Argentinian—this desire, wanting to be European, being ashamed to be American. In the novel, one official states, "I'm surprised by so many Americans who do not want to be Americans."

G&S: The soundscape is always very important in your films, but it seems even more prominent and audacious in *Zama*.

LM: The audio is loud and screechy and creates the sensation of close proximity. And we used the Shepard tone, which is an auditory illusion

Interviews | 145

that creates the false impression of a continuously swelling sound, a bit like the optical illusions of M. C. Escher.

G&S: Initially, Lita Stantic, with whom you worked on your first three features, was set to produce *Zama*. What led to the split with her?

LM: Lita wanted to produce this film the way she had produced films before, when the market for auteurist cinema was still more favorable and when films could be made with four coproducers. (*Zama* has almost thirty producers—it's crazy.) But these three young guys from Rei Cine—Benjamin Doménech, Matías Roveda, and Santiago Gallelli—had so much enthusiasm, it was infectious. They are very talented and they really fought for the film, as did Danny Glover and Gael García Bernal. With all the difficulties we had, they could have left on many occasions, and I consider myself very fortunate that they never abandoned me. I was also really lucky to have Daniel Giménez Cacho, the only actor who was present during the entire shoot, and the only actor I considered for the role. It would have been impossible to make the film without him.

I believe *Zama* can be an important precedent for Latin American cinema for how to produce films. We have to find a way of being more ambitious. We cannot only make films about today and what's close to us, nor can we make films in English, just to guarantee the financing. We have to find a way to tell our history, both past and future, without being confined by the market.

G&S: Did you ever think that just like Zama is waiting in vain, the world, too, would have to wait in vain for this film?

LM: Well, *Zama* was almost not completed. I was diagnosed with cancer during postproduction and was bedridden for almost eight months. But I was never afraid. And if you're not afraid, the process can be very interesting. My treatment was in Buenos Aires, but my family lives in Salta, so each week one of my siblings would come to help. And my brothers, who had never cooked, even learned how to cook.

It's almost embarrassing to say this, because it sounds like a cliché, but because of the experience of my illness, my relation to the film changed completely. And I don't mean only individual changes, which often happen in postproduction, but my overall relation to the entire film. Individual elements took on a new order, and I inserted several scenes that I had eliminated earlier. For example, I reinserted the scene

146 | **Lucrecia Martel**

of Luciana's servant walking away painfully, because her feet had been mutilated.

G&S: The Argentine filmmaker Nicolás Sarquis, a friend of Antonio Di Benedetto and his companion in exile in Madrid, had begun filming a version of *Zama* in 1984, but the actor who played the protagonist, Mario Pardo, abandoned the project after a fallout with Sarquis, and the film was never completed. Did you believe at some point that there was a curse on *Zama*?

LM: When I got sick I began to think that I had been rather naive not to believe in this pernicious aura and that there might be a world in which I had not believed. I then realized that the story of Zama became also my own story—the tremendous effort it took to make this film. When I now watch the film, I see a man who feels trapped, gets sick, is mutilated, and who at the very end says, "Yes, I want to live." That's me—I want to live.

Filomography |

El 56 (1988)
Animated short
Codirected by Lucrecia Martel, Carlos Belenda, Alberto Fasce, Jorge Lumbreras, Pedro Stelkic
1:30 min.
Link: https://www.youtube.com/watch?v=n9s51X5ZtL0&feature=youtu.be

Piso 24 / Floor 24 (1989)
Animated short

No te la llevarás, maldito / Don't You Dare Take Her (1989)
Producer: Lucrecia Martel
Director: Lucrecia Martel
Writer: Lucrecia Martel
Cinematography: Diego Lublinsky
Editor: Nicanor Barnia
2 min.

La otra / The Other (1989)
Production: Centro Experimental y de la Realización Cinematográfica
Producer: Diego S. Kaplan
Director: Lucrecia Martel
Camera: Diego Lublinsky
Sound: Andrés Foswil
9 min.
Link: https://www.youtube.com/watch?v=AbuosfcMolM&t=32s

Besos rojos / Red Kisses (1991)
Director: Lucrecia Martel
Music: Ruy Folguera
24 min.

Rey Muerto / Dead King (1995)
Producer: Alejandro Arroz
Director: Lucrecia Martel
Writer: Lucrecia Martel
Music: Lía Crucet, Maria Laura Ruggiero
Cinematography: Esteban Sapir
Editor: Fernanda Rossi
Sound Design: Horacio Almada, Pablo Barbieri Carrera
Costume Design: Alejandra Crespo
Principal Cast: Roly Serrano, Sandra Ceballos, Carlos Aldana, Marcelo Machuca
12 min.

D.N.I. (1995)
Argentina Televisora Color (ATC)
Producer: Lucrecia Martel
Director: Lucrecia Martel
60 min.

Magazine for Fai (1995)
Producer: Álvara Urtizberea
Directors: Lucrecia Martel, Nora Moseinco, Mex Urtizberea
Writers: Alberto Muñoz, Mex Urtizberea
30 min.

Las dependencias: Silvina Ocampo / The Servants (1999)
Producers: Ana de Skalon, Lita Stantic
Director: Lucrecia Martel
Screenplay: Graciela Esperanza, Adriana Mancini
Editor: Mario Pavéz
Cinematography: Marcelo Iaccarino
50 min.
Link: http://www.marienbad.com.ar/video/silvina-ocampo-las-dependencias

La ciénaga / The Swamp (2001)
Production: 4k Films, Wanda Visíon S.A., Cuatro Cabezas, TS Productions
Distribution: Cowboy Booking International
Executive Producers: Mario Pergolini, Diego Guebel
Producer: Lita Stantic
Director: Lucrecia Martel
Screenplay: Lucrecia Martel
Cinematography: Hugo Colace
Editor: Santiago Ricci
Sound Design: Guido Berenblum

Principal Cast: Graciela Borges (Mecha), Mercedes Morán (Tali), Martín Adjemián (Gregorio), Juan Cruz Bordeu (José), Sofia Bertoletto (Momi), Silvia Baylé (Mercedes), Leonora Balcarce (Verónica), Andrea López (Isabel), Sebastián Montagna (Luciano), Fabio Villafane (Perro)
103 min.

La niña santa / The Holy Girl (2004)
Production: La Pasionaria, R&C Produzioni, Teodora Fil, El Deseo
Distribution: Fine Line Features
Executive Producers: Esther García
Producers: Lita Stantic, Agustín Almodóvar, Pedro Almodóvar
Director: Lucrecia Martel
Screenplay: Juan Pablo Domenech, Lucrecia Martel
Cinematography: Félix Monti
Editor: Santiago Ricci
Music: Andres Gerszenzon
Sound Design: Guido Berenblum
Costumes: Julio Suárez
Principal Cast: María Alche (Amalia), Mercedes Morán (Helena), Carlos Belloso (Dr. Jano), Alejandro Urdapilleta (Freddy), Julieta Zylberberg (Josefina), Mía Maestro (Inés), Marta Lubos (Mirta), Arturo Goetz (Dr. Vesalio), Mónica Villa (Josefina's mother), Rodolfo Ceja (Josefina's father), Manuel Schaller (Theremin player)
106 min.

*La ciudad que huye / * The City that Runs Away (2006)
Director: Lucrecia Martel
Producers: Fabián Berenblum, Vanina Berghella, Santiago Leiro
Editor: Ariel Ledesma Becerra
Principal Cast: Marina Ferraro (narrator), Lucrecia Martel (herself)
5 min.
Link: https://www.youtube.com/watch?v=LeUvjPIJm_s

La mujer sin cabeza / The Headless Woman (2008)
Production: Aquafilms, El Deseo, R&C Prouzioni, Slot Machine, Teodora Film
Distribution: Strand Releasing
Producers: Lita Stantic, Agustín Almodóvar, Pedro Almodóvar, Verónica Cura, Esther García, Cesare Petrillo, Lucrecia Martel
Director: Lucrecia Martel
Screenplay: Lucrecia Martel
Cinematography: Barbara Alvarez
Editor: Miguel Schverdfinger
Music: Roberta Ainstein

Filmography | 151

Sound Design: Guido Berenblum
Costumes: Julio Suárez
Casting: Natalia Smirnoff
Principal Cast: María Onetto (Verónica), Claudia Cantero (Josefina), Inés Efron (Candita), César Bordón (Marcos), Daniel Genoud (Juan Manuel), Guillermo Arengo (Marcelo), María Vaner (Aunt Lala)
87 min.

Nueva Argirópolis / New Argiropolis (2010)
Production: Magma Cine
Producers: María Onis, Marcelo Schapces
Director: Lucrecia Martel
Screenplay: Lucrecia Martel
Cinematography: Alejandro Millán Pastori
Editor: Pablo Barbieri Carrera
Music: María Onis
8 min.
Link: https://www.youtube.com/watch?v=X-UKTNW3CJo

Pescados / Fishes (2010)
Director: Lucrecia Martel
Editor: María Onis
Sound Design: María Onis
Composer: Juana Molina
4 min.
Link: https://www.youtube.com/watch?v=2Bok-jJK2ck

Muta / It (or She) Mutates (2011)
Production: Miu Miu
Producers: Max Brun, Lita Stantic, Gabriela Sabaté
Director: Lucrecia Martel
Screenplay: Lucrecia Martel, Alejandro Ros
Cinematography: Hugo Colace
Editor: Ariel Ledesma Becerra
Music: María Onis
Sound Design: Guido Berenblum
Models: María Alché, Julia Anderson, Cecilia Barrios, Emilienne de Souza, Piren Larrieu Iturre, Rocío Nuñez, Florencia Ramaccioni, Rocío Somoza
7 min.
Link: http://www.youtube.com/watch?v=nAC-k8PThzk
See also: *Muta—Behind the Scenes* (Making-Of): http://youtu.be/ZlwgonmPRX8

152 | Filmography

Leguas / Leagues (2015)
Production: Marta Núñez Porto
Producer: María Onis
Director: Lucrecia Martel
Screenplay: Lucrecia Martel
Cinematographer: Alejandro Millán Pastori
Editor: Ariel Ledesma Becerra
Sound Design: Guido Berenblum
Principal Cast: Facundo Gabriel Seguí, Jésica Herrera, Salomé Solana Lezcano, Alfredo Castillo, Juan Manuel Castillo Martel, Facundo Castillo Martel, Juan Alberto Ruíz, Darío Fernando Ruíz, Adalberto Ruíz
12 min.
Part of the omnibus film *El aula vacía/The Empty Classroom* (2015, 108 min.), creative director Gael García Bernal. Other directors include Flávia Castro, Mariana Chenillo, Pablo Fendrik, Carlos Gaviria, Tatiana Huezo, Nicolás Pereda, Eryk Rocha, Pablo Stoll, Daniel, Diego Vega

Zama (2017)
Production: Rei Cine, Bananeira Filmes
Distribution: Strand Releasing
Executive Producers: Gael García Bernal, Angelisa Stein, Diego Luna, Pablo Cruz
Producers: Benjamín Doménech, Santiago Gallelli, Matias Roveda, Vania Catani, Agustín Almodóvar, Pedro Almodóvar, Joslyn Barnes, Alejandro Cacetta
Director: Lucrecia Martel
Screenplay: Lucrecia Martel
Cinematography: Rui Poças
Editor: Miguel Schverdfinger
Music: Gustavo Montenegro
Sound Design: Guido Berenblum
Costumes: Julio Suárez
Principal Cast: Daniel Giménez Cacho (Zama), Lola Dueñas (Luciana), Matheus Nachtergaele (Vicuña Porto), Juan Minujín (Ventura Prieto), Nahuel Cano (Fernández), Mariana Nunes (Malemba), Carlos Defeo (the Oriental), Rafael Spregelburd (Captain Parilla), Carlos Cano (guard), Gustavo Böhm (1st Governor), Daniel Veronese (2nd Governor), Rodolfo Prantte (3rd Governor), Massamba Seye (messenger), Germán de Silva (Indalecio), Vincenzo Navarro Rindel (son of the Oriental), Juan Pablo Gómez (Bermudez), María Etelvina Peredez (Emilia), Milo Alberto Gutiérrez (Zama's son), Silvia Luque (Zumala/Tora), Francisca Domínguez (blind Indian woman), Edgar Acosta (Indian boy in canoe)
115 min.

Julieta Laso: Fantasmas / Julieta Laso: Ghosts (2018)
Director: Lucrecia Martel
Cinematography: Federico Lastra
Principal Cast: Julieta Laso, Fidela Carrizo, Jorgelina Contrera
4 min.
Link: https://www.youtube.com/watch?v=xPnuVimbj8o

Bibliography

Abramovich, Manuel. *Años luz/Light Years*. Documentary. Bananeira Filmes, 72 min. 2017.

———. *Soldado/Soldier*. Documentary. GemaFilms, 72 min. 2017.

Aftab, Kaleem. "I Used to Hate the Western—But Now Women Are Riding in to Save the Genre." *Independent*, April 13, 2018. https://www.independent.co.uk/arts-entertainment/films/features/western-movies-films-white-privilege-power-women-directors-save-genre-lucrecia-martel-a8302676.html. Accessed 04/16/18.

Aguilar, Gonzálo. *Other Worlds: New Argentine Film*. Translated by Sarah Ann Wells. New York: Palgrave, 2008.

Aguzzi, Juan. "'El deseo es algo que fluye, evitarlo es una actitud muy clase media': Entrevista con Lucrecia Martel." *El eclipse* 3.4 (2001): 25–27.

———. "*Zama* es un film alucinado y exquisito." *El ciudadano*, October 1, 2017. http://www.elciudadanoweb.com/zama-es-un-film-alucinado-y-exquisito/. Accessed 10/03/17.

Alániz, Daniel. "Bajo este sol tremendo." *Haciendo cine*, June 22, 2015. http://www.haciendocine.com.ar/content/bajo-este-sol-tremendo. Accessed 02/15/16.

Aldazábal, Carlos J. "Desdomesticar la percepción." *Revistateína* 6 (October–November–December 2004). http://www.revistateina.es/teina/web/teina6/cine4.htm. Accessed 3/12/14.

Allen, Esther. Preface to *Zama*, by Antonio Di Benedetto. Translated by Esther Allen. New York: New York Review of Books, 2016.

———. "The Crazed Euphoria of Lucrecia Martel's *Zama*." *New York Review of Books*, April 14, 2018a. http://www.nybooks.com/daily/2018/04/14/the-crazed-euphoria-of-lucrecia-martels-zama/. Accessed 04/15/18.

———. Interview with Lucrecia Martel. Film Society of Lincoln Center, April 2018b. https://www.youtube.com/watch?v=JtdLaF5tlVs. Accessed 05/31/18.

Almada, Selva. *El mono en el remolino: Notas del rodaje de "Zama" de Lucrecia Martel*. Buenos Aires: Random House, 2017.

Almodóvar, Pedro. "Colocar la cámara, llenar la pantalla de sonidos." In Panozzo, *La propria voz*, 8–9.

Alonso, Luciano. "*Zama* de Antonio Di Benedetto no es *Zama* de Lucrecia Martel." *Revista kunst*, October 5, 2017. https://revistakunst.com/2017/10/05/zama-de-antonio-di-benedetto-no-es-zama-de-lucrecia-martel/. Accessed 10/06/17.

Amado, Ana. "Cine argentino: Cuando todo es margen." *Pensamiento de los confines* 11 (September 2002): 87–94.

———. "Velocidades, generaciones y utopías: A propósito de la *La ciénaga*, de Lucrecia Martel." *Alceu* 6.12 (January–July 2006): 48–56.

———. *La imagen justa: Cine argentino y política (1980–2007)*. Buenos Aires: Ediciones Colihue, 2009.

Amatriain, Ignacio, ed. *Una década de nuevo cine argentino (1995–2005): Industria, crítica, formación, estéticas*. Buenos Aires: Ediciones Ciccus, 2009.

Ames, Eric. *Ferocious Reality: Documentary According to Werner Herzog*. Minneapolis: University of Minnesota Press, 2012.

Andermann, Jens. *New Argentine Cinema*. New York: Tauris, 2012.

Andermann, Jens. "Argentine Cinema after the New: Territories, Languages, Medialities." *Senses of Cinema* 89 (December 2018). http://sensesofcinema.com/2018/latin-american-cinema-today/argentine-cinema-after-the-new-territories-languages-medialities/. Accessed 12/20/2018.

———, and Álvaro Fernández Bravo, eds. *New Argentine and Brazilian Cinema: Reality Effects*. New York: Palgrave, 2013.

Anderson, Jeffrey. "The Nature of Water: Interview with Lucrecia Martel." *Combustible Celluoid*, April 22, 2005. http://www.combustiblecelluloid.com/interviews/martel.shtml. Accessed 10/01/14.

Anderson, Matthew. "London Film Festival Review *Zama*." *Cinevue*, October 20, 2017. http://www.cine-vue.com/2017/10/lff-2017-zama-review.html?m=1. Accessed 10/22/17.

Aprea, Gustavo. *Cine y políticas en Argentina: Continuidades y discontinuidades en 25 años de democracia*. Buenos Aires: Biblioteca Nacional, 2008.

Arboleda Ríos, Paola: "From National Allegory to Autobiography: Un-Pleasure and Other Family Pathologies in Two Films by Lucrecia Martel." In *Latin American Cinemas: Local Views and Transnational Connections*, edited by Nayibe Bermúdez Barrios, 47–78. Calgary: University of Calgary Press, 2011.

Aufderheide, Pat. "Awake, Argentina." *Film Comment*, March 1986, 51–55.

Azara, Félix de. *Voyage dans l'Amérique méridionale: Depuis 1781 jusq'en 1801*. Paris: Dentu, 1809.

Babino, Ernesto. "Mi límite es el pudor, no lo que va a pensar el público: Lucrecia Martel, director de *La ciénaga*." *Sin cortes*, May 2001, 40–42.

———. "Lucrecia Martel y las interioridades de *La ciénaga*." *Cineasta: Portal de cine y el audiovisual latinoamericano y caribeño*. N.d. http://www.cinelatinoamericano.org/texto.aspx?cod=2737. Accessed 12/03/14.

Backstein, Karen. "The Headless Woman." *Cineaste*, Winter 2009, 64–65.

Balsom, Erika. "Breaking Time's Arrow: Lucrecia Martel and *Zama* at the 2017 LFF." *BFI: Film Forever*, October 20, 2017. http://www.bfi.org.uk/news-opinion/sight-sound-magazine/comment/festivals/breaking-time-s-arrow-lucrecia-martel-zama-london-film-festival. Accessed 10/20/17.

Barfield, Charles. "*Zama* Filmmaker Lucrecia Martel to Team with Björk on a New Stage Production." *Playlist*, February 6, 2019. https://theplaylist.net/lucrecia-martel-bjork-concert-20190206/. Accessed 02/06/2019.

Battle, Diego. "*La ciénaga* revela el talento de una joven directora salteña." *Lanacion.com*, April 12, 2001. http://www.lanacion.com.ar/59684-la-cienaga-revela-el-talento-de-una-joven-directora-saltena. Accessed 06/28/13.

———. "Crítica de *Zama*, de Lucrecia Martel." *Otroscines*, August 31, 2017a. https://www.otroscines.com/nota-12487-critica-de-zama-de-lucrecia-martel-venezia74. Accessed 09/06/17.

———. "*It* (Eso) sigue primera en Argentina y *Zama* hizo historia." *Otroscines*, October 2, 2017b. https://www.otroscines.com/nota-12587-it-eso-sigue-primera-en-argentina-y-zama-hizo-historia. Accessed 10/03/17.

Bazin, André. "An Aesthetic of Realism: Neorealism." In *What Is Cinema? Essays Selected and Translated by Hugh Gray*, 2:16–22. Translated by Hugh Gray. Berkeley: University of California Press, 1971.

Bell, Nicholas. "Mortal Transfer: Martel Returns with Lush, Dark Comedy on Colonial Maneuvering." *Ioncinema*, September 9, 2017. http://www.ioncinema.com/news/zama-lucrecia-martel-review. Accessed 09/12/17.

Berghella, Vanina. "La ciudad que huye, por Lucrecia Martel." *La Propaladora*, May 3, 2007. http://www.lapropaladora.com.ar/2007/05/03/la-ciudad-que-huye-por-lucrecia-martel/. Accessed 01/16/14.

Bermúdez Barrios, Nayibe, ed. *Latin American Cinemas: Local Views and Transnational Connections*. Calgary: University of Calgary Press, 2011.

Bermúdez, Juan Antonio. "Hiperrealismo tropical." *Cineasta: Portal de cine y el audiovisual latinoamericano y caribeño*. N.d. http://www.cinelatinoamericano.org/texto.aspx?cod=1099. Accessed 03/12/14.

Bernades, Horacio. "La cuestión de la identidad es inapresable: Entrevista a Lucrecia Martel." *Página/12*, September 28, 2017. https://www.pagina12.com.ar/65610-la-cuestion-de-la-identidad-es-inapresable. Accessed 09/30/17.

———, Diego Lerer, and Sergio Wolf, ed. *New Argentine Cinema: Themes, Auteurs and Trends of Innovation*. Buenos Aires: Ediciones Tatanka, 2002.

Bernini, Emilio, Domin Chois, Mariano Dupont, and Daniela Googi. "Tres cineastas argentinas: Conversación con Lucrecia Martel, Lisandro Alonso y Ariel Rotter." *Kilometro* 111.2 (2001): 125–50.

Bertoni, María. "El sucesor de Aguirre." *Espectadores*, April 10, 2017. https://espectadores.com.ar/2017/10/04/zama-lucrecia-martel/. Accessed 08/08/2018.

———. "Martel en tiempos de *Zama*." *Espectadores*, August 5, 2018. https://espectadores.com.ar/2018/08/05/anos-luz-manuel-abramovich-lucrecia-martel-estreno-malba/amp/?__twitter_impression=true. Accessed 08/08/2018.

Bettendorf, Paulina, and Agustina Pérez Rial. "Artilugios de pensamiento: Entrevista a Lucrecia Martel." In *Tránsitos de la mirada*, edited by Paulina Bettendorf and Agustina Pérez Rial, 179–96. Buenos Aires: Librería, 2014a.

Bettendorf, Paulina, and Agustina Pérez Rial, eds. *Tránsitos de la mirada.* Buenos Aires: Libreria, 2014b.

Beycero, Raúl, Rafael Filipelli, David Oubiña, and Alan Pauls. "Estética del cine, nuevos realismos, representación." *Punto de vista* 67 (2000): 1–9.

Bobillo, Gabriel, and Fernando Martín Peña. "Lucrecia Martel." In *Generaciones 60/90: Cine argentino independiente*, edited by Fernando Martín Peña, 117–25. Buenos Aires: Fundación Eduardo F. Costantini, 2003.

Bolaño, Roberto. "Sensini." In *Last Evenings on Earth*, 1–18. Translated by Chris Andrews. New York: New Directions, 2006.

Bordón, Juan Manuel. "Estoy sumergida en el mundo de *Zama*." *Los Andes*, March 2, 2013. www.losandes.com.ar/notas/2013/3/2/lucrecia-martel-estoy-sumergida-mundo-zama-699393.asp. Accessed 06/06/13.

Bresson, Robert. *Notes on the Cinematographer*. Translated by Jonathan Griffin. New York: Quartet Books, 1986.

Brodersen, Diego. "Lejana tierra mía." *Página/12*, September 21, 2017. https://www.pagina12.com.ar/63274-lejana-tierra-mia. Accessed 09/21/17.

———. "*Zama*: Lucrecia Martel golpea con un trip colonial y filosófico." *Rolling Stone* (Argentina), September 28, 2017. http://www.rollingstone.com.ar/2067302-zama-lucrecia-martel-golpea-con-un-trip-colonial-y-filosofico?platform=hootsuite. Accessed 09/30/17.

Brody, Richard. "Zama." *New Yorker*, April 23, 2018, 12. https://www.newyorker.com/goings-on-about-town/movies/zama. Accessed 04/20/18.

Brooks, Brian. "Argentine Filmmaker Lucrecia Martel in Sarajevo: 'Avoiding Obviousness I Discover Other Things.'" *Indiewire*, July 29, 2011. www.indiewire.com/article/argentine_filmmaker_lucrecia_martel_in_sarajevo_avoiding_obviousness_i_disc. Accessed 01/23/13.

Brooks, Xan. "Lucrecia Martel Emerges from the Wilderness with a Strange, Sensual Wonder." *Guardian*, August 31, 2017. https://www.theguardian.com/film/2017/aug/31/zama-review-lucrecia-martel-emerges-from-the-wilderness-with-a-strange-sensual-wonder. Accessed 08/31/17.

Calavera, Emmanuel. "Lucrecia Martel habla de *El Eternauta*." *Facultad de Periodismo y Comunicación Social UNLP*, November 13, 2008. https://www.youtube.com/watch?v=u8OPy2AloLA. Accessed 02/14/16.

Camia, Giovanni Marchini. "'The Narrative Model Used in TV Series Brings Us Back to a Stage That We Long Surpassed in Cinema': Lucrecia Martel's Rotterdam Masterclass." *Filmmaker Magazine*, February 12, 2018. https://filmmakermagazine.com/104839-tv-series-brings-us-back-to-a-stage-that-we-long-surpassed-in-cinema-lucrecia-martels-rotterdam-masterclass/#.WvGp162ZOr8. Accessed 02/14/18.

Campero, Agustín. *Nuevo cine argentino: De "Rapado" a "Historias extraordinarias."* Buenos Aires: Biblioteca Nacional, 2009.

Canclini, Néstor García. "Will There Be Latin American Cinema in the Year 2000? Visual Culture in a Postnational Era." In *Framing Latin American Cinema: Contemporary Critical Perspectives*, edited by Ann Marie Stock, 246–58. Translated by Adriana X. Tatum and Ann Marie Stock. Minneapolis: University of Minnesota Press, 1997.

Carballa, Matías. "Crítica de *Zama*." *Cinescondite*, September 28, 2017. http://www.cinescondite.com/2017/09/28/critica-de-zama/. Accessed 09/30/17.

Cavagna, Manon. "*Zama*—Kritik." *Critic.de*, June 18, 2018. https://www.critic.de/film/zama-10964/. Accessed 07/17/18.

Centenera, Marc. "La directora Lucrecia Martel indaga el territorio misterioso de sus actrices." *El País*, April 22, 2017. https://elpais.com/cultura/2017/04/21/actualidad/1492810817_928404.html. Accessed 07/18/17.

———. "*Zama*, atrapado en la esperanza." *El País*, October 8, 2017. https://elpais.com/cultura/2017/10/07/actualidad/1507401583_261239.html. Accessed 10/09/17.

Chang, Dustin. "Lucrecia Martel's *Zama* Is the Cinematic Highlight of the Year." *Screen Anarchy*, October 4, 2017. http://screenanarchy.com/2017/10/new-york-2017-review-lucrecia-martels-zama-is-the-cinematic-highlight-of-the-year.html. Accessed 10/06/17.

———. "Quiet Catharsis." *Floating World*, October 5, 2017. http://www.dustinchang.com/2017/10/quiet-catharsis.html?spref=tw. Accessed 10/06/17.

———. "*Zama* Offers a Withering Critique of Colonialism from Within." *NPR*, April 24, 2018. https://www.npr.org/2018/04/24/605249336/-zama-offers-a-withering-critique-of-colonialism-from-within. Accessed 04/26/18.

Chen, Phoebe. "Fragments of Lucrecia Martel's *The Headless Woman*." *Another Gaze* 2 (2018): 87–90.

Chiaravalli, Veronica. "Una argentina en Berlín." *La Nación*, February 4, 2001.

Choi, Domin, and Emilio Bernini. "*La ciénaga* o el arte de la infancia." *Kilómetro 111.2* (2001): 151–53.

Christofoletti Barrenha, Natalia. "*La mujer sin cabeza* (Lucrecia Martel, 2008) y el mecanismo del olvido en el pasado y el presente." *Revista comunicación* 10.1 (2012): 643–52.

Coetzee, J. M. "A Great Writer We Should Know." *New York Review of Books*, January 19, 2017. https://www.nybooks.com/articles/2017/01/19/antonio-di-benedetto-great-writer/. Accessed 01/20/2017.

Collins, Austin K. "*Zama* Review: This Surreal Period Piece Is 2018's Best Film So Far." *Vanity Fair*, April 20, 2018. https://www.vanityfair.com/hollywood/2018/04/zama-movie-review-lucrecia-martel. Accessed 04/20/18.

Constantini, Gustavo. "La banda sonora en el nuevo cine argentino." *Cuadernos hispanoamericanos* 679 (2007): 7–17.

Copertari, Gabriela. *Desintegración y justicia en el cine argentino contemporáneo*. Rochester, NY: Tamesis, 2009.

"Cortes: El estilo de Antonio Di Benedetto." *Radiaciones*, April 6, 2014. https://blogderadiaciones.wordpress.com/2014/04/06/cortes-el-estilo-de-antonio-di-benedetto/. Accessed 10/10/17.

Costa, Jordi. "Era un espejismo." *El País*, January 19, 2018. https://elpais.com/cultura/2018/01/19/actualidad/1516367811_921629.html. Accessed 04/20/18.

Cozarinsky, Edgardo. "Letter from Buenos Aires." *New Left Review* 26 (2004): 105–16.

Croll, Ben. "Lucrecia Martel's Long-Awaited Epic Is a Serious Achievement That Will Keep You Guessing." *IndieWire*, August 30, 2017. https://www.theguardian.com/film/2017/aug/31/zama-review-lucrecia-martel-emerges-from-the-wilderness-with-a-strange-sensual-wonder. Accessed 08/31/17.

Cruz Carvajal, Isleni. "He sentido mucho dolor haciendo *La ciénaga*." *El Kinetoscopio* 61 (2001): 14–17.

Cutler, Aaron. "La Ciénaga." DVD review. *Cineaste*, summer 2015, 66–67.

Dargis, Manohla. "Men, Women, Cinema: No Longer the Same Old Story." *New York Times*, September 15, 2017. https://www.nytimes.com/2017/09/15/movies/toronto-international-film-festival-lady-bird-i-love-you-daddy.html?mcubz=0. Accessed 09/21/17.

———. "A Cinematic Marvel, *Zama* Brilliantly Tackles Colonialism in the New World." *New York Times*, April 12, 2018. https://www.nytimes.com/2018/04/12/movies/review-zama-lucrecia-martel.html. Accessed 04/12/18.

"Debemos converser, ser valientes y afrontar este tema tan doloroso." *El tribuno*, July 16, 2018. https://www.eltribuno.com/salta/nota/2018-7-16-0-0-0-lucrecia-martel-debemos-conversar-ser-valientes-y-afrontar-este-tema-tan-doloroso/amp?__twitter_impression=true. Accessed 07/16/18.

Delgado, Maria. "The Headless Woman." *Sight and Sound* 20.3 (March 2010): 64.

———. "*Zama* Makes Slow Jest of a Mouldering Colonial Mandarin." *BFI: Film Forever*, May 27, 2018. http://www.bfi.org.uk/news-opinion/sight-sound-magazine/reviews-recommendations/zama-lucrecia-martel-colonial-mandarin. Accessed 05/28/18.

Dennison, Stephanie, ed. *Contemporary Hispanic Cinema: Interrogating the Transnational in Spanish and Latin American Film*. Rochester, NY: Tamesis, 2013.

"Desde de los 18 me siento vieja." *Clarín.com*, February 2, 2004. http://edant.clarin.com/suplementos/mujer/2004/03/02/m-00401.htm. Accessed 10/02/14.

D'Espósito, Leonardo M. "La estructura siniestra: *La mujer sin cabeza* de Lucrecia Martel." *Kinetoscopio* 84 (December 2008a): 105–9.

———. "*La mujer sin cabeza*: Viaje al principio del horror." In Panozzo, *La propria voz* (2008b), 51–52.

———. "Los noventa son el plan maestro de la dictadura: Entrevista con Lucrecia Martel." *Crítica de la Argentina*, August 20, 2008c.

———. "Hemos demostrado que podemos competir con una industria million-aria: Entrevista a Lucrecia Martel." *Noticias*, October 12, 2017. http://noticias.perfil.com/2017/10/12/lucrecia-martel-hemos-demostrado-que-podemos-competir-con-una-industria-millonaria/. Accessed 10/13/17.

De Valck, Marijke. *Film Festivals: From European Geopolitics to Global Cinephilia*. Amsterdam: University of Amsterdam Press, 2007.

"Días de hotel y película para Lucrecia Martel." *Lanacion.com*, August 29, 2008. http://www.lanacion.com.ar/1044288-dias-y-hotel-de-pelicula-para-lucrecia-martel. Accessed 06/28/13.

Di Benedetto, Antonio. *Escritos periodísticos, 1943–1986*. Edited by Liliana Reales. Buenos Aires: Adriana Hidalgo, 2016a.

———. *Zama*. Translated by Esther Allen. New York: New York Review of Books, 2016b.

Di Tella, Andrés. "Memories of New Argentine Cinema." In *The Film Edge: Contemporary Filmmaking in Latin America*, edited by Eduardo A. Russo, 199–212. Buenos Aires: Teseo, 2010.

Diz, Javier, and Diego Lerer. "Lucrecia Martel habla de *Zama*, su nueva película." *Los inrockuptibles*, August 31, 2017. https://losinrocks.com/lucrecia-martel-zama-do95abf57edf. Accessed 09/30/2017.

D'Lugo, Marvin. "Pedro Almodóvar's Latin American 'Business.'" In *Contemporary Hispanic Cinema: Interrogating the Transnational in Spanish and Latin American Film*, edited by Stephanie Dennison, 113–36. Rochester, NY: Tamesis, 2013.

Duclós Sibuet, Victoria, "*Zama*, exponente de immersión sonora." *Puntocero*, September 26, 2017. http://puntocero.me/zama-exponente-inmersion-sonora/. Accessed 09/27/2017.

Dupont, Joan. "A Director Examines the Abuse of Power." *New York Times*, May 21, 2004.

Ďurovičová, Nataša, and Kathleen Newman, eds. *World Cinemas, Transnational Perspectives*. New York: Routledge, 2010.

Ebert, Roger. "La ciénaga." *RogerEbert.com*, October 19, 2001. http://www.rogerebert.com/reviews/la-cienaga-2001. Accessed 06/28/13.

Elena, Alberto, and Marina Díaz López, eds. *The Cinema of Latin America*. New York: Wallflower Press, 2003.

"El extraño mundo de Lucrecia Martel." *La nación*, August 19, 2008. http://www.lanacion.com.ar/1040986-el-extrano-mundo-de-lucrecia-martel. Accessed 06/28/13.

"El nuevo libro de Selma Almada sobre la película de Martel." *Entre ríos ahora*, August 27, 2017. http://entreriosahora.com/el-nuevo-libro-de-selva-almada-sobre-la-pelicula-de-martel/. Accessed 08/28/17.

Elsaesser, Thomas. "Film Festival Networks: The New Topographies of Cinema in Europe." In *European Cinema: Face to Face with Hollywood*, 82–107. Amsterdam: Amsterdam University Press, 2005.

Enríquez, Mariana. "Ese oscuro objeto es deseo." *Página/12*, May 2, 2004. http://www.pagina12.com.ar/. Accessed 10/02/14.

———. "La mala memoria: Entrevista a Lucrecia Martel." Radar, *Página/12*, August 17, 2008. http://www.pagina12.com.ar/. Accessed 07/07/13.

Eseverri, Máximo, and Fernando Martín Peña. *Lita Stantic: El cine es automóvil y poema*. Buenos Aires: Eudeba, 2013.

"Esperando a *Zama*: El cine de Lucrecia Martel." *Otro Cines*, September 7, 2017. https://www.otroscines.com/nota?idnota=12519. Accessed 09/08/2017.

Escribano, Martín. "Desde el exilio." *Artezeta*, October 30, 2017. http://artezeta.com.ar/desde-el-exilio/. Accessed 10/31/17.

Ezra, Elizabeth, and Terry Rowden, eds. *Transnational Cinema: The Film Reader*. New York: Routledge, 2006.

Falicov, Tamara L. "Los Hijos de Ménem: The New Independent Argentine Cinema, 1995–1999." *Framework* 44.1 (spring 2003): 49–63.

———. *The Cinematic Tango: Contemporary Argentine Film*. New York: Wallflower Press, 2007.

———. "Migrating from South to North: The Role of Film Festivals in Funding and Shaping Global South Film and Video." In *Locating Migrating Media*, edited by Greg Elmer et al., 3–21. Lanham, MD: Lexington Books, 2010.

———. "Argentine Cinema and the Crisis of Audience." In Ingruber and Prutsch, *Filme in Argentinien*, 207–18.

Fear, David. "Lucrecia Martel's Imperialism Takedown Is a Slow-Burn Masterpiece." *Rolling Stone*, April 13, 2018. https://www.rollingstone.com/movies/reviews/zama-movie-review-w518905. Accessed 04/16/18.

Feenstra, Pietsie, Esther Gimena Ugalde, and Kathrin Sartingen, eds. *Directoras de cine en España y América Latina*. Frankfurt am Main: Peter Lang, 2014.

Feijoo, Sebastián. "'Con las actuales políticas del INCAA hubiera sido imposible hacer *Zama*': Entrevista a Lucrecia Martel." *Tiempoar*, September 30, 2017. https://www.tiempoar.com.ar/articulo/view/71202/con-las-actuales-pola-ticas-del-incaa-hubiera-sido-imposible-hacer-zama?utm_content=buffer67587&utm_medium=social&utm_source=facebook.com&utm_campaign=buffer#.WdOBFoTOoQD.twitter. Accessed 10/06/17.

Felperin, Leslie. "*The Headless Woman*." Review, *Variety* 411 (2008): 22–23.

Felten, Uta. "Subversive Strategien im Kino von Lucrecia Martel." In *Lateinamerikanisches Kino der Gegenwart: Themen, Genres, Stile, RegisseurInnen*, edited by Christian von Tschilke, Maribel Cedeño Rojas, and Isabel Maurer Queipo, 325–34. Tübingen: Stauffenberg, 2015.

Fernandez, Migue. "*El Eternauta* no tiene quien lo filme (Parte I)." *Cinescondite*, May 22, 2013. http://www.cinescondite.com/. Accessed 02/16/16.

Filer, Malva E. *La novela y el diálogo de los textos: Zama de Antonio di Benedetto*. Mexico, DF: Editorial Oasis, 1982.

Finchelstein, Federico. *The Ideological Origins of the Dirty War: Fascism, Populism, and Dictatorship in Twentieth Century Argentina*. Oxford: Oxford University Press, 2014.

Finkielman, Jorge. *The Film Industry in Argentina: An Illustrated Cultural History*. Jefferson, NC: McFarland, 2004.

Fiorucci, Flavia, and Marcus Klein, eds. *The Argentine Crisis at the Turn of the Millenium: Causes, Consequences and Explanations*. Amsterdam: Aksant, 2004.

Flanagan, Matthew. "Towards an Aesthetic of Slow in Contemporary Cinema." *16:9: Danmarks klogeste filmtidsskrift* 6.29 (November 2008). http://www.16-9.dk/2008-11/side11_inenglish.htm. Accessed 12/05/14.

Forcinito, Ana. "Mirada cinematográfica y género sexual: Mímica, erotismo y ambigüedad en Lucrecia Martel." *Chasqui* 35.2 (2006): 109–30.

Foster, David William. "Contemporary Argentine Cinema." In *New Latin American Cinema*, edited by Michael T. Martin, 2:464–79. Detroit: Wayne State University Press, 1997.

———. *El Eternauta, Daytripper and Beyond: Graphic Narrative in Argentina and Brazil*. Austin: University of Texas Press, 2016.

François, Cécile. "El cine de Lucrecia Martel: Una estética de la opacidad." *Espéculo* 43 (2009): 1–13.

Frodon, François. "Le cinema comme espace collectif: Rencontre Lucrecia Martel." *Cahiers du cinema* 593 (September 2004): 30–31.

de la Fuente, Anna Maria. "Lucrecia Martel on Adapting a Soliloquy, *Zama*." *Variety*, October 27, 2017. http://variety.com/2017/film/festivals/lucrecia-martel-on-adapting-a-soliloquy-zama-1202600826/. Accessed 10/27/17.

Fuller, Graham. "Shots in the Dark." *Interview* 35.3 (April 2005): 106.

Gallego, Rolando. "'Ir a un festival es una pesadilla': Entrevista a Lucrecia Martel." *Cinemaboutique*, September 26, 2017. http://www.cinemaboutiquela.com/2017/09/26/lucrecia-martel/. Accessed 10/03/17.

Galt, Rosalind. "Default Cinema: Queering Economic Crisis in Argentina and Beyond." *Screen* 54.1 (spring 2013): 62–81.

García, Jorge. "Argentina 6, resto del mundo 4." *El amante cine* 200 (2009): 14.

García, Jorge, and Eduardo Rojas. "Desbordes del deseo: Entrevista con Lucrecia Martel." *El amante cine* 145 (May 2004): 12–14.

García, Jorge, and Eduardo Rojas. "Para mí el cine es un lugar de percepción." *El amante cine* 195 (August 2008): 8–10.

Gemünden, Gerd. "The Making of Now: New Wave Cinema in Berlin and Buenos Aires." In *A Transnational Art Cinema: The Berlin School and Its Global Contexts*, edited by Marco Abel and Jaimey Fisher, 293–312. Detroit: Wayne State University Press, 2018.

Gemünden, Gerd, and Silvia Spitta. "'I Was Never Afraid': An Interview with Lucrecia Martel." *Film Quarterly* 71.4 (2018): 33–40.

Getino, Octavio. *Entre lo posible y lo deseable*. Buenos Aires: Ediciones Ciccus, 2005.

———, ed. *Cine latinoamericano: Producción y mercados en la primera década del siglo xxi*. Buenos Aires: Ediciones Ciccus, 2012.

Giménez Cacho, Daniel. "Martel." *Letras libres*, April 1, 2018. http://www.letraslibres.com/mexico/revista/martel. Accessed 05/28/18.

Girish, Devika. "Lucrecia Martel's Next Film." *Film Comment*, April 23, 2018. https://www.filmcomment.com/blog/news-week-april-23/. Accessed 04/23/18.

Gómez, Leila. "El cine de Lucrecia Martel: La medusa en lo recóndito." *Ciberletras* 13 (July 2005). http://www.lehman.cuny.edu/ciberletras/v13/gomez.htm. Accessed 12/05/12.

González, David. "'I Am Not Crazy about Filming, and Nor Is It the Most Interesting Thing to Me': Interview with Lucrecia Martel." *Cineuropa*, September 3, 2017. http://cineuropa.org/it.aspx?did=325392&l=en&t=interview. Accessed 09/04/2017.

Granero, Lucas. "Colchones de fe: Tres aproximaciones a *Zama*." *Las pistas*, October 2, 2017. https://las-pistas.com/2017/10/02/colchones-de-fe-tres-aproximaciones-a-zama/. Accessed 10/06/17.

Grater, Tom. "Sundance Institute, UK's ICA Team for Lucrecia Martel Documentary *Chocobar*." *Screendaily*, November 5, 2018. https://www.screendaily.com/news/sundance-institute-uks-ica-team-for-lucrecia-martel-documentary-chocobar-exclusive/5134269.article. Accessed 11/05/18.

Grissemann, Stefan. "Lucrecia Martel: Argentiniens scharfsinnigste Regisseurin." *Profil*, July 7, 2018. https://www.profil.at/kultur/lucrecia-martel-zama-regisseurin-10184392. Accessed 08/01/18.

Guerreiro, Leila. "El optimismo de la decadencia." *Cineasta: Portal de cine y el audiovisual latinoamericano y caribeño*. N.d. http://www.cinelatinoamericano.org/texto.aspx?cod=4905. Accessed 12/03/14.

Guest, Haden. "Interview with Lucrecia Martel." *Bomb* 106 (2009). Translated by Phillip Penix-Tadsen. http://bombsite.com/issues/106/articles/3220. Accessed 04/24/12.

Guillen, Michael. "Argentine Cinema: *The Headless Woman*—Onstage Conversation between Lucrecia Martel and B. Ruby Rich." *Screenanarchy*, August 30, 2009. http://screenanarchy.com/2009/08/argentine-cinema-the-headless-womanonstage-conversation-between-lucrecia-ma.html. Accessed 10/10/14.

Gundermann, Christian. "The Stark Gaze of New Argentine Cinema: Restoring Strangeness to the Object in the Perverse Age of Commodity Fetishism." *Journal of Latin American Cultural Studies* 14.3 (December 2005): 241–61.

Guzzante, Marina. "Quería ser invisible: Entrevista a Selva Almada." *Los Andes*, September 23, 2017. http://www.losandes.com.ar/article/selva-almada-queria-ser-invisible. Accessed 09/26/17.

Hades, Martin. "The Navigator of Eternity." Preface to *The Eternaut*, by H. G. Oesterheld, drawings by Francisco Solano López, i–ii. Translated by Erica Mena. Seattle: Fantagraphics Books, 2016.

Halligan, Fionnuala. "*Zama*: Venice Review." *Screendaily*, August 31, 2017. https://www.screendaily.com/reviews/zama-venice-review/5121861.article?utm_medium=email&utm_campaign=US%20Daily%20September%201%20actual&utm_content=US%20Daily%20September%201%20actual+CID_

ob4a392bf7f02318fb4aecb246b5f329&utm_source=Newsletter&utm_term =Zama%20Venice%20Review. Accessed 08/31/17.

Hart, Stephen M. *A Companion to Latin American Film*. Rochester, NY: Tamesis, 2004.

———. *Latin American Cinema*. London: Reaktion Books, 2015.

Haywood Ferreira, Rachel. "*Más Allá, El Eternauta*, and the Dawn of the Golden Age of Latin American Science Fiction (1953–59)." *Extrapolation* 51.2 (2010): 281–303.

Higuinen, Erwan. "La boue des damnés: *La ciénaga* de Lucrecia Martel." *Cahiers du cinema* 564 (January 2002): 72–75.

Hoberman, Jim. "Far from Heaven: Argentine Writer-Director Artfully Plumbs Sexual and Religious Obsession." *Village Voice*, April 19, 2005. http://todd haynes.wolfzen.com/text/reviews/ffh_voice.shtml. Accessed 05/03/12.

———. "Lucrecia Martel: A Director Who Confounds and Thrills." *New York Times*, April 13, 2018. https://www.nytimes.com/2018/04/13/movies/lucrecia -martel-zama-argentina.html. Accessed 04/13/18.

Hochhäusler, Christoph, and Nicolas Wackerbarth. "Lucrecia Martel: Revolver Live + Meisterklasse." *Revolver* 39 (2018): 6–42.

Holden, Stephen. "Summertime, and the Living Is Near Unbearable." *New York Times*, October 1, 2001. http://www.nytimes.com/2001/10/01/movies/01CIEN .html. Accessed 05/03/12.

———. "What It Hurts to Remember Becomes Convenient to Forget." *New York Times*, August 18, 2009. http://www.nytimes.com/2009/08/19/ movies/19headless.html?_r=0. Accessed 05/03/12.

Holmes, Amanda. "Landscape and the Artist's Frame in Lucrecia Martel's *La ciénaga/The Swamp* and *La niña santa/The Holy Girl*." In Rego and Rocha, *New Trends*, 131–46.

Horton, Robert. "The Conquistador Fever Dream of *Zama*." *Seattle Weekly*, April 25, 2018. https://www.seattleweekly.com/film/the-conquistador-fever -dream-of-zama/. Accessed 04/26/18.

Ingruber, Daniel, and Ursula Prutsch, eds. *Filme in Argentinien—Argentine Cinema*. Berlin: Lit Verlag, 2012.

"Interview with Lucrecia Martel." *La niña santa* (official website). N.d. http:// www.laninasanta.com/entrevista.html. Accessed 10/01/14.

Isabelinho, Domingo. "Héctor Gérman Oesterheld: Ethics and Aesthetics of a Humanist." *European Comic Art* 7.1 (2014): 31–55.

Jaffe, Ira. *Slow Movies: Countering the Cinema of Action*. New York: Wallflower, 2014.

Jagoe, Eva-Lynn, and John Cant. "Vibraciones encarnadas en *La niña santa* de Lucrecia Martel." In Rangil, *El cine argentino*, 169–90.

James, Nick. "Divine Innocence: *La niña santa*." *Sight and Sound* 15.2 (2005): 18–20.

Jones, Kent. "In the Thick of It." *Film Comment*, March/April 2005, 22–24.

Jubis, Oscar. "The Salta Trilogy of Lucrecia Martel." MA thesis, University of Miami, 2009.

Kadritzke, Till. "Verstörte Kamera: Retrospektive Lucrecia Martel. *Critic.de*, March 7, 2018. https://www.critic.de/special/verstoerte-kamera-retrospektive -lucrecia-martel-4231/. Accessed 07/12/18.

Kaganski, Serge. "Lucrecia Martel: Pour l'Argentine." *Les Inrocks.com*, January 8, 2002. http://www.lesinrocks.com/2002/01/08/cinema/actualite-cinema/ lucrecia-martel-pour-largentine-11217793/. Accessed 03/03/15.

Kairuz, Mariano. "Rizos en blanco y negro sobre rojo furioso." In Panozzo, *La propria voz*, 53–55.

Kalmanovitz, Manuel. "'The Vanity of Being Productive: An Interview with Lucrecia Martel." *Terremoto* 8 (February 2017). http://terremoto.mx/article/ the-vanity-of-being-productive/ Accessed 07/31/17.

Karstulovich, Federico. "Los otros, los clásicos, los cuentos: *La mujer sin cabeza*." *El amante cine* 195 (August 2008): 7.

Karstulovich, Frederico, Marcos Rodríguez, Sebastián Rosal, and Hernán Schell. "Cuatro voces hablan sobre *Zama*." *Perro Blanco*, September 29, 2017. https://www.perroblanco.net/dialogo-cuatro-voces-hablan-zama/. Accessed 10/03/2017.

Katunaric, Boris. "Lucrecia Martel y *Zama*: El Óscar por encima de Darín." *APU* (Agencia Paco Urondo: Periodismo Militante), September 30, 2017. http://www.agenciapacourondo.com.ar/cultura/lucrecia-martel-y-zama-el -oscar-por-encima-de-darin. Accessed 10/03/17.

King, Jessica. "Lucrecia Martel's *Zama* Is Difficult, Beautiful, and Cruel." *Playlist*, August 30, 2017. http://theplaylist.net/lucrecia-martel-zama-review -20170830/. Accessed 08/31/17.

King, John, Ana M. López, and Manuel Alvarado, eds. *Mediating Two Worlds: Cinematic Encounters in the Americas*. London: BFI, 1993.

King, John, Sheila Whitaker, and Rosa Bosch, eds. *An Argentine Passion: María Luisa Bemberg and Her Films*. New York: Verso, 2000.

Knol, Matthijs Wouter. "In the Limelight: Conversation with Lucrecia Martel." Berlinale Master Class 2013. http://www.berlinale-talents.de/bt/program/ telelecture/1333. Accessed 04/04/13.

Knörer, Ekkehard. "Hier waren wir: Zu Lucrecia Martels *Zama*." *Cargo* 38 (June 2018): 4–9.

Koch, Tomasso. "*Zama*, el hermoso regreso de Lucrecia Martel, fascina fuera de concurso." *El País*, August 31, 2017. http://link.crwd.fr/2WbN#https:// elpais.com/cultura/2017/08/31/actualidad/1504202425_689873.html?utm _campaign=crowdfire&utm_content=crowdfire&utm_medium=social&utm _source=facebook_page. Accessed 09/06/17.

Koepnick, Lutz P. *On Slowness: Toward an Aesthetic of the Contemporary*. New York: Columbia University Press, 2014.

Kohn, Eric. "How Pedro Almodóvar Pushed Argentina's Greatest Filmmaker to Make Her Best Movie Ever." *IndieWire*, November 21, 2017. http://www.indiewire.com/2017/11/lucrecia-martel-zama-interview-pedro-almodovar-1201899907/. Accessed 11/22/17.

Kolesnicov, Patricia. "*Zama* o por qué no ir hacia la propria vida." *Clarín*, October 2, 2017. https://www.clarin.com/opinion/zama-ir-propia-vida_0_SJtWAgenZ.html. Accessed 10/03/17.

Koza, Roger. "El oído de Lucrecia: Una conjetura sonora sobre el cine de Martel." *Con los ojos abiertos*, July 10, 2017. http://www.conlosojosabiertos.com/oido-lucrecia-una-conjetura-sonora-cine-martel/. Accessed 08/29/17.

———. "Crítica de *Zama*." YouTube, posted October 6, 2017. https://www.youtube.com/watch?v=DnmmaBZ2E24. Accessed 02/02/18.

Kozak, Daniela. "Lucrecia Martel: Hay algo en la literatura de Di Benedetto que en el cine puede estallar." *Diario Clarín*, January 1, 2013. http://www.revistaenie.clarin.com/escenarios/cine/Entrevista-Lucrecia-Martel-Hay-algo-en-la-literatura-de-Di-Benedetto_0_857914400.html Accessed 02/16/16.

Kracauer, Siegfried. *Theory of Film: The Redemption of Physical Reality*. Princeton, NJ: Princeton University Press, 1997 [1960].

———. *History, the Last Things Before the Last*. New York: Oxford University Press, 1969.

Kulfas, Matías. *La industria cinematográfica en la Argentina:Entre los límites del mercado y el fomenta estatal*. Buenos Aires: CEDEM, 2003.

Kunkel, Benjamin. "Voyage to the Interior." *New Yorker*, January 23, 2017, 72–75.

La Ferla, Jorge. "Argentine Cinema: A State of Affairs." In *The Film Edge: Contemporary Filmmaking in Latin America*, edited by Eduardo A. Russo, 173–98. Buenos Aires: Teseo, 2010.

Lalanne, Jean-Marc. "'Le film s'enracine dans des peurs d'enfant': Rencontre Lucrecia Martel." *Cahiers du cinéma* 564 (2002): 74–75.

Lazic, Elena. "You Only Address Colonialism with Solemn Seriousness If You Don't Experience It Daily." *Seventh Row*, April 24, 2018. https://seventh-row.com/2018/04/24/lucrecia-martel-zama/. Accessed 05/01/18.

Lerer, Diego. "'All that Heroic Past and Brave Macho Stuff Makes Me Ill': An Interview with Lucrecia Martel." *BFI: Film Forever*, July 27, 2017. Translated by Mar Diestro-Dópido.http://www.bfi.org.uk/news-opinion/sight-sound-magazine/interviews/lucrecia-martel-interview-zama?utm_content=buffer031a1&utm_medium=social&utm_source=twitter.com&utm_campaign=buffer. Accessed 07/31/17.

———. "El desafío de filmar la angustia." *La agenda*, August 31, 2017. http://laagenda.buenosaires.gob.ar/post/164824456850/el-desaf%C3%ADo-de-filmar-la-angustia. Accessed 05/24/18.

————. "Estrenos: Crítica de 'Zama,' de Lucrecia Martel." *Microposia: Un blog de Diego Lerer*, September 27, 2017. http://www.micropsiacine.com/2017/09/estrenos-critica-zama-lucrecia-martel/. Accessed 09/27/17.

"Ley del Aborto: Lucrecia Martel y actrices argentinas le escribieron una carta a Urtubey." *La Gaceta Salta*, June 19, 2018. https://www.lagacetasalta.com.ar/nota/106563/actualidad/ley-aborto-lucrecia-martel-actrices-argentinas-le-escribieron-carta-urtubey.html. Accessed 06/20/18.

Link, Daniel. "Tres mujeres." *Página/12*, March 1, 2001. http://www.pagina12.com.ar/2001/suple/Radar/01-03/01-03-18/nota1.htm. Accessed 03/03/15.

————. "Aspectos sobre el fin del mundo y la vida después de mañana en algunas películas argentinas." Unpublished paper, presented at CRIC Buenos Aires, August 2015.

Lodge, Guy. "Venice Film Review: *Zama*." *Variety*, August 30, 2017. http://variety.com/2017/film/reviews/zama-review-1202543356/. Accessed 08/31/17.

Lorenz, Günter W. *Dialog mit Lateinamerika: Panorama einer Literatur der Zukunft*. Tübingen: Erdmann, 1970.

Losada, Matt. "Lucrecia Martel's *La mujer sin cabeza*: Cinematic Free Indirect Discourse, Noise-Scape and the Distraction of the Middle Class." *Romance Notes* 50.3 (2010): 307–13.

Lucca, Violet. "Lucrecia Martel's *Zama*." Podcast with Esther Allen and Dennis Lim. *Film Comment*, October 24, 2017. https://www.filmcomment.com/blog/film-comment-podcast-lucrecia-martels-zama/. Accessed 10/25/2017.

"Lucrecia Martel llevó su esperada *Zama* a Venecia." *La Nación*, September 1, 2017. http://www.lanacion.com.ar/2058500-lucrecia-martel-llevo-su-esperada-zama-a-venecia. Accessed 09/04/2017.

"Lucrecia Martel prepara *Zama*." *Haciendo cine*, September 3, 2012. http://www.haciendocine.com.ar/content/lucrecia-martel-prepara-zama. Accessed 02/15/16.

"Lucrecia Martel's Closet Picks." *Criterion Collection*, September 18, 2018. https://www.criterion.com/current/posts/5927-lucrecia-martel-s-closet-picks. Accessed 09/18/18.

"Lucrecia Martel se manifestó ante las fuertes ofensas que recibió." *La Gaceta Salta*, March 30, 2018. https://www.lagacetasalta.com.ar/nota/101922/actualidad/lucrecia-martel-se-manifesto-ante-fuertes-ofensas-recibio.html. Accessed 04/11/18.

Lusnich, Ana Laura, and Pablo Piedras, eds. *Una historia del cine político y social en Argentina: Formas, estilos y registros, 1969–2009*. Buenos Aires: Nueva Librería, 2011.

Macnab, Geoffrey. "*The Holy Girl*." Review, *Sight and Sound* 15.2 (February 2005): 53.

Macovsky, Pablo. "Historias de crímenes de clase." *La capital*, December 13, 2009. http://www.lacapital.com.ar/ed_senales/2009/12/edicion_60/contenidos/noticia_5001.html. Accessed 05/05/15.

Magary, John. "A Woman under the Influence: Interview with Lucrecia Martel." *Reeler*, October 8, 2008. http://www.thereeler.com/the_blog/a_woman_under_the_influence.php. Accessed 04/14/15.

Maranghello, César, ed. *El cine argentino y su aporte a la identidad nacional.* Buenos Aires: Federación de la Industria Gráfica y Afines, 1999.

———. *Breve historia del cine argentino.* Barcelona: Laertes, 2004.

Marchini Camia, Giovanni. "'It's Not Literary Adaptation, It's Literary Infection': An Interview with Lucrecia Martel." *Cineaste* 43.3 (summer 2018a): 45–46.

———. "Zama." *Cineaste* 43.3 (summer 2018b): 53–55.

Martel, Lucrecia. Director's statement. *La ciénaga.* 2001. http://www.litastantic.com.ar/lacienaga/ (dead).

———. Director's statement. *La niña santa.* 2004. http://www.litastantic.com.ar/laninasanta/ (dead).

———. "El sonido en la escritura y la puesta en escena." Workshop for the Festival Vivamérica at the Casa de América, Madrid, 2009. Posted January 26, 2011. https://www.youtube.com/watch?v=mCKHzMzMlZo. Accessed 11/03/14.

———. "La Confederación de ríos." *Página/12*, October 3, 2010. https://www.pagina12.com.ar/diario/suplementos/radar/9-6511-2010-10-03.html. Accessed 05/30/18.

———. "Manifesto." *Las naves* 1 (April 2013): 14.

———. "Llevar al cine una obra maestra." *El País*, March 31, 2017. https://elpais.com/cultura/2017/03/31/babelia/1490954491_002830.html. Accessed 04/20/18.

———. "Voyage of Time." *Film Comment*, March–April 2018a, 6.

———. "Carta abierta por el aborto legal." *Página/12*, July 14, 2018b. https://www.pagina12.com.ar. Accessed 07/16/18.

Martin, Deborah. "Wholly Ambivalent Demon-Girl: Horror, the Uncanny and the Representation of Feminine Adolescence in Lucrecia Martel's *La niña santa.*" *Journal of Iberian and Latin American Studies* 17.1 (April 2011): 59–76.

———. *The Cinema of Lucrecia Martel.* Manchester: Manchester University Press, 2016a.

———. "Lucrecia Martel's *Nueva Argirópolis*: Rivers, Rumours and Resistance." *Journal of Latin American Cultural Studies* 25.3 (2016b): 449–65.

———. "*Planeta ciénaga*: Lucrecia Martel and Contemporary Argentine Women's Filmmaking." In *Latin American Women Filmmakers: Production, Politics, Poetics*, edited by Deborah Martin and Deborah Shaw, 241–62. London: Tauris, 2017.

Martin, Leticia. "Una historia que se repite: La incomunicación." *Baires digital*, October 30, 2017. https://bairesdigitalweb.wordpress.com/2017/10/30/cine-zama-por-leticia-martin/. Accessed 10/31/17.

Martin, Michael T., ed. *New Latin American Cinema*. 2 vols. Detroit: Wayne State University Press, 1997.

Martinez, Javier. "Entrevista a Lucrecia Martel." *Esto no es una revista 07*. N.d. http://www.estonoesunarevista.com.ar/martel.html. Accessed 02/14/16.

Martín Morán, Ana. "*La ciénaga/The Swamp*: Lucrecia Martel, Argentina, 2001." In *The Cinema of Latin America*, edited by Albert Elena and Marina Díaz López, 231–39. New York: Wallflower Press, 2003.

Martins, Laura. "Bodies at Risk: On the State of Exception." In *Argentinean Cultural Production during the Neoliberal Years (1989–2001)*, edited by Hugo Hortiguera and Carolina Rocha, 205–15. Lewiston, NY: Edwin Mellen Press, 2007.

Masnatta, Clara. "Lucrecia Martel's *The Holy Child* (2004)." Unpublished paper, Harvard University, n.d.

Matheou, Demetrios. *The Faber Book of New South American Cinema*. London: Faber and Faber, 2010a.

———. "Vanishing Point: Interview with Lucrecia Martel." *Sight and Sound* 20.3 (2010b): 28–32.

Maurer Queipo, Isabel, ed. *Directory of World Cinema: Latin America*. Chicago: Intellect, 2013.

Mazzini, Martín. "No puedo avalar con mis películas las fantasias violatorias: Entrevista a Lucreca Martel." *La Nación*, September 27, 2017. http://www.lanacion.com.ar/2066908-lucrecia-martel-no-puedo-avalar-con-mi-pelicula-las-fantasias-violatorias. Accessed 09/30/17.

Mendonça Filho, Kleber. "La dama de oro." *Haciendocine*, September 27, 2017. http://www.haciendocine.com.ar/content/la-dama-de-oro. Accessed 09/27/2017.

Merolla, Daniel. "Lucrecia Martel filmará 'El Eternauta.'" *Perfil.com*, May 13, 2008. http://www.perfil.com/contenidos/2008/05/13/noticia_0021.html. Accessed 05/05/15.

Midding, Gerhard. "Bild ist ein Geräusch." *Der Freitag* 26 (2018). https://www.freitag.de/autoren/der-freitag/bild-ist-ein-geraeusch. Accessed 07/12/18.

Milsztajn, Fernando. "Tan Martel: *La mujer sin cabeza*." *Haciendo cine* 13.84 (August 2008): 34.

———. "La mujer con cabeza: Entrevista a María Onetto." *Haciendo cine* 13.84 (August 2008): 18–20.

Monteagudo, Luciano. "Lucrecia Martel: Whispers at Siesta Time." In *New Argentine Cinema: Themes, Auteurs and Trends of Innovation*, edited by Horacio Bernades, Diego Lerer, and Sergio Wolf, 69–78. Buenos Aires: Ediciones Tatanka, 2002.

———. "Cuando lo místico se vuelve erótico." *Cineasta: Portal de cine y el audiovisual latinoamericano y caribeño*. N.d. http://www.cinelatinoamericano.org/texto.aspx?cod=219. Accessed 12/03/14.

————. "Exiliado en su subjetividad." *Página/12*, September 28, 2017. https://www.pagina12.com.ar/65611-exiliado-en-su-subjetividad. Accessed 09/30/17.

Montenegro, Fabiana. "Confusión que provoca la falta de información o el olvido voluntario." *Cineasta: Portal de cine y el audiovisual latinoamericano y caribeño*. N.d. http://www.cinelatinoamericano.org/texto.aspx?cod=4719. Accessed 12/04/14.

Moore, María José, and Paula Wolkowicz, ed. *Cines al margen: Nuevos modos de representación en el cine argentino contemporáneo*. Buenos Aires: Librería, 2007.

Mora, Adriana. "Cannes 2008: Ecos de un festival." *Kinetoscopio* 83 (August–October 2008): 106–12.

Morla, Jorge. "Lucrecia Martel: 'A leer *Zama* comprendí algo que no sé explicar.'" *El País*, January 18, 2018. https://elpais.com/cultura/2018/01/18/actualidad/1516287430_701460.html. Accessed 04/20/18.

Moscoso, Rodrigo. "Desangrándonos: Entrevista con Lucrecia Martel y Lita Stantic." *Haciendo cine*, March 22, 2001, 22–26.

Moseguí, Carlota. "Lucrecia Martel: "El cineasta es el guardián de la incertidumbre." *Otros Cines Europa*, January 25, 2018. http://www.otroscineseuropa.com/lucrecia-martel-cineasta-guardian-la-incertidumbre/. Accessed 01/29/2018.

Mugica, María Fernanda. "*Zama*: Una obra de arte que recompensa con creces al espectador." *La Nación*, September 28, 2017. https://www.lanacion.com.ar/espectaculos/cine/zama-una-obra-de-arte-que-recompensa-con-creces-al-espectador-nid2067024. Accessed 03/18/2019.

Mullaly, Laurence H. "La autoría del cuerpo en el cine de Lucrecia Martel." *Estudios* 21.42 (July–September 2013): 159–71.

————. "Silvina Ocampo y Lucrecia Martel: Dependencias y promesas." Unpublished paper, Congreso del IILI: La Literatura Iberoamericana Entre Dos Orillas, 2015.

Murthi, Vicram. "TIFF 2017: *The Day After, Prototype, Zama, Let the Corpses Tan*." *Rogerebert.com*, September 15, 2017. https://www.rogerebert.com/festivals-and-awards/tiff-2017-the-day-after-prototype-zama-let-the-corpses-tan. Accessed 01/18/18.

Naymann, Adam. "Stuck in a Moment." *Reverse Shot*, September 28, 2017. http://reverseshot.org/reviews/entry/2356/zama. Accessed 09/30/17.

Néspolo, Jimena. *Ejercicios de pudor: Sujeto y escritura en la narrativa de Antonio Di Benedetto*. Buenos Aires: Adriana Hidalgo, 2004.

————. "Antonio Di Benedetto, el escritor 'anti-boom.'" *El País*, April 3, 2017. https://elpais.com/cultura/2017/03/31/babelia/1490969475_189144.html?rel=mas. Accessed 04/20/18.

Nick, James. "Divine Innocence." *Sight and Sound* 15.2 (2005): 18–20.

"'No hay que filmar tanto, no tengo tanto para decir': Lucrecia Martel en Venecia." *La Nación*, August 31, 2017. http://www.lanacion.com.ar/2058298-lucrecia-martel-en-venecia-no-hay-que-filmar-tanto-no-tengo-tanto-para-decir?utm_term=Autofeed&utm_campaign=Echobox&utm_medium=Echobox&utm_source=Twitter#link_time=1504187047. Accessed 09/06/17.

Nord, Cristina. "Das eigene Land neu entdecken." *Taz*, June 25, 2003. http://www.taz.de/1/archiv/?dig=2003/06/25/a0162. Accessed 04/27/11.

Noriega, Gustavo. "Los jóvenes viejos." *El amante cine* 108 (2001): 8–9.

Oesterheld, H. G. *Oesterheld en primera persona*. Buenos Aires: La Bañadera del Cómic, 2005.

———. *The Eternaut*. Translated by Erica Mena. Seattle: Fantagraphics Books, 2016.

O'Hehir, Andrew. "Why the Cannes Boo-Birds Are Wrong (as Usual)." *Salon.com*, May 25, 2008. http://www.salon.com/2008/05/25/martel/ Accessed 06/28/13.

Olsen, Mark. "Lucrecia Martel Fuses the Mystical and the Historical with Bold Adventure in *Zama*." *Los Angeles Times*, April 20, 2018. http://www.latimes.com/entertainment/movies/la-et-mn-lucrecia-martel-zama-20180420-story.html. Accessed 04/20/18.

Orea, Verónica. "Problemas personales de Lucrecia Martel impiden la presencia en Cannes de *Zama*." *Noticine*, March 23, 2016. http://noticine.com/festivales/24373-problemas-personales-de-lucrecia-martel-impiden-la-presencia-en-cannes-de-zama.html. Accessed 03/28/16.

Oubiña, David. "Between Breakup and Tradition: Recent Argentinean Cinema." *Senses of Cinema* 31 (April 2004). http://sensesofcinema.com/2004/feature-articles/recent_argentinean_cinema/. Accessed 04/08/14.

———. "Un mapa arrasado: *Silvia Prieto, La ciénaga* y el nuevo cine argentino des los '90." *Sinopse* 8.11 (2006): 10–17.

———. "Entrevista a Lucrecia Martel: El cine como intención amorosa." In *Estudio crítico sobre "La ciénaga": Entrevista a Lucrecia Martel*," 67–81. Buenos Aires: Picnic, 2009a.

———. *Estudio crítico sobre "La ciénaga": Entrevista a Lucrecia Martel*. Buenos Aires: Picnic, 2009b.

———. "Shipwreck in the Middle of the Mountain: *La Ciénaga*." In *The Ten Best Latin American Films of the Decade (2000–2009)*, edited by Carlos Gutiérrez, 1–10. New York: Jorge Pinto, 2010.

———. "Un realismo negligente (El cine de Lucrecia Martel)." In *Tránsitos de la mirada*, edited by Paulina Bettendorf and Agustina Pérez Rial, 69–82. Buenos Aires: Libraría, 2014.

Oumano, Elena. *Cinema Today: A Conversation with Thirty-Nine Filmmakers from Around the World*. New Brunswick, NJ: Rutgers University Press, 2011.

Page, Joanna. "The Nation as the Mise-en-scène of Film-Making in Argentina." *Journal of Latin American Cultural Studies* 13.3 (December 2005): 305–24.

———. "Espacio privado y significación en el cine de Lucrecia Martel." In Rangil, *El cine argentino*, 157–68.

———. *Crisis and Capitalism in Contemporary Argentine Cinema*. Durham, NC: Duke University Press, 2009.

———. "Intellectuals, Revolution and Popular Culture: A New Reading of *El Eternauta*." *Journal of Latin American Cultural Studies* 19.1 (March 2010): 45–62.

———. "Folktales and Fabulation in Lucrecia Martel's Films." In *Latin American Popular Culture: Politics, Media, Affect*, edited by Geoffrey Kantaris and Rory O'Bryen, 71–87. London: Boydell & Brewer, 2013.

———. *Science Fiction in Argentina: Technologies of the Text in a Material Multiverse*. Ann Arbor: University of Michigan Press, 2016.

Palavecino, Santiago. "Lucrecia Martel: El cine, un pensamiento sin cabeza." *Otra Parte* 10 (summer 2006–2007). http://revistaotraparte.com/no-10-verano -2006-verano-2007/lucrecia-martel-el-cine-un-pensamiento-sin-cabeza. Accessed 10/10/12.

Palleja, Tònio. "Desidia estival, tedio existential." *Cineasta: Portal de cine y el audiovisual latinoamericano y caribeño*. N.d. http://www.cinelatinoamericano. org/texto.aspx?cod=1006. Accessed 03/12/14.

Panozzo, Marcelo. "La dificultad no es el propósito de nadie." *Clarín.com*, November 27, 2000. www.clarin.com. Accessed 02/25/14.

———, ed. *Cine argentino 99-08: Bafici 10 años*. Buenos Aires: Ministerio de Cultura, 2008.

———, ed. *La propria voz: El cine sonoro de Lucrecia Martel*. Gijón: Festival Internacional de Cine de Gijón, 2008.

Parmo, Guido Fernández. "El cine de Lucrecia Martel y las cicatrices perceptivos." *Unión de Trabajadores de Prensa de Buenos Aires*, November 2, 2017. http://www.utpba.org/2017/11/02/el-cine-de-lucrecia-martel-y-las-cicatrices -perceptivos/. Accessed 05/23/18.

Pécora, Paulo. "Lucrecia Martel muestra en *Zama* que hay una necesidad de demencia para pertecener a la sociedad." *Télam*, September 25, 2017. http://www .telam.com.ar/notas/201709/207047-lucrecia-martel-muestra-en-zama-que -hay-una-necesidad-de-demencia-para-pertenecer-a-la-sociedad.html#.Wck ZYY5KUW4.twitter. Accessed 09/27/17.

Peluffo, Ana. "Staging Class, Gender and Ethnicity in Lucrecia Martel's *La Ciénaga/The Swamp*." In Rego and Rocha, *New Trends*, 211–23.

Peña, Fernando Martín. "Entrevista a Lucrecia Martel." In Peña, *Generaciones 60/90*, 116–25.

———. *Cien años de cine argentino*. Buenos Aires: Biblos, 2012.

———, ed. *Generaciones 60/90: Cine argentino independiente*. Buenos Aires: Fundación Eduardo F. Costantini, 2003.

Peña, Francisco. "*La ciénaga*, de Lucrecia Martel." *Cinevisiones*, January 1, 2010. http://cinevisiones.blogspot.com/2010/04/la-cienaga-de-lucrecia-martel .html Accessed 06/28/13.

Peña, Isabel. "*Zama.*" *La gaceta literaria*, October 29, 2017. http://www.lagaceta.com.ar/nota/749748/la-gaceta-literaria/zama.html?utm_source=twitter&utm_medium=social&utm_campaign=botonamp. Accessed 10/31/2017.

Peña, Jaime, ed. *Historias extraordinarias: Nuevo cine argentino, 1999–2008.* Madrid: T & B Editores, 2009.

Perucca, Pedro. "¿Hacia un eternauta salvaje?" *Notas: Periodismo popular,* September 4, 2014. https://notas.org.ar/2014/09/04/szifron-eternauta-relatos-salvajes-nippur/ Accessed 03/06/16.

Pescara, Luis Alberto. "*Zama*: Vivir es esperar." *Revistamutt,* October 4, 2017. http://revistamutt.com/letras/zama-antonio-di-benedetto-lucrecia-martel/. Accessed 10/10/2017.

Peters, Patrick. "*The Headless Woman.*" Review, *Empire,* March 2010, 72.

Podalsky, Laura. "Out of Depth: The Politics of Disaffected Youth and Contemporary Latin American Cinema." In *Youth Culture in Global Cinema,* edited by Timothy Shary and Alexandra Seibel, 109–30. Austin: University of Texas Press, 2007.

———. *The Politics of Affect and Emotion in Contemporary Latin American Cinema: Argentina, Brazil, Cuba, and Mexico.* New York: Palgrave, 2011.

Pomeraniec, Hinde. "'Hay que usar palabras indio, torta, puta, darles la vuelta y que sean palabras felices': Entrevista a Lucrecia Martel." *Infobae,* September 24, 2017. http://www.lanacion.com.ar/2065855-lucrecia-martel-el-heroe-tradicional-es-necesariamente-una-mentira. Accessed 09/27/17.

Porta Fouz, Javier. "El arte de los planificadores." *El amante cine* 108 (2001): 5–7.

———. "El cine de Lucrecia Martel y las palabras." In Panozzo, *La propria voz,* 18–22.

"Premios Cóndor de Plata 2018: *Zama*, de Lucrecia Martel, fue la gran ganadora." *Diario de cultura,* August 14, 2018. http://www.diariodecultura.com.ar/cine-y-artes-visuales/premios-condor-de-plata-2018-zama-de-lucrecia-martel-fue-la-gran-ganadora/. Accessed 08/15/2018.

Prividera, Nicolás. *El país del cine: Para una historia política del nuevo cine argentino.* Córdoba: Los Ríos Editorial, 2014.

Punte, Maria José. "Mirada y voz en el cine de Lucrecia Martel: Aportes desde la teoría crítica feminista." *Letras* 63–64 (2011): 101–13.

Quandt, James. "Art of Fugue." *Artforum* 47.10 (summer 2009): 95–96.

———. "In the Realm of the Senses." *Artforum* 56.8 (April 2018): 144–53.

Quintín. "Es de Salta y hace falta: Entrevista con Lucrecia Martel." *El amante cine* 100 (July 2000): 24–28.

———. "The Headless Woman." *Cinema Scope* 35 (summer 2008): 42–43.

———. "Lucrecia Martel, autora del Quijote." *La lectora provisoria,* October 15, 2017. https://lalectoraprovisoria.wordpress.com/2017/10/15/lucrecia-martel-autora-del-quijote/. Accessed 10/22/2017.

————— and Horacio Bernades. "Conversación en el Maxi: Entrevista con los realizadores de *Historias breves*." *El amante cine* 40 (June 1995): 23–25.

Quirós, Daniel. "'La época está en desorden': Reflexiones sobre la temporalidad en *Bolivia* de Adrián Caetano y *La mujer sin cabeza* de Lucrecia Martel." *A contracorriente* 8.1 (2010): 230–58. http://www.ncsu.edu/acontracorriente/fall_10/articles/Quiros.pdf. Accessed 07/04/13.

Rangil, Viviana. *Otro punto de vista: Mujer y cine en la Argentina*. Rosario: Beatriz Viterbo Editora, 2005.

—————. "En busca de la salvación: Sexualidad y religión en las películas de Lucrecia Martel." In *El cine argentino de hoy: Entre el arte y la política*, 209–20. Buenos Aires: Biblos, 2007.

—————, ed. *El cine argentino de hoy: Entre el arte y la política*. Buenos Aires: Biblos, 2007.

Ranzani, Oscar. "Lucrecia Martel hace cine para todo el mundo." *Cineasta: Portal de cine y el audiovisual latinoamericano y caribeño*. N.d. http://www.cinelatinoamericano.org/texto.aspx?cod=3098 Accessed 03/12/14.

Rapán, Elecnora. "Sound Continuity and Tragedy in *La ciénaga*." Translated by Gustavo Costantini. *Filmwaves* 33 (2009): 42–45.

Ravaschino, Guillermo. "La ciénaga." *Cineismo.com*, 2001. http://www.cineismo.com/criticas/cienaga-la.htm. Accessed 06/28/13.

Rego, Cacilda, and Carolina Rocha, eds. *New Trends in Argentine and Brazilian Cinema*. Chicago: Intellect, 2011.

Rich, Ruby. "An/Other View of New Latin American Cinema." In *New Latin American Cinema*, edited by Michael T. Martin, 1:273–97. Detroit: Wayne State University Press, 1997.

—————. "Making Argentina Matter Again." *New York Times*, September 30, 2001. http://www.nytimes.com/2001/09/30/movies/film-making-argentina-matter-again.html. Accessed 07/05/13.

—————. *New Queer Cinema: The Director's Cut*. Durham, NC: Duke University Press, 2013.

—————. "In Conversation with Lucrecia Martel." *Film Quarterly*, August 31, 2018. https://filmquarterly.org/2018/08/31/lucrecia-martel-in-conversation-with-b-ruby-rich/. Accessed 09/09/18.

Ríos, Hugo. "La poética de los sentidos en los filmes de Lucrecia Martel." *Atenea* 28.2 (2008): 9–22.

Rocha, Carolina. "Contemporary Argentine Cinema during Neoliberalism." In Rego and Rocha, *New Trends*, 17–34.

————— and Elizabeth Montes Garcés, eds. *Violence in Argentine Literature and Film (1989–2005)*. Calgary: University of Calgary Press, 2010.

Rodríguez Marcos, Javier. "'La gente no se da cuenta de que las series son un retroceso': Entrevista a Lucrecia Martel." *El País*, January 16, 2018. https://

elpais.com/cultura/2018/01/16/actualidad/1516125674_495994.html. Accessed 03/20/18.

Rohter, Larry. "Floating Below Politics." *New York Times*, May 1, 2005. http://www.nytimes.com/2005/05/01/movies/01roht.html?module=Search&mab Reward=relbias%3Ar&_r=0. Accessed 06/28/13.

Rojas, Eduardo. "Tocar y quedarse: *La niña santa.*" *El amante cine* 145 (May 2004): 10–11.

Romero, María Eugenia. "Un barco atraviesa las montañas: Lucrecia Martel/A Ship Sails Across the Mountains: Lucrecia Martel." In *Escritores Argentinos: Entrevistas/Argentine Writers: Interviews*, 149–67. Translated by Luciano Camio. Buenos Aires: Patricia Rizzo Editora, 2005.

Rooney, David. "*Zama* Film Review, Venice 2017." *Hollywood Reporter*, August 31, 2017. http://www.hollywoodreporter.com/review/zama-venice-2017-1034312. Accessed 08/31/17.

Rosenblatt, Adam. "The Making and Remaking of *El Eternauta.*" *International Journal of Comic Art* 9.2 (fall 2007): 81–92.

Rothe, E. Nina. "'Being a Woman I See as a Great Advantage': Lucrecia Martel on *Zama*, Quentin Tarantino and Avoiding Gender Violence in Films." *Huffington Post*, October 2, 2017. http://www.huffingtonpost.com/entry/being-a-woman-i-see-as-a-great-advantage-lucrecia_us_59d0dcd6e4b034ae778d4b66. Accessed 10/03/17.

Ruimy, Jordan. "Lucrecia Martel Talks *Zama*, Her Lost Sci-Fi Project and More." *Playlist*, October 9, 2017. https://theplaylist.net/lucrecia-martel-zama-nyff-2017 1009/?utm_source=dlvr.it&utm_medium=twitter. Accessed 10/10/2017.

Ruoff, Jeffrey, ed. *Coming to a Festival Near You: Programming Film Festivals.* Edinburgh: St. Andrews Press, 2012.

Russell, Dominique. "Lucrecia Martel: A Decidedly Polyphonic Cinema." *Jump Cut* 50 (spring 2008). https://www.ejumpcut.org/archive/jc50.2008/LMarte lAudio/. Accessed 04/12/12.

Russo, Eduardo A. "Materia y forma." *El amante cine* 145 (May 2004): 11.

———, ed. *The Film Edge: Contemporary Filmmaking in Latin America.* Buenos Aires: Teseo, 2010.

Ryzik, Melena. "How Björk Brought Her Sci-Fi, Feminist Fairy Tale to Life." *The New York Times*, May 8, 2019. https://www.nytimes.com/2019/05/08/arts/music/bjork-cornucopia.html. Accessed 05/09/2019.

Sabat, Cynthia. "Lucrecia Martel: *La mujer sin cabeza.*" Liberamedia. N.d. http://www.liberamedia.tv/. Accessed 05/14/13.

Sachs, Ben. "An Interview with Lucrecia Martel, Argentina's Greatest Filmmaker." *Chicago Reader*, April 16, 2018. https://www.chicagoreader.com/Bleader/archives/2018/04/16/an-interview-with-lucrecia-martel-argentinas-greatest-filmmaker?media=AMP%20HTML&__twitter_impression=true. Accessed 04/18/18.

Saer, Juan José. "Zama." In *El concepto de ficción*, 47–54. Buenos Aires: Ariel, 1997.

————. "Antonio di Benedetto." In *El concepto de ficción*, 55–57. Buenos Aires: Ariel, 1997.

Sánchez, Matilde. "'*Zama*, una película como reescritura virtuosa': Entrevista a Lucrecia Martel." *Clarín*, September 15, 2017. https://www.clarin.com/revista -enie/escenarios/zama-pelicula-reescritura-virtuosa_0_SkPlW6Fqb.html. Accessed 09/19/17.

Sandberg, Claudia, and Carolina Rocha, eds. *Contemporary Latin American Cinema: Resisting Neoliberalism?* Cham: Palgrave, 2018.

Sartora, Josefina. "La niña santa." *Cineimso.com*, 2004. http://www.cineismo.com/ criticas/nina-santa-la.htm. Accessed 03/03/15.

————. "They and the Others, in a Country Gone Mad: *The Headless Woman*." In *The Ten Best Latin American Films of the Decade (2000–2009)*, edited by Carlos Gutiérrez, 60–67. New York: Jorge Pinto, 2010.

Sasturain, Juan. *El domicilio de la aventura*. Buenos Aires: Ediciones Colihue, 1995.

————. *El aventurador: Una lectura de Oesterheld*. Buenos Aires: Aquilina, 2010.

Schell, Hernán. "Un cine distinto y con formas proprias: Las películas de Lucrecia Martel." *Infobae*, September 19, 2017. http://www.infobae.com/ cultura/2017/09/19/un-cine-distinto-y-con-formas-propias-las-peliculas-de -lucrecia-martel/. Accessed 09/21/17.

Schindel, Dan. "*Zama*: TIFF Review." *Vague Visages*, September 13, 2017. https://vaguevisages.com/2017/09/13/tiff-2017-review-lucrecia-martels-zama/. Accessed 10/03/17.

Schlickers, Sabine. "San(t)idad y aberración en *La niña santa* (2004) de Lucrecia Martel." In *Directoras de cine en España y America Latina*, edited by Pietsie Feenstra, Esther Gimena Ugalde, and Kathrin Sartingen, 201–18. Frankfurt am Main: Peter Lang, 2014.

Scholz, Pablo O. "'Quedé atrapada en su mundo': Entrevista a Lucrecia Martel." *Clarín.com*, June 23, 2015. http://www.clarin.com/extrashow/cine/ Lucrecia_Martel-Almodovar-Zama-Antonio_Di_Benedetto-Gimenez_Cacho -Spregelburd-Veronese_0_1381062302.html. Accessed 06/24/15.

————. "*Zama*: Sí, es cautivante." *Clarín*, September 27, 2017. https://www .clarin.com/espectaculos/cine/zama-cautivante_0_SJuP-nKjZ.html. Accessed 09/27/17.

Schroeder Rodríguez, Paul A. "After New Latin American Cinema." *Cinema Journal* 51.2 (winter 2012): 87–112.

————. *Latin American Cinema: A Comparative History*. Berkeley: University of California Press, 2016.

Schulze, Peter W., ed. *Junges Kino in Lateinamerika.* Munich: Text + Kritik, 2010.

Schwarzböck, Silvia, and Hugo Salas. "El verano de nuestro descontento." *El amante cine* 108 (2001): 10–13.

Scolari, Carlos. "*El Eternauta*: Brief Story of a Classic." In *Transmedia Archeology: Storytelling in the Borderlines of Science Fiction, Comics and Pulp*

Magazines, edited by Carlos Scolari, Paolo Bertetti, and Matthew Freeman, 56–62. New York: Palgrave Macmillan, 2014.

Scott, A. O. "The Stirrings of Sensuality for a Pilgrim on the Road." *New York Times*, October 9, 2004. http://www.nytimes.com/2004/10/09/movies/09girl.html?_r=0. Accessed 03/12/13.

———. "Strangeness, Daring and Provocations." *New York Times*, September 28, 2018. https://www.nytimes.com/2018/09/27/movies/new-york-film-festival-highlights.html. Accessed 09/28/18.

Seitz, Alexandra. "Lucrecia Martels neues Meisterwerk *Zama*." *Berliner Zeitung*, July 11, 2018. https://amp.berliner-zeitung.de/kultur/film/film-der-woche-lucrecia-martels-neues-meisterwerk—zama—30944598?__twitter_impression=true. Accessed 07/12/18.

Selimovic, Inela. *Affective Moments in the Films of Martel, Carri, and Puenzo*. Basingstoke, UK: Palgrave Macmillan, 2018.

Serra de Renobales, Fátima, and Helena Talayo-Manso, eds. *Agentes de cambio : Perspectivas cinematográficas de España y Latinoamérica en el siglo XXI*. Madrid: Editoiral Pliegos, 2014.

Shaw, Deborah. *Contemporary Cinema of Latin America: Ten Key Films*. New York: Continuum, 2003.

———, ed. *Contemporary Latin American Cinema: Breaking into the Global Market*. Lanham, MD: Rowman & Littlefield, 2007.

"Siento que tengo que superarme." *Página/12*, February 19, 2004. http://www.pagina12.com.ar/diario/espectaculos/6-31663-2004-02-19.html. Accessed 03/03/15.

Sims, David. "*Zama* Is a Surreal Satire of Colonialism." *Atlantic*, April 19, 2018. https://www.theatlantic.com/amp/article/558398/?__twitter_impression=true. Accessed 04/20/18.

Sinagra, Laura. "Hearing Voices: Argentine Director Lucrecia Martel Explores Carnality and Sacred Solitude in *The Holy Girl*." *Village Voice*, February 2, 2005. http://www.villagevoice.com/2005-02-22/film/hearing-voices/full/. Accessed 06/28/13.

Skye, Sherwin. "*La niña santa* Interview: Director Lucrecia Martel Confesses." *BBC*. N.d. http://www.bbc.co.uk/. Accessed 10/01/14.

Slobodian, Jennifer. "Analyzing the Woman *Auteur*: Female/Feminist Gazes of Isabel Coixet and Lucrecia Martel." *Comparatist* 36 (2012): 160–77.

Smith, Paul Julian. "*La ciénaga*." *Sight and Sound*, December 2001, 45.

Sontag, Susan. *Against Interpretation*. New York: Farrar, Straus & Giroux, 1964.

Sosa, Cecilia. "A Counter-Narrative of Argentine Mourning: *The Headless Woman* (2008), directed by Lucrecia Martel." *Theory, Culture and Society* 267.8 (2009): 250–62.

Stantic, Lita. "On My Relation to *Zama* and Martel." *Cine el Cairo*, July 10, 2015. https://www.youtube.com/watch?v=9zYEW1iqXTI. Accessed 09/09/2017.

178 | Bibliography

Stiletano, Marcelo. "'El héroe tradicional es necesariamente una mentira.': Entrevista a Lucrecia Martel." *La Nación*, September 24, 2017. http://www.lanacion.com.ar/2065855-lucrecia-martel-el-heroe-tradicional-es-necesariamente-una-mentira. Accessed 09/27/17.

Stites Mor, Jessica. "Transgresión y responsabilidad: Desplazamiento de los discursos feministas en cineastas argentinas desde Maria Luisa Bemberg hasta Lucrecia Martel." In Rangil, *El cine argentino*, 137–53.

———. *Transition Cinema: Political Filmmaking and the Argentine Left since 1968*. Pittsburgh: University of Pittsburgh Press, 2012.

Stock, Ann Marie, ed. *Framing Latin American Cinema: Contemporary Critical Perspectives*. Minneapolis: University of Minnesota Press, 1997.

Su, Zhuo-Ning. "*Zama* Venice 2017 Review." *Film Stage*, September 2, 2017. https://thefilmstage.com/reviews/zama-review-lucrecia-martel-venice/. Accessed 09/06/17.

Svampa, Maristella. *La sociedad excluyente: La Argentina bajo el signo del neoliberalismo*. Buenos Aires: Taurus, 2005.

Taubin, Amy. "Temples of the Familiar." *Village Voice*, October 2, 2001. http://www.villagevoice.com/2001-10-02/film/temples-of-the-familiar/full/. Accessed 06/28/13.

———. "Vocational Education: An Interview with Lucrecia Martel." *Artforum* 43.8 (April 2005): 172–75.

———. "Identification of a Woman." *Film Comment*, July/August 2009a, 20–23.

———. "Shadow of a Doubt: Lucrecia Martel Interviewed." *Film Comment*, July/August 2009b. http://www.filmcomment.com/article/shadow-of-a-doubt-lucrecia-martel-interviewed. Accessed 04/15/15.

"Tenemos el mundo que hemos querido, no el único possible: Conversación con Lucrecia Martel." *La ventana*, June 7, 2005. http://laventana.casa.cult.cu. Accessed 10/01/14.

Teodoro, José. "Interview: Lucrecia Martel." *Film Comment*, September 26, 2017. https://www.filmcomment.com/blog/interview-lucrecia-martel/. Accessed 09/27/17.

Thomas, Kevin. "Faith and Longing Thicken the Plot." Review. *Los Angeles Times*, May 13, 2005.

Thompson, Kristin, and David Bordwell. "Venice 2017: Martel's Drama of Expectations." David Bordwell's Website on Cinema, September 9, 2017. http://www.davidbordwell.net/blog/2017/09/09/venice-2017-martels-drama-of-expectations/. Accessed 09/12/17.

Thrift, Matt. "'History Is More Arbitrary than Science Fiction': Interview with Lucrecia Martel." *Little White Lies*, May 23, 2018. http://lwlies.com/interviews/lucrecia-martel-zama/. Accessed 05/28/18.

Tierney, Dolores. "The Link between Funding and Text: Transnational Aesthetics in Lucrecia Martel's Films." *Mediático*, March 2014. http://reframe.sussex

.ac.uk/mediatico/2014/03/23/the-link-between-funding-and-text-transnational -aesthetics-in-lucrecia-martels-films/ Accessed 03/26/2014.

Toal, Andrea. *"The Holy Girl." Sight and Sound*, October 2005, 97.

Toledo, Teresa. *Miradas: El cine argentino de los noventa*. Madrid: Casa de América, 2000.

Torrents, Nissa. "One Woman's Cinema: Interview with María Luisa Bemberg." In *Knives and Angels: Women Writers in Latin America*, edited by Susan Bassnett, 171–75. London: Zed Books, 1990.

Tracy, Andrew. "Cutes Too Narrow." *Reverse Shot*, October 2004. http://reverse-shot.org/reviews/entry/317/holy_girl. Accessed 05/05/15.

Trerotola, Diego. "Esplendor argentino." *El amante cine* 145 (May 2004): 8–9.

Trillo, Carlos. "Las muchas lecturas de un clásico." Preface to *El Eternauta* by H. G. Oesterheld, 7–12. Barcelona: Norma Editorial, 2013.

Tripodero, José. *"Zama." A sala llena*, September 27, 2017. http://www.asalallena .com.ar/cine/zama-segun-jose-tripodero/. Accessed 09/30/17.

Tsai, Martin. *"The Holy Girl."* Review, *Cineaste* 30.4 (fall 2005): 54–56.

Ulrich, Esteban. "Ama y haz lo que quieras: Conversación entre Lucrecia Martel y Leonardo Favio." *Haciendo cine*, January 24, 2011. http://www.haciendocine .com.ar/article/ama-y-haz-lo-que-quieras. Accessed 10/17/14.

Urraca, Beatriz. "Independent Cinema in Argentina: The Role of the BAFICI." In Ingruber and Prutsch, *Filme in Argentinien*, 219–323.

———, and Gary M. Kramer, eds. *Directory of World Cinema: Argentina*. Chicago: Intellect, 2014.

Urrutia, Belén Raca. "'Las mujeres estamos en la periferia del orden, por lo tanto le somos molestas y peligrosas': Entrevista a Lucrecia Martel." *El desconcierto*, June 15, 2018. http://www.eldesconcierto.cl/2018/06/15/lucrecia -martel-cineasta-las-mujeres-estamos-en-la-periferia-del-orden-por-lo-tanto -le-somos-molestas-y-peligrosas/. Accessed 06/20/18.

Uzal, Marcos. *"Caniba* et *Zama*, au plus près de la folie." *La liberation*, September 5, 2017. http://next.liberation.fr/cinema/2017/09/05/caniba-et-zama -au-plus-pres-de-la-folie_1594368. Accessed 09/08/17.

Valens, Grégory. *"La ciénaga*: Familles, je vous . . ." *Positif*, January 2002, 41–42.

Valladares, Carlos. "Argentine Director Lucrecia Martel to Attend Berkeley Retrospective of Her Work." *San Francisco Chronicle*, April 17, 2018. https:// www.sfchronicle.com/movies/amp/Argentine-director-Lucrecia-Martel-to -attend-12838201.php?__twitter_impression=true. Accessed 04/18/18.

Vara, Patricia, and Robert C. Dash. "(Re)imaginando la nación argentina: Lucrecia Martel y *La ciénaga*." In Rangil, *El cine argentino*, 191–207.

Vázquez, Cristian. "Eterno Resplandor." *Clarín.com*, April 20, 2007. http://edant .clarin.com/diario/2007/04/20/conexiones/t-01403713.htm. Accessed 01/18/16.

Vázquez, Débora. *"Zama* versus *Zama*: La piedad de Lucrecia Martel." *Otra parte*, October 17, 2017. http://revistaotraparte.com/semanal/discusion/zama -versus-zama-la-piedad-de-lucrecia-martel/. Accessed 10/27/17.

Verardi, Malena. "El nuevo cine argentino: Claves de lectura de una época." In *Una década de nuevo cine argentino (1995–2005): Industria, crítica, formación, estéticas*, edited by Ignacio Amatriain, 171–89. Buenos Aires: Ediciones Ciccus, 2009.

Vespa, Mariano. "Notas de un largo viaje llamado *Zama*." *La Nación*, September 24, 2017. http://www.lanacion.com.ar/2064838-notas-de-un-largo-viaje -llamado-zama. Accessed 09/27/17.

Vieytes, Marcos. "Lucrecia Martel: La mujer del cuadro." In *Historias extraordinarias: Nuevo cine argentino, 1999–2008*, edited by Jaime Pena, 129–38. Madrid: T & B Editores, 2009.

Villani, Ramiro. "La mujer sin cabeza." *Cineismo.com*, 2008. http://www.cineismo .com/criticas/mujer-sin-cabeza-la.htm. Accessed 03/03/15.

Vivarelli, Nick. "Argentina's Lucrecia Martel Named Venice Jury President." *Variety*, June 24, 2019. https://variety.com/2019/film/news/lucrecia-martel -venice-film-festival-jury-president-argentina-director-1203251250/. Accessed 06/24/2019.

Von Sprecher, Robert. *El Eternauta: La sociedad como imposible: Modelos de sociedad en las obras de Héctor Germán Oesterheld*. Córdoba: Alto Verde, 1998.

Von Tschilke, Christian, Maribel Cedeño Rojas, and Isabel Maurer Queipo, eds. *Lateinamerikanisches Kino der Gegenwart: Themen, Genres, Stile, RegisseurInnen*. Tübingen: Stauffenberg, 2015.

Wain, Martín. "Tan cercano al thriller: *La mujer sin cabeza*." *La Nación*, April 2, 2006.

White, Patricia. *Women's Cinema, World Cinema: Projecting Contemporary Feminisms*. Durham, NC: Duke University Press, 2015.

Williams, Blake. "Those You Call Mutants: The Films of Lucrecia Martel." *Cinemascope* 72 (fall 2017). http://cinema-scope.com/features/those-you-call -mutants-the-films-of-lucrecia-martel/. Accessed 10/08/2017.

———. "Zama." *Cinemascope* 72 (fall 2017). http://cinema-scope.com/cinema -scope-online/zama-lucrecia-martel-argentinabrazilspainfrancenetherlands mexicoportugalusa-masters/. Accessed 09/05/17.

Wisniewski, Chris. "When Worlds Collide: An Interview with Lucrecia Martel, director of *The Headless Woman*." *Reverse Shot* 25 (August 17, 2009). http:// www.reverseshot.com/article/interview_lucrecia_martel. Accessed 04/12/12.

———. "Shades of Grey." *Reverse Shot*, October 20, 2010. http://reverseshot .org/symposiums/entry/1377/la_cienaga. Accessed 05/05/15.

———. "Layers of Evidence." *Reverse Shot* 33 (April 4, 2013). http://www .reverseshot.com/article/headless_woman_0. Accessed 04/15/13.

Wolf, Sergio. "Que aparezca un accidente." In Panozzo, *La propria voz*, 42–45.

Wood, Jason. "Lucrecia Martel." In *Talking Movies: Contemporary Filmmakers in Interview*, 166–72. London: Wallflower, 2006.

Wood, Michael. "Vileness." *London Review of Books*. 40.7 (April 5, 2018): 35–36.

Woznicki, Krystian. "Hinter dem Rücken des Kolonialherren: Wie die Regisseurin Lucrecia Martel das Kino revolutioniert." *Berliner Gazette*, July 21, 2018. https://berlinergazette.de/lucrecia-martel-kino/. Accessed 07/25/18.

Yañes, Manu. "*Zama* de Lucrecia Martel: Algo salvaje." *Fotogramas*, August 31, 2017. http://www.fotogramas.es/Festival-de-Venecia/2017/Zama-Lucrecia-Martel. Accessed 08/31/17.

Yáñez Murillo, Manuel. "Perdiendo la cabeza: *La mujer rubia*." *Fotogramas*, December 2008, 148–49.

———. "Voyage of Time: Lucrecia Martel's Masterful *Zama* Broaches the Strangest of Strange Lands: The Colonial Past." *Film Comment*, March/April 2018, 6.

Yemayel, Mónica. "El ojo extraterrestre." *Gatopardo*, June 19, 2018. https://gatopardo.com/reportajes/entrevista-lucrecia-martel/. Accessed 06/20/18.

Yency Martell, María. "Cuatro directoras lationamericanas: Otros puntos de vista." PhD diss., Arizona State University, May 2008.

Yuszczuk, Marina. "Imán visual." *Página/12*, October 6, 2017. https://www.pagina12.com.ar/67393-iman-visual. Accessed 10/10/17.

"*Zama*, la pelicula más nominada a los premios Condor de Plata." *La Nación*, March 12, 2018. https://www.lanacion.com.ar/2116261-zama-la-pelicula-mas-nominada-a-los-premios-condor-de-plata. Accessed 03/12/18.

Index

Aballay/Six Shooters (Spiner), 103
Abramovich, Manuel: *Años luz/Light Years*, 6; *Soldado/Soldier*, 6
absurdism: *Pescados*, 98; *Zama*, 98, 127
Acción Católica, 67
actorship, costumbrismo, 12
Adjemián, Martín, 29
adolescent girls and horror films, 59
Aguirre, der Zorn Gottes/Aguirre, The Wrath of God (Herzog), 125–26
Álamos talados (Di Benedetto), 103
Alché, María, 51, 102; facial expressions, 55; *Muta*, 96
Allen, Esther, 5
Almada, Selva: *El mono en el remolino: Notas del rodaje de "Zama" de Lucretia Martel*, 124
Almodóvar, Agustín, 51
Almodóvar, Pedro, 10, 51, 78; *La mujer sin cabeza*, 86
Alonso, Lisandro, 11; *Jauja*, 126
ambiguity: critics on, 68–69; *La mujer sin cabeza*, 75; unanswered, 66–67
analogue *versus* digital, 145
Andermann, Jens, 86, 87
Años luz/Light Years (Abramovich), 6
Antonioni, Michelangelo, 17
Argentine Ministry of Culture, 98
Atallah, Niles, 126
AVEX (Escuela de Cine de Animación de Avellaneda), 10–11
awards, 10; *La ciénaga*, 10, 11, 13; *La niña santa*, 10; *Zama*, 105
Azara, Félix de, 119–20

Backstein, Karen, 75–76
Baenas, Diego, 29
BAFICI (Buenos Aires International Independent Film Festival), 14
Baylé, Silvia, 37
Belloso, Carlos, 51
Bemberg, María Luisa: *Camila*, 18; *Miss Mary*, 18, 34, 67; *Momentos*, 18, 34; *Señora de nadie/Nobody's Wife*, 18; *Yo, la peor de todas/I, Worst of All*, 18
Bernal, Gael García, 146; *El aula vacía*, 100–101
Bertoletto, Sofía, 29
Bertuccelli, Valeria, 28
Besos rojos/Red Kisses, 11, 149
Bielinsky, Fabián, 13–14; *El aura/The Aura*, 13; *Nueva reinas/Nine Queens*, 13
The Blair Witch Project (Myrick and Sánchez), 59
Bolaño, Roberto: "Sensini," 104
Bolivia (Caetano), 15–16, 17
Böll, Heinrich, 104
Bordeau, Juan Cruz, 37, 38
Borges, Graciela, 18, 29, 34, 38, 79; ·
Heroína, 57; *La mujer sin cabeza*, 79–80
Borges, Jorge Luis, 23, 102
bourgeoisie, *La ciénaga and*, 34–35
Breccia, Alberto, 93
Bresson, Robert, 17, 31
Buñuel, Luis: *El ángel exterminador/The Exterminating Angel*, 46–47
Burman, Daniel, 19

Cabezas, Cuatro, 19

Cacho, Daniel Giménez, 106, 116–17
Caetano, Adrián, 11, 15–16; *Bolivia,* 15–16, 17
Cafrune, Jorge, 25
Cama adentro/Live-In Maid (Gaggero), 15, 46
Cámara Argentina de la Industria Cinematográfica/Board of Argentine Industrial Cinematography, 18
camera work: angles, 24
Camila (Bemberg), 18
Campanella, Juan José, 13–14; *El hijo de la novia/Son of the Bride* (Campanella), 14; *El secreto de sus ojos/The Secret in Their Eyes,* 14; *Luna de Avellaneda/ Avellaneda's Moon,* 14
Cannes Film Festival 2004: *La niña santa,* 68
Carlos III (King), 119
Carnival of Souls (Harvey), 82
Carri, Albertina, 28
Casares, Adolfo Bioy, 23
Cassavetes, John, 17
Castellari, Enzo G., *Keoma,* 141
Castillo, Dominga Sotomayor, 28
casting, 139–40; nonprofessionals in *Zama,* 143
Catholic Church/Catholicism: hope and, 142–43; *La niña santa,* 51, 53, 61–62, 67; Martel as "Catholic without God," 61; post-Catholicism, 8–9; *Zama,* 118, 126, 142
Chiquilines (Mittelman), 103
Chocobar, 101–2; *Zama and,* 102
Chocobar, Javier, 101–2
cigars, 124
Cine Liberación, 19
cinema trouvé, 36
Cinemascope, 72–73; collision in *La mujer sin cabeza,* 78; disorienting nature, 13; establishing shots, 52; height in *La ciénaga,* 47; *La ciénaga,* 31, 140; *La mujer sin cabeza,* 72–73; *La niña santa,* 60, 65–66; *Las dependencias,* 23–24; montage techniques, 24; real time sensation, 26; sound and, 25; spatial orientation and, 52; spying with a lot of curiosity, 47; *Zama,* 109–12

class: dictatorship and, 72; *La mujer sin cabeza,* 72, 80, 83–84
Coetzee, J. M., 117
collective as hero in *El Eternauta,* 91
colonialism: *Aguirre, der Zorn Gottes/ Aguirre, The Wrath of God* (Herzog), 125–26; *El abrazo de la serpiente/ The Embrace of the Serpent* (Guerra), 126; *Fitzcarraldo* (Herzog), 125–26; *Jauja* (Alonso), 126; *Joaquím* (Gomez), 126; postcolonial rewriting of history, 126; race in *La ciénaga,* 46; *Rey/King* (Atallah), 126; *Vazante* (Thomas), 126; *Zama,* 105
color: in *Zama,* 114–15
Cóndor de Plata competition, 105
Cortázar, Julio, 41, 102
costumbrismo, 12
crazy aunts, 80–81
Cronenberg, David, 17; *The Dead Zone,* 82

Darín, Ricardo, 14
The Dead Zone (Cronenberg), 82
death: *La ciénaga,* 137–38
de Ávila, Teresa: *The Ecstasy of Saint Teresa* (Bernini), 53; "Vuestra soy"/"I Am Yours," 53
de la Torre, Raúl: *Heroína,* 56–57, 79–80
Delgado, María, 77, 87
desire, 7–8; *La ciénaga,* 37–39; Salta trilogy, 87; same-sex *La mujer sin cabeza,* 79
D'Espósito, Leonardo M., 81
de Tella, Andrés, 14
dialogue, 26; *La ciénaga,* 42–43; storytelling and, 42–43; uses, 62–63
Di Benedetto, Antonio, 2, 89, 106, 115, 118, 119, 125; *Álamos talados,* 103; cinema and, 103; *El juicio de Dios,* 103; imprisonment, 103–4; *Los suicidas,* 103; writing of *Zama,* 102–3
dictatorship: class and, 72; *El Eternauta* and, 93–94; *La mujer sin cabeza,* 72, 84; post-dictatorship Argentine cinema, 16; *Un muro de silencio,* 18
digital *versus* analogue, 145
Dirty War: *La mujer sin cabeza,* 84–85
D.N.I., 150

Doménech, Benjamin, 146
Dueñas, Lola, 106, 117–18

economy, the arts and, 15–16
El 56, 11, 149
El abrazo de la serpiente/The Embrace of the Serpent (Guerra), 126
El amante, 14
El ángel exterminador/The Exterminating Angel (Buñuel), 46–47
El aula vacía/ The Empty Classroom, 100–101
El aura/The Aura (Bielinsky), 13
El Eternauta, 88, 89, 144–45; collective as hero, 91; dictatorship and, 93–94; installments, 90; modernist narrative, 92; Paraná River and, 102; sound, 94; technology in, 90–91
El Eternauta II, 93
El hijo de la novia/Son of the Bride (Campanella), 14
El juicio de Dios (Di Benedetto), 103
elliptical storytelling, 42–43
El mono en el remolino: Notas del rodaje de "Zama" de Lucrecia Martel (Almada), 124
El niño pez/The Fish Child (Puenzo), 28
El secreto de sus ojos/The Secret in Their Eyes (Campanella), 14
El ultimo verano de la boyita/The Last Summer of La Boyita (Solomonoff), 28
Encarnación Ezcurra, 11, 22–23
epistemology, certainties and, 61
Escuela de Cine de Animación de Avellaneda (AVEX), 10–11
Escuela Nacional de Experimentación y Realización Cinematográfica/National School of Experimental Film Direction, 10–11, 14
establishing shots: avoidance, 52; *La mujer sin cabeza*, 70

Fantasmas, 90
Favio, Leonardo, 17
Festival del Cine y Mujer/Festival of Women Filmmakers, 19
Filho, Kleber Mendonça, 102, 114

filmmaking: economic crisis and, 15–17; filmmakers as genres, 28; *Las Naves* "manifesto," 5–6; perception, 6–7; script and, 6
film schools, 14–15
Filmoteca: Temas de Cine, 14
Fin de fiesta/The Party Is Over (Nilsson), 34
Fitzcarraldo (Herzog), 125, 126
forced labor, 119
foreshadowing: *La ciénaga*, 137
Fundación Universidad del Cine (FUC), 14

Gaggero, José, 15; *Cama adentro/Live-In Maid* (Gaggero), 15, 46; *Vida en Falcon*, 15
Gallelli, Santiago, 146
Gatti, Juan, 78
gaze, objectification and, 54–55
Gemünden, Gerd, interview, 141–47
gender identity: *La otra/The Other*, 22
gender roles: pursuer/pursued in *La niña santa*, 56
genre: filmmaker as, 28; Martel's approach, 18
ghosts: *La mujer sin cabeza/The Headless Woman*, 80–81
girl saint: *La niña santa*, 58–59
Glover, Danny, 146
Gomes, Miguel, 145
Gomez, Marcelo, 126
Guerra, Ciro, 126
Guido, Beatriz, 33–34

"Habanera" from *Carmen* (Bizet), 54
Haciendo cine, 14
hair: *La mujer sin cabeza*, 79, 85; *La niña santa*, 66
Harvey, Herk: *Carnival of Souls*, 82
Havana Film Festival, 19
hearing/listening: *La niña santa*, 50–51; Helena in the pool, 56
Heroína (de la Torre), 56–57, 79–80
Herzog, Werner: *Aguirre, der Zorn Gottes/Aguirre, The Wrath of God*, 125–26; *Fitzcarraldo*, 125, 126; Minnesota declaration, 125–26

Index | 185

Historias breves/Short Histories, 19
Hitchcock, Alfred: *Vertigo,* 82
Hoberman, J., 52
Hochhäusler, Chrisoph, 95
home movies, 10
hope, 142–43; post-Catholicism and, 9
horror films: adolescent girls and, 59;
  Argentine terror, *La mujer sin cabeza,*
  82; car accident in *La niña santa,* 60;
  epistemology and, 61; *La niña santa*
  and, 59–61; *Psycho* (Hitchcock), 59;
  reality and, 61; *The Shining* (Kubrick),
  59; theremin and, 59
hospital: *La niña santa,* 63
hotel: as character in *La niña santa,* 63;
  and economic decline *(La niña santa),*
  59; erotic fantasies *(La niña santa),*
  59; *La mujer sin cabeza,* 81; *La niña*
  santa, 63

INCAA (Instituto Nacional de Cine y
  Artes Audiovisuales/National Institute
  of Cinema and Audiovisual Arts), 13
indigenous groups: Catholic Church
  and, 142–43; language, 100; *Leguas,*
  100–101; Martel and, 124; the Qom,
  124; *Zama,* 122–24
Indulto, 18
Infamous Decade, 34
interpretation in *La niña santa*: dialogue,
  62–63; medical conference, 61–62;
  religion, 61–62
Italian neorealism, New Argentine Cinema and, 17–18

Janus, god of beginnings and transitions,
  59
Joaquim (Gomez), 126
Jones, Kent, 68
Julieta Laso: Fantasmas/Julieta Laso:
  Ghosts, 153

Kairuz, Mariano, 78
Keoma (Castellari), 141
King, Jessica, 111
kisses, stolen: *La niña santa,* 64
Knol, Matthijs Wouter, 25
Kohn, Eric, 28

Kracauer, Siegfried: *Theory of Film,* 24
Kramer, Oscar, 89
Kubrick, Stanley: *The Shining,* 59

La caída/The Fall (Nilsson), 33
La casa del angel/The House of the Angel
  (Nilsson), 33
La ciénaga/The Swamp, 150–51; African
  rat, 41–42; awards, 10; bed, 38–39;
  blood, 31; Borges, Graciela, 29, 34;
  camera work, 31, 47, 140; children,
  47–48; class relationships, 44–45; collos, 45; color palette, 31–32; current
  events, 35; death, 137–38; desire,
  37–39; dialogue, 42–43; El gringo, 50;
  foreshadowing, 137; framing, 32; La
  Mandrágora, 30, 31; *La niña santa* and,
  50, 140–41; locations, 29–30; matriarch, 34–35; Menem presidency, 35–
  36; *Miss Mary* (Bemberg) and, 34–35;
  narrative, 26; narrative *versus* plot,
  32; opening sequences, 29–31; oral
  narration and, 41–42; orientation, 31;
  polytemporality, 39; post-Catholicism,
  8; premonition, 29, 30; race, 45–46;
  religion, 48–49; repetition, 137; *Rey*
  Muerto and, 140–41; skin, 7; sound,
  139; storytelling, 39–40; synopsis,
  Martel's, 33; taboos, 37–39; time, 39,
  41; vignettes *versus* plot, 36; violence,
  children and, 48; Virgin's appearance,
  48–49; water, 36–37; water in, 2, 4
La ciudad que huye/The City That Runs
  Away, 151; Paraná River, 98
La mujer sin cabeza/The Headless
  Woman, 151–52; 1970s references,
  84; ambiguity, 75, 76; appearances,
  80; awards, 10; camera work, 72–73;
  Cannes critics, 86–87; car accident in
  La niña santa, 60–61; central character,
  75; class differences, 72, 80, 83–84;
  collision, camera work, 78; confession,
  77–78; consciousness, 74; contradictions, 76; contrast, 75; crazy aunts,
  80–81; dictatorship and, 72, 84; Dirty
  War, 84–85; enigmas, 76; establishing
  shots, 70; film poster, María Onetto,
  78–79; genre conventions, 83; ghosts,

186 | Index

80–81; hair, 79, 85; hotel, 81; *La mujer rubia/The Blonde Woman,* 79; Martel's nightmares, 82; matriarchs, 79–80; narrative *versus* random scenes, 74; Onetto, María, 78; opening, 69–71; patriarchy, 84; post-Catholicism, 9; reviews, 86–87; shallow focus, Vero's awareness and, 73; skin, 7; soundtrack, 84; state of mind of protagonist, 75–76; stylistic innovations, 72–73; suspense, 75; water in, 4, 70

La otra/The Other, 11, 149; gender identity, 22

La reina del miedo/The Queen of Fear (Said), 28

Lang, Fritz: *Metropolis,* 14

language: new cinema, 136; *Nueva Argirópolis,* 100; *Zama,* 113–14, 121–22, 143

La niña santa/The Holy Girl, 151; Alché's gaze, 54–55; Amalia's paradoxical mission, 56; assualt on Amalia, 51–52, 54; awards, 10; camera work, 60, 65–66; Cannes Film Festival 2004, 68; car accident, *La mujer sin cabeza,* 60; Catholic Church/Catholicism, 51, 53, 61–62, 67; choreography of, 52; director's statement, 50; doctor character, 50–51; Dr. Jano, Janus (god) and, 59; female self-empowerment, 54; gaze, 54–55; girl saint, 58–59; "Habanera" from *Carmen* (Bizet), 54; hair, 66; hearing/listening, 50–51, 56–57; heat in, 7; horror films and, 59–61; hotel as character, 63; hotel setting, 52, 59; hygiene, 66; Inés's hymn, 52–54; interpretation issues, 61–63; *La ciénaga* and, 50, 140–41; mirror images, 58; post-Catholicism, 8, 67; private areas, blurring with public, 63–65; pursuer and pursued, gender roles and, 56; rationalism, 62–63; religion, 52–54; reviews, 68–69; sexuality, 52–53; smell, 66; sound, 52; Stantic, Lita, 51; stolen kisses, 64; theremin music, 54; touch, 65–66; triangle, 55–56, 58; visual style, 52; "Vuestra soy"/"I Am Yours," 53; water in, 2

Larralde, José, 25

Las dependencias: Silvina Ocampo/The servants, 11, 23–24, 150; camera work, 23–24

Las Naves, statement on filmmaking, 5–6

Laso, Julieta, 90

Leguas/Leagues, 153; indigenous groups, 100–101

Lerman, Diego, 19

Ley del Cine (film law), 13

Linklater, Richard, 17

López, Andrea, 29

Los guantes mágicos/The Magic Gloves (Rejtman), 16

Los Indios Tabajara, 108, 128

Los Perros/The Dogs (Said), 28

Los suicidas (Di Benedetto), 103

Los suicidas (Villega), 103

Luna de Avellaneda/Avellaneda's Moon (Campanella), 14

Lynch, David, 17

Magazine for Fai, 150

magical realism, 41–42

Margary, John, 87

Marks, Laura: visuality, 51

Márquez, Gabriel García, 38

Martel, Lucrecia: Amalia and, similarities, 67; Catholic without God, 61; on colonial adventure, 118; Escuela de Cine de Animación de Avellaneda (AVEX), 10–11; home movies, 10; illness, 146–47; indigenous groups and, 124; on new cinema, 136; personal Jano experience, 68; post-Catholicism, 8; on science fiction, 118; on storytelling in television series, 5

Martin, Deborah, 99

Mathé, Alfredo, 125

matriarchs: crazy aunts, 80–81; *La mujer sin cabeza,* 79–80

May Revolution: *Nueva Argirópolis,* 98–100

Menem, Carlos: film industry and, 13; neoliberal economy, 15–16

Metropolis (Lang), 14

minimalism, narrative, 27

Ministry of Culture, 99; *Nueva Argirópolis,* 98–99

Index | 187

Minujín, Juan, 108
mise-en-scène, storyboarding and, 138
missed opportunities, 2
Miss Mary (Bemberg), 18, 34–35, 67
Mittleman, Mario A.: *Chiquilines,* 103
Miu Miu, 96
Molina, Juana, 97
Momentos (Bemberg), 18
monkey: in *Zama,* 124
Mora, Adriana, 86
moral fables, 8
Morán, Mercedes, 78; *La ciénaga,* 18; *La niña santa,* 51
Mundo grua/Crane World (Trapero), 17
Murga, Celina, 28
Muta, 9, 96, 152; Paraná River, 98; sound, 96
Myrick, Daniel, 59

Nachtergaele, Matheus, 106
narrative, 26; minimalism, 27; omniscience and, 27; orality and, 139; *versus* scenes in *La mujer sin cabeza,* 74; *Zama* adaptation, 115–16
neoliberalism: countries, Tigre, 98; *La mujer sin cabeza,* 84–85; New Argentine Cinema and, 36
neorealism, New Argentine Cinema and, 17–18
New Argentine Cinema, 9–17, 19; Italian neorealism and, 17–18; neoliberalism and, 36
new cinema, 136
Nilsson, Leopoldo Torre, 17, 34; *Fin de fiesta/The Party Is Over,* 34; *La caída/The Fall,* 33; *La casa del angel/The House of the Angel,* 33
No te la llevarás, maldito/Don't You Dare Take Her, 149
Nueva Argirópolis/New Argiropolis, 98–100, 152; language, 100; sound *versus* visual, 100
Nueva reinas/Nine Queens (Bielinsky), 13
Nunes, Mariana, 108

objectification of female body: *La niña santa,* 54; Helena, 58
Ocampo, Silvina, 23

Oesterheld, Héctor Germán, 144; disappearance, 93–94; *El Eternauta,* 88–93; *El Eternauta II,* 93; eternauta, 90; Montoneros, 93
off-screen space, 52
O'Hehir, Andrew, 87
omniscience in narrative, 27
Onetto, María, 78
óperas primas, funding, 13
oral narration, 139; *La ciénaga,* 41–42
oral traditions, 136–37
Oubiña, David, 35; *Estudio crítico sobre "La ciénaga": Entrevista a Lucrecia Martel,* 135; interview, 135–41

Paraná River, 98; *El Eternauta* and, 102; *Nueva Argirópolis,* 99; *Voyage dans l'Amerique meridionale depuis 1781 jusqu'en 1801* (Azara), 120; *Zama* and, 102
Pardo, Mario, 125
patriarchy: *La mujer sin cabeza/The Headless Woman,* 84
Peña, Fernando Martín, 14
perception, cinema and, 6–7
Pescados/Fishes, 9, 97, 109, 152; absurdism, 98
physicality of films, 7
Piso 24/Floor 24, 11, 149
plot, 5
Poças, Ruy, 118, 145
Polanski, Roman: *Rosemary's Baby,* 81
polytemporality: *La ciénaga/The Swamp,* 39
post-Catholicism, 8; hope and, 9; *La ciénaga,* 8; *La mujer sin cabeza,* 9; *La niña santa,* 8; Salta trilogy, 8; surrealism and, 9; *Zama,* 9
post-dictatorship Argentine cinema, 16, 18
Premios Fénix, 105
private areas: blurring with public, 63–65; *La ciudad que huye,* 98
Psycho (Hitchcock), 59
public areas, 98; blurring with private, 63–65; *La ciudad que huye,* 98
Puenzo, Lucia, 28

Quandt, James, 75, 83, 87

queer cinema, 7–8
Quintín, 13, 75, 115
Quiroga, Horacio, 26, 41–42, 60
Quiros, Daniel, 75, 80

racism, *Zama*, 119
Rapado/Cropped Head (Rejtman), 17
rationalism: *La niña santa*, 62–63
Rejtman, Martín, 11, 16, 17; *Los guantes mágicos/The Magic Gloves*, 16; *Rapado/Cropped Head*, 17
Relatos salvajes/Wild Tales (Szifrón), 43
religion: girl saint, 58–59; interpretation and, 61–62; *La niña santa*, 52–54; sexuality and, 67. *See also* Catholic Church/Catholicism
Rey/King (Atallah), 126
Rey Muerto/Dead King, 10, 19–22, 54, 150; Havana Film Festival, 19; *La ciénaga* and, 140–41
Ríos, Paola Arboleda, 35
Rosemary's Baby (Polanski), 81
Rosenblatt, Adam, 93
Roveda, Matías, 146
ruralism, 18

Saer, Juan José, 118
Said, Marcela, 28; *La reina del miedo*, 28; *Los Perros/The Dogs*, 28
Salta region: *La ciénaga*, 43–44
Salta trilogy, 2; desire, 87; economic crisis and, 16; impact, 28; as one piece, 87–88; post-Catholicism, 8; props, 88; settings, 87–88
Sánchez, Eduardo, 59
Sarmiento, Domingo Faustino, 99
Sarquis, Nicolás, 125, 147
Schindel, Dan, 127
Scott, A. O., 28, 68
script, film and, 6
security, lack of: horror and, 61
Señora de nadie/Nobody's Wife (Bemberg), 18
"Sensini" (Bolaño), 104
sexuality: *La niña santa*, 52–53; religion and, 67
shallow focus: *La mujer sin cabeza*, 73
The Shining (Kubrick), 59

shorts: *Chocobar*, 101–2; *El 56*, 149; *Leguas (El aula vacía/ The Empty Classroom)*, 100–101; *El Eternauta* (Oesterheld), 88–94; *Fantasmas*, 90; *Muta*, 96, 98; *Nueva Argirópolis*, 98–101; *Pescados/Fishes*, 97; *Piso 24/ Floor 24*, 149
Sincortes, 14
social media, 89
Solanas, Fernando, 12
Solano López, Francisco, 88; *El Eternauta* drawings, 90
Soldado/Soldier (Abramovich), 6
Solomonoff, Julia, 28
Sosa, Cecilia, 83
sound: camera work and, 25; *El Eternauta*, 94; *La ciénaga*, 139; *La niña santa*, 52, 54; language in *Nueva Argirópolis*, 100; Molina, Juana, 97; *Muta*, 96; primacy, 24–25; theremin, 54; *Zama*, 113, 145
soundtrack: choosing, 139; *La mujer sin cabeza*, 84; *La niña santa*, 50–51; Molina, Juana, 97; *Zama*, 113, 145
Spiner, Fernando, *Aballay/Six Shooters*, 103
Spitta, Silvia, interview, 141–47
stagnant water, 4–5
Stagnaro, Bruno, 19
Stantic, Lita, 11, 18–19, 22, 146; Bemberg, María Luisa and, 18; *La niña santa*, 51; *Un muro de silencio/A Wall of Silence*, 18
storyboarding, 138
storytelling: dialogue and, 42–43; elliptical, 42–43; foreshadowing, 137; *La ciénaga*, 39–40; Martel on, 136–37; oral traditions, 136–37; television series and, 5
Subiela, Eliseo, 12
surrealism, post-Catholicism and, 9
suspense: *La mujere sin cabeza*, 75
swimming pools, 4; *Zama*, 1
Szifrón, Damián: *Relatos salvajes/Wild Tales* (Szifrón), 43

Taubin, Amy, 74, 76, 86
technology, in *El Eternauta*, 90–91
television work, 11

Index | 189

Teodoro, José, 118
Theory of Film (Kracauer), 24
theremin: horror films, 59; *La niña santa,* 54
Thomas, Daniela, 126
Thomas, Kevin, 68
thriller movies: Martel on, 82
time: *La ciénaga,* 39, 41; passage, 26; setting, 26
Tiscornia, Fabiana, 28
topics, political, 8
transformistas: *La otra,* 22
Trapero, Pablo, 11, 17; *Mundo grua/ Crane World,* 17
Trerotola, Diego, 69
Tsai, Martin, 68–69

universalism, *Zama,* 127–28
Un muro de silencio/A Wall of Silence (Stantic), 18
Urdapilleta, Alejandro, 51

Vaner, María, *La mujer sin cabeza,* 79–80
Vazante (Thomas), 126
Vertigo (Hitchcock), 82
Vespa, Mariano, 125
viceroyalty, 120–21
Vida en Falcon (Gaggero), 15
Villegas, Juan: *Los suicides,* 103
Viñoly, Román, 125
Voyage dans l'Amerique meridionale depuis 1781 jusqu'en 1801 (Azara), 119–20
"Vuestra soy"/"I Am Yours" in *La niña santa,* 53

Wackerbarth, Nicolas, 95
water, 2; EICTV profile, 4; *La ciénaga,* 2, 4, 36–37; *La mujer sin cabeza,* 4, 70; *La niña santa,* 2; stagnant, 4–5; swimming pools, 4; *Zama,* 1

Wolf, Sergio, 81
Women's Tales, 96

Yemayel, Mónica, 8
Yo, la peor de todas/I, Worst of All (Bemberg), 18
YouTube: *Fantasmas,* 90; Martel on, 89–90; *Nueva Argirópolis,* 99–100

Zama, 1, 89, 94–95, 153; absurdism, 98, 127; adaptation, 115–16, 125, 144; americanos, 119; awards, early, 105–6; blind men and women, 122; Bolaño, and, 104; bureaucracy, 127; Cacho, Daniel Giménez, 116–17; Carlos III, 119; casting of nonprofessionals, 143; Catholic Church/Catholicism, 118, 126, 142; *Chocobar* and, 102; cinematography, 118; colonial hero in Zama, 106–7; colonialism and, 105; color in, 114–15; composition, 111–12; Dueñas, Lola, 117–18; female characters, 127–28; as frontier story, 127; hope, 142; identity crises of Zama and Argentina, 117–18; indigenous groups, 122–24; language, 113–14, 121–22, 143; male protagonist, 142; monkey, 124; narrative, 115–16; novel compared to film, 107; opening, 105, 108–9; Paraná River and, 102; Porto, Vicuña, 121–22; positive reception, 141–42; post-Catholicism, 9; racism, 119; real events, references to, 119; rhythm, 111; setting, 2, 97; skin and, 7; slaves, 122–24; sound, 113, 145; soundtrack, 145; timeline, 107; universalism, 127–28; unlikable protagonist, 111; vignette style, 111; violence, 110–11; visuals, 110; water in, 1. *See also* Di Benedetto, Antonio
Zylberberg, Julieta, 51

Gerd Gemünden is professor of German studies, film and media studies, and comparative literature at Dartmouth College. His books include *Continental Strangers: German Exile Filmmakers in Hollywood, 1933–1950* and *A Foreign Affair: Billy Wilder's American Films*.

Books in the series Contemporary Film Directors

Nelson Pereira dos Santos
Darlene J. Sadlier

Abbas Kiarostami
Mehrnaz Saeed-Vafa and Jonathan Rosenbaum

Joel and Ethan Coen
R. Barton Palmer

Claire Denis
Judith Mayne

Wong Kar-wai
Peter Brunette

Edward Yang
John Anderson

Pedro Almodóvar
Marvin D'Lugo

Chris Marker
Nora Alter

Abel Ferrara
Nicole Brenez, translated by Adrian Martin

Jane Campion
Kathleen McHugh

Jim Jarmusch
Juan Suárez

Roman Polanski
James Morrison

Manoel de Oliveira
John Randal Johnson

Neil Jordan
Maria Pramaggiore

Paul Schrader
George Kouvaros

Jean-Pierre Jeunet
Elizabeth Ezra

Terrence Malick
Lloyd Michaels

Sally Potter
Catherine Fowler

Atom Egoyan
Emma Wilson

Albert Maysles
Joe McElhaney

Jerry Lewis
Chris Fujiwara

Jean-Pierre and Luc Dardenne
Joseph Mai

Michael Haneke
Peter Brunette

Alejandro González Iñárritu
Celestino Deleyto and Maria del Mar Azcona

Lars von Trier
Linda Badley

Hal Hartley
Mark L. Berrettini

François Ozon
Thibaut Schilt

Steven Soderbergh
Aaron Baker

Mike Leigh
Sean O'Sullivan

D.A. Pennebaker
Keith Beattie

Jacques Rivette
Mary M. Wiles

Kim Ki-duk
Hye Seung Chung

Philip Kaufman
Annette Insdorf

Richard Linklater
David T. Johnson

David Lynch
Justus Nieland

John Sayles
David R. Shumway

Dario Argento
L. Andrew Cooper

Todd Haynes
Rob White

Christian Petzold
Jaimey Fisher

Spike Lee
Todd McGowan

Terence Davies
Michael Koresky

Francis Ford Coppola
Jeff Menne

Emir Kusturica
Giorgio Bertellini

Agnès Varda
Kelley Conway

John Lasseter
Richard Neupert

Paul Thomas Anderson
George Toles

Cristi Puiu
Monica Filimon

Wes Anderson
Donna Kornhaber

Jan Švankmajer
Keith Leslie Johnson

Kelly Reichardt
Katherine Fusco and Nicole Seymour

Michael Bay
Lutz Koepnick

Abbas Kiarostami, Expanded Second Edition
Mehrnaz Saeed-Vafa and Jonathan Rosenbaum

Lana and Lilly Wachowski
Cáel M. Keegan

Todd Solondz
Julian Murphet

Lucrecia Martel
Gerd Gemünden

The University of Illinois Press
is a founding member of the
Association of University Presses.

———————————————

University of Illinois Press
1325 South Oak Street
Champaign, IL 61820-6903
www.press.uillinois.edu